River Books Guides

KHMER TEMPLES
IN THAILAND & LAOS

Written and Photographed
by
Michael Freeman

WEATHERHILL
New York • Tokyo

A New Map of
EAST INDIA.

Sold by Tho. Basset in Fleetstreet.
and Richard Chiswell in St Pauls
Church yard.

First edition, 1996
First Weatherhill edition, 1998
Published by Weatherhill, Inc., of
New York and Tokyo, with editorial
offices at 568 Broadway, Suite 705,
New York, N.Y. 10012, USA
by special arrangement with
River Books.

Text and Photographs
© 1996 Michael Freeman

Collective Work
© 1996 River Books, Bangkok

The author and River Books would like to
acknowledge the important contribution to
Khmer studies made by Assistant Professor
Smitthi Siribhadra

Editor Narisa Chakrabongse
Design Supadee Ruangsak
Production Paisarn Piemmettawat

Printed and bound in Thailand by
Amarin Printing and Publishing Public
Co. Ltd.

ISBN 0-8348-0450-6

C O N

T E N T S

INTRODUCTION

"The domain of Khmer archaeology comprises on the one hand the alluvial plains of the Mekong and the basin of the Grand Lac Tonlé Sap, and on the other the plateau of Khorat. As will be seen, the attempt to unite these two parts, so different from every point of view, resulted in a political unit which was never stable. The whole history of Cambodia is dominated by the struggle between the peoples of the highlands north of the Dongrek mountains and of the lowlands to the south."

George Coedès: Angkor, An Introduction.

The Khmer Empire, which for about 500 years was the most powerful on the mainland of Southeast Asia, was ruled for the greater part of its history from Angkor, on the shores of Cambodia's Great Lake, the Tonlé Sap. A pattern of conquests under successive kings, however, took the frontiers way beyond the immediate limits of the city. At its height, the Empire stretched west to what is now Burma, south onto the Malay Peninsula, east to the Vietnamese coast, and north almost as far as Vientiane.

Not all of this territory was under direct military control, and as more inscriptions are found and translated, a picture is emerging of an empire that was quite complex in its organisation, and by no means stable. There were patterns of allegiances, fiefdoms, semi-independent provinces, and periods of intense struggle. A great deal of Khmer history remains unknown, particularly the disputes of kingship and civil wars, but hints of these can be found in inscriptions and on a few historical bas-reliefs, such as on the gallery walls of the Bayon at Angkor and Banteay Chhmar in the far north-west of Cambodia.

In fact, geography made it almost inevitable that there would be political and social differences. Angkor lies on the fertile plain bordering the Great Lake in lowland Cambodia, yet one of the major parts of the Empire occupied the large Khorat Plateau to the north, separated from the plains by the Dongrek Mountains. For much of their length they form a wall that can be crossed only through a few passes. Beyond these mountains, in present-day Thailand, the broad, shallow valley of the Mun River was an independent centre of civilisation, and it seems likely that the Khmers moved south into the lowlands from here. Far from being a provincial backwater, this region furnished Cambodia and Angkor with two kings directly – Jayavarman VI and Suryavarman II – while Jayavarman VII, the last great Khmer ruler, was a cousin of Suryavarman II.

A large part of this book is, in fact, a guide to what used to be upland Cambodia. The political frontiers have changed considerably since the time of the Khmer Empire, but the monuments remain – some 300 in what is now Thailand. Indeed, the southern part of the Khorat Plateau where most of the Khmer temples are situated, is essentially Khmer-speaking. The dialect, however, is distinct from the Khmer spoken in present-day Cambodia, and the Thais distinguish between the two forms — and the two peoples — as *'Khmer soong'* (high, or upland Khmer from the plateau) and *'Khmer tam'* (low Khmer from the plains).

For the visitor, the Khmer temples of Thailand and Laos contain works of the first rank, both artistically and architecturally, and have their own special character, set in a distinctive environment. Apart from museums, this guide covers 40 temples and related sites — essentially those where there is still something to see. Virtually all are in Thailand, but the importance and beauty of Wat Phu in Southern Laos demand its inclusion. Besides, it is not inconveniently far from the sites close to Ubon in Northeast Thailand, and marks the eastern end of the main string of Khmer temples on the plateau. Another mountain temple is Preah Vihear, known to the Thais as Khao Phra Viharn. Although in Cambodia (just — the border begins on its lower steps), it is only practicable to visit it from the Thai side, and for this reason is also included in the guide.

Wat Phu and Preah Vihear are just two of several major Khmer temples covered here — major, that is, by the highest standards of Khmer architecture, including the monuments at Angkor itself. To give some perspective to the many sites, we have ranked them according to their size, importance and condition. This mixture is necessarily based on personal judgement, but is designed to help the first-time visitor plan a trip. Sites marked with 🔥🔥🔥 merit a complete journey, are of the first rank architecturally, and contain sufficient interest for a visit of at least an hour. Sites with 🔥🔥 are of great interest and are worth devoting a half-day of travelling time, while those with a 🔥 are worth an hour or two of journey time. Monuments with no ranking are worth stopping for if en route. This said, however, all the sites covered in this guide are worth visiting for anyone with a specific interest in Khmer art and architecture. Those monuments that are also situated in pleasant surroundings (such as in attractive countryside, or with a mountain view), are highlighted with a 🍃 symbol. The delight of these monuments, most of them in a continuous swathe across the Northeast of Thailand and across into Southern Laos, lies in discovery. Few people have seen any but a handful of them. The combination of restoration programmes and changes in political circumstances have essentially opened up a new art and architectural experience.

HISTORY

Statue of King Jayavaraman VII, National Museum, Bangkok.

The history of the Khmer Empire, and in particular the Angkorean period from 802 to c.1431, has traditionally been seen from the standpoint of lowland Cambodia. For an overall perspective, there is considerable justification for this, given what we know of its government. From George Coedès: "The whole political organisation of the country was centred on the king, who, in theory, was the source and sum of all authority, the custodian of the established order, the final judge of disputes between his subjects, the defender of the faith and the protector of the religious foundations entrusted to his care." Power flowed outwards from the capital — which for most of the time was at Angkor — administered by a hierarchy of officials and priests, and maintained by the army. Lands and fiefdoms were dispensed to favoured priests and princes, who kept allegiance to the king.

The centralisation of the empire went further than just its administration. The temple mountain that almost every new king built represented Mount Meru, the home of the gods in Hindu cosmology, and so the capital itself was in effect a microcosm of the centre of the universe (↦ 21-22). By the time of Jayavarman VII (1181-c.1220), the entire capital at Angkor was rebuilt to symbolise this; even the entrance causeways to the city were conceived as part of a gigantic model.

Nevertheless, communications were slow over what became a very large empire, reaching west to Burma, north as far as present-day Vientiane, and east to the delta of the Mekong, and the amount of real control exercised over the provinces is incompletely known. The evidence of certain inscriptions, such as at Phnom Rung, and above all, differences in the architecture and decorative carvings, suggest that the further Khmer provinces had some significant independence.

The majority of these further provinces is in what is now Thailand, and the most important temple remains lie on the Khorat Plateau in the country's Northeast. Seen from Angkor and lowland Cambodia, these provincial centres lie beyond a real physical barrier – the range of mountains running west-east a little over 100 km north of Angkor, known as the Dongrek range. This natural frontier, which forms such a decisive break in the landscape that today it defines part of the border between Cambodia and Thailand, separates the lowland plains from the Khorat Plateau. From the Thai side, which already lies at an average elevation of about 200 metres, the 500- to 700-metre peaks of the Dongreks appear quite low, but from the Cambodian plain they rise as a steep wall, abrupt and sheer in some places.

To the west, access to the lower and middle Chao Phraya valley was a relatively easy, if long journey, via routes passing close to the modern border town of Aranyaprathet. To the north, only a few passes cross the Dongreks, and this physical restriction must have had some effect on the way in which Khmer civilisation developed on the plateau. Local records are sparse, and mainly in the form of later local chronicles, such as the *Chamadevivamsa* written in the early 15th century. The earliest Khmer inscription is from Ayutthaya, dated 937, and refers to a succession of princes whose names are unknown from Cambodian records. There is even less evidence for what happened on the Khorat Plateau, even though it is here that the major temples of Phimai, Phnom Rung and Preah Vihear were built. An inscription from Ban Bung Ke, near Ubon, dates to 886 and shows that the Khmers were well established in the Mun Valley by this time.

The scarcity of written history in the Khmer provinces is compounded by the progress of Khmer archaeology. The French colonisation of Cambodia provided the opportunity for an illustrious line of French scholars to excavate, reconstruct and study the temples and inscriptions of the Khmer heartland. When the art historians of the École Française d'Extrême Orient set to work on the chronology of the styles of architecture and sculpture, the models they used were, naturally enough, in lowland Cambodia and, for the most part, from the Angkor area. In Thailand, which remained an independent kingdom, there was no such concerted effort to investigate its Khmer past until fairly recently.

As a result, the history of the Khmer Empire has been written from the perspective of Angkor. Only now is it becoming clear that this does not completely correspond with the development of Khmer temples beyond the Dongrek range. One notable anomaly is the dating of the different Angkorean styles. For obvious reasons, these have been named after the major locations to have been studied, such as the Bakheng, Angkor Wat and Bayon styles, and the models for the lintels, sculptures, architectural methods and so on are, for the most part, temples at Angkor.

Now, according to this system, the style known as Baphuon, named after the colossal temple mountain near the centre of the capital, lasted from about 1010 to 1080 AD. At Angkor, it is represented by the eponymous temple mountain that was the most ambitious structure attempted to that date – but by very little else. On the Khorat Plateau, however, the Baphuon style assumes much more importance. It is by far the most common form of architectural decoration and sculpture, despite the fact that the period at Angkor lasted only about 70 years. This suggests that between the capital and the further provinces the periods may have lasted for different lengths of time. Perhaps provincial tastes were slower to change.

Stele with 13th century inscription, from Samnak Nangkhao, Mahasarakham.

Not surprisingly, Khmer history beyond Cambodia has largely been relegated to passing references and footnotes. Certainly, Angkor has been centre-stage for most of the important centuries of the civilisation, from the 9th to the early 15th centuries, yet the artistic and architectural achievements at Phimai and Phnom Rung, among others, show that these provincial centres were extremely important in their own right. Exceptional finds have been made just within the last few years – witness the bronze guardian discovered at Kamphaeng Yai – and with the excavation and reconstruction programme begun in the 1960s by Thailand's Fine Arts Department, some old assumptions are being challenged and Khmer provincial history is being re-examined.

The history of Khmer civilisation in Thailand and Laos is not entirely that of the empire based at Angkor. The most influential reigns were those of the three kings responsible for the major territorial conquests – Indravarman I, Suryavarman I and Suryavarman II – and the king who undertook the largest building programme of any, Jayavarman VII.

Even before this, excavations at one particular site, Wat Phu in Southern Laos, still under archaeological investigation, show it to have been one of the oldest in Indochina. The Khmer Empire was heir to the earlier kingdom now known only by its Chinese name, Funan, founded probably sometime in the 1st century AD and occupying the lower Mekong valley. Funan became the most powerful kingdom in the Indochinese peninsula, until it was conquered by a northern vassal state, Chenla, at the end of the 6th century. Chenla, by which name the Chinese continued to refer to Cambodia, had its centre at present-day Champasak on the Mekong River. Overlooking the Chenla capital is a mountain with a monolith on its summit – a natural rock *linga* (a phallus ➡ p.19) that gave it its Sanskrit name Lingaparvata, 'the mountain of the *linga*'. A 6th century Chinese account records that a temple was constructed on the mountain, and was the site of an annual human sacrifice performed by the king. Wat Phu, the surviving buildings of which date to the 11th and 12th centuries, was built on the lower slopes of this mountain, on a site with even earlier origins. Local tradition, backed by epigraphic evidence, suggests that the area around Champasak was originally ruled by the Chams.

Near the beginning of the Angkorean period, Indravarman I (877-889) ruled from Hariharalaya, some 16 km south-east of Angkor, and even in this short reign of 12 years pushed his territory beyond the limits of modern Cambodia, onto the Khorat Plateau. An inscription found north-west of Ubon Ratchathani mentions him in 886. At his capital in 879 he had the brick temple of Preah Ko built, giving the name to the style that lasted about 20 years at the end of the century. On the plateau its influence can be seen at the temple of Phnom Wan, near Khorat.

The second Khmer ruler to make his power felt beyond the lowlands was Suryavarman I (1002-1050). His reign marked the end of a nine-year war, about which little is known, and under his rule Khmer authority was extended into the Chao Phraya valley and the uninhabited lowlands west of the Great Lake. Louvo (present-day Lopburi), the former Mon centre, became a Khmer provincial capital, and later chronicles from the 15th and 16th centuries recount a war in this region with the Mon kingdom of Haripunjaya (present-day Lamphun). Although these chronicles are not completely reliable, they give a picture of the expanding Khmer influence in what is now central Thailand, at the expense of the Mons. The Thais themselves had not at this point settled in the region. An inscription of 1022-25 from Lopburi confirms Suryavarman I's control. The style associated with his reign is that of the Khleangs, marked by the appearance of complete surrounding galleries with vaulted roofs. In Thailand, the temples of Muang Tam and Preah Vihear date partly from this time.

It was another king to take the title 'protégé of the sun', Suryavarman II, who pushed the Empire to its furthest limits. Reigning from 1113 to at least 1150 (the exact date of his death is unknown), Suryavarman II was both the greatest conqueror in Khmer history and the builder of the largest and most famous of all temple-mountains, Angkor Wat. He too was from the dynasty that started in the Mun valley, and came to power as a result of a struggle in which he defeated two other kings (one of them his great-uncle Dharanindravarman I); an inscription found at Wat Phu mentions that he had "taken the royalty by unifying a double kingdom". He immediately began a series of campaigns, in the east and north against the Chams and the Dai Viet (the first Vietnamese empire), and in the west and north-west against the Mons of the Chao Phraya valley. The wars against Haripunjaya, conducted from

the regional capital of Louvo, were renewed, although ultimately without success. The Chinese *History of the Sung* mentions not only that he sent embassies to China in 1116 and 1120, but records the limits of his empire – specifically, the western frontier by the middle of the century had reached the kingdom of

Louvo troops in the army of Suryavarman II on a bas-rellief from the south gallery of Angkor Wat.

Pagan. The exact status of Louvo is obscure, and the later chronicles can be interpreted as referring to the ruler of Louvo as a Khmer governor or as Suryavarman II himself. From the *History of the Sung*, it appears that at the beginning of his reign, in 1115, Louvo had sent its own embassy to China (where it was known as Lo-hu), which may possibly have been an assertion of independence .

It is at this time that we have a remarkable picture of the provincial Khmer army. The western half of the bas-reliefs carved on the south outer gallery of Angkor Wat depicts the great personalities of the time, and the linking theme for this series of portraits is a march-past of the Khmer troops. At their head, an exotic and disorderly troop represents Thai mercenaries, called here on the gallery's inscription 'Syam Kuk', meaning 'Siamese people', and the origin of the name Siam. Behind them march the contingent from Louvo, in appearance completely Khmer.

The architectural culmination of Suryavarman II's reign was Angkor Wat, but considerably more was built, or initiated. In the provinces, most of Phimai and Phnom Rung were built, Wat Phu was added to considerably, and several smaller sanctuaries were constructed.

The style of the reign is that of Angkor Wat, characterised in its architecture by large constructions, concentric series of enclosures and, most memorable of all, the ogival, corn-cob tower. In this feature, the Khorat Plateau plays an important role. The major settlement of the region was Vimayapura (Phimai), to the north of modern Nakhon Ratchasima, and its temple pre-dates Angkor Wat by a little. Its sanctuary towers clearly influenced the towers of the capital.

The death of Suryavarman II sometime around 1150 heralded a new round of revolts and struggles within the Empire. The ultimate decline of Khmer power began at this point. Provincial history is marked by attempts to break the ties with Angkor, and in 1155 a new embassy was sent to China by Louvo. The name of a king of Louvo, Dharmashoka, is mentioned in an inscription of 1167 found near Nakhon Sawan, suggesting that this provincial state may have quickly declared its independence.

The foreign campaigns that Suryavarman II and some of his predecessors had waged now began to turn against the Khmers. The Chams, following a treaty with their other enemy the Dai Viet, attacked. After inconclusive fighting to begin with, they succeeded in 1177 in taking the capital at Angkor by means of a naval attack up the Great Lake. Only the appearance of an outstanding Khmer king stemmed the decline of the Empire. Jayavarman VII, a legitimate heir to the throne whose absence from the country had prevented his accession, returned to liberate the capital. It took four years to drive the Chams out, and in 1181 he was crowned, in his fifties. Two major achievements mark Jayavarman VII's reign of more than 30 years, and both were felt in the northern provinces. One was the massive building programme, not only of temples, but of more utilitarian and beneficial constructions – roads, travellers' rest-houses and hospitals. The other was the widespread introduction of Mahayana Buddhism, the religion of his father and his two consecutive wives. In fact, Buddhism was the inspiration for the building programme, and the hospitals and rest-houses were an expression of the compassionate element of the faith.

However, here as in other instances, neither the history nor the architectural legacy of Jayavarman VII was the same from the provincial perspective as from that of the capital. At Angkor, his outstanding, even bizarre, masterpieces of construction were the Bayon, with its more than 200 benign giant faces, and the modelling of the entire city of Angkor Thom as a microcosm of the universe, complete with *naga* 'bridges' at the city gates and the full range of religious symbolism. More temples were built around the city – at great speed, from which the construction and decoration suffered. One of the most impressive features was the level to which Jayavarman VII raised the cult of his personality; it is generally agreed that the faces carved on the towers not only at Angkor but across lowland Cambodia are an idealised portrait of him as the compassionate Bodhisattva Lokesvara. The temple-city of Banteay Chhmar in the north-west of the country also has some of these face-towers, and is included in this guide because of its proximity to present-day Thailand.

North of the Dongreks, however, there is little evidence of all of this, and the architectural mark of the reign is the use of laterite instead of stone. There are no face towers, no complex symbolism in stone, and the demotic bas-reliefs of the Bayon, which give such a fascinating picture of Khmer daily life at the turn of the 13th century, have no counterpart in what is now Thailand. Nevertheless, though the remains are sparse, Jayavarman VII managed to expand the Empire's frontiers. An inscription of 1186 from Sai Fong, on the Mekong near Vientiane, is the most northerly known. 12th and 13th century Chinese accounts (the *Ling-wai Tai-ta* of 1178, and that of Chao Ju-kua of 1225) relate that Khmer control extended into

'Syam Kuk' Siamese mercenaries in Suryavarman II's army, south gallery of Angkor Wat.

present-day Burma and part of the Malay Peninsula. The last large Khmer settlement discovered in Thailand is that of Muang Singh, west of the Chao Phraya near present-day Kanchanaburi. Although hastily built in laterite, with only traces remaining of the stucco work with which it was decorated, the sanctuary and surrounding earthen ramparts indicate that this was an important foundation, its settlement no doubt guarding the western frontier.

Other constructions of the period, for which the style is that of the Bayon, are hospitals and rest-houses along the major roads. The 1191 stele at Preah Khan, the temple consecrated to the memory of Jayavarman VII's father, describes 121 "houses with fire" – the rest-houses or way-stations built a day's walk apart from each other (approximately 15 km). In addition, the stele of Ta Prohm, consecrated to the memory of Jayavarman VII's mother, mentions 102 hospitals. One of the principal routes of the Empire was the road leading north-west from Angkor to Phimai, passing the important temples of Ta Muen Thom, Muang Tam and Phnom Rung. Along this road 17 rest-houses were built, of which eight have been found. At the Ta Muen Pass are two of the best-preserved chapels of these constructions: that of Ta Muen from the rest-house and that of Ta Muen Toch from the hospital.

The art of this Bayon period is Buddhist in inspiration, and the statuary found in Thailand is extensive. One very distinctive form of statue is of a seated heavy-set man, hair pulled back into a chignon, with closed eyes and a faint smile indicating an inner Buddhist peace – not dissimilar from the expression on the face-towers. Several such statues – or parts – have been found, one of them in Thailand, and they are clearly an idealised portrait of the king. In addition, stone Buddhas under nagas abound, and numerous bronzes of the Buddha, bodhisattvas and Buddhist deities. From Muang Singh are two important stone statues of the so-called 'radiating' Lokesvara.

The end of Jayavarman VII's reign effectively marks the end of Khmer building in permanent materials, and thus the end of the remains known to us. Even more significant in the Chao Phraya valley and on the Khorat Plateau is that Jayavarman VII's death around 1220 coincides with the break-away from Angkor. Although the dates are uncertain, the beginnings of what Louis Finot called the Tai "inundation" were about this time. The start of the century saw the foundation of small Tai principalities in present-day Laos and the Shan States of Burma; by its end the Tai had moved into, and taken control of, the northern and central parts of the Chao Phraya valley and its tributaries. In 1287, the three Tai rulers Mengrai of Chiangmai, Ngan Muang of Phayao and Ramkhamhaeng of Sukhothai concluded their famous treaty, and the Siamese era had begun. Sukhothai, which had been a provincial Khmer seat, must have fallen to the Siamese around the time of the death of Jayavarman VII. During this period Louvo also must have been taken, or else declared its independence from Angkor, for it sent its own embassies once more to China between 1289 and 1299. The last account to report the Khmers in control of provinces beyond lowland Cambodia is Chao Ju-kua's Chu-fan-chih in 1225, which includes Lo-hu (Louvo) and P'u-kan (Pagan) among its dependencies. What happened on the Khorat Plateau is unknown, but linguistically at least, a belt of Khmer speakers still occupies the southern part of the plateau.

The Angkorean period continued for two more centuries, and while the provinces had gained their independence, and there was no further building of significance in Cambodia after Jayavarman VII, the Empire still flourished. The famous account of Angkor at the end of the 13th century, written by Chou Ta-Kuan, records the life of a prosperous city, dominated by magnificent temples "which have caused merchants from overseas to speak so often of 'Cambodia the rich and noble' "

However, the end of Angkor was already in sight, as the Siamese , with their newly consolidated power in the central Chao Phraya valley, began to harass the Khmers. In his same account, Chou Ta-Kuan mentions "I have heard it said that in war with the Siamese universal military service was required". Siamese chronicles, though of suspect reliability, give two dates, 1352 and 1394, on which Ayutthayan armies succeeded in taking Angkor. Thereafter, nothing is known of the wars between the two nations until the final indisputable sacking of Angkor in 1431, when the Khmer king Dhammashokaraja was killed. The city was abandoned after this forever as being too difficult to defend.

The Khmer legacy in Thailand was considerable. Some Khmer sites, such as Sukhothai and Si Satchanalai, were retained by the Siamese as foundations for their own cities and temples. The immediate response in the 13th century appears to have been a reaction against Khmer design. Under Ramkhamhaeng at Sukhothai, Siamese art, architecture and political systems seem to have developed in deliberate contrast to Khmer authoritarianism, although Siamese script, the invention of which is attributed to Ramkhamhaeng, was derived directly from the more complex Khmer system. When Ayutthaya became the centre of Siamese power, the pendulum began to swing back with a full-blown Khmer Revival, which coincided with the campaigns against Angkor (1350 to 1430). This deliberate return to Khmer influence was felt in sculpture (the U Thong school), architecture (the evolution of the Tai *prang* from the Khmer sanctuary towers) and in the political and administrative system, focused on a monarchy that revived the claims for divine power.

Khmer Rulers

Ruler	Dates
Jayavarman II	802-850
Jayavarman III	850-877
Indravarman I	877-889
Yasovarman I	889-900
Harshavarman I	900-c.922
Isanavarman II	925
Jayavarman IV	928-942
Harshavarman II	942-944
Rajendravarman	944-968
Jayavarman V	968-1001
Udayadityavarman I	1001-1002
Suryavarman I	1002-1050
Udayadityavarman II	1050-1066
Harshavarman III	1066-1080
Jayavarman VI	1080-1107
Dharanindravarman I	1107-1113
Suryavarman II	1113-1150
Dharanindravarman II	c.1160
Yasovarman II	c.1160-c.1165
Jayavarman VII	1181-1219
Indravarman II	1219-1243
Jayavarman VIII	1243-1295
Srindravarman	1295-1307
Srindrajayavarman	1307-1327
Jayavarmadiparamesvara	1327-?

Comments

Founder of the Khmer Empire at Mt. Mahendra in the Kulen Mts. Later moved the capital to Hariharalaya (Roluos).

No building known.

Temples and irrigation projects at Hariharalaya (Roluos).

Moved the capital (Yasodharapura) to Angkor, built the East Baray.

Succeeded to the throne very young; very little known.

Very little known about the short reign.

Revolted against his nephew Harshavarman II in 921, moved the capital to Koh Ker.

Successor at Koh Ker.

Moved the capital back to Angkor. Successful war against the Chams.

Succeeded to the throne as a child; a peaceful reign, largely under the guidance of the priest Yajñavaraha.

A period of troubles and revolt.

Took the throne by force, becoming the undisputed ruler by 1010. Expanded the empire to the north and west.

More revolts. Expanded the empire even further to the west. Built the West Baray.

Devastation from the previous reign's troubles and a new war with the Chams prevented new building.

First king from the Mahidharapura dynasty; though not of royal blood, his accession was legitimised by the priest Divakarapandita. His authority probably only recognised in the north.

Younger brother of Jayavarman VI. Killed by Suryavarman II, who disputed the throne.

Grand-nephew of Jayavarman VI and Dharanindravarman I. Ambitious, war-like and a great builder. Extended the empire, fought the Dai-Viet, Chams and Mons, and built Angkor Wat.

Little known about the reign. Continued the war against the Chams. A Mahayana Buddhist.

Chosen to succeed because the heir (Dharanindravarman II's son) was fighting in Champa. Killed by a usurper, who in turn was killed during the 1177 Cham invasion.

The legitimate heir of Dharanindravarman II. Fought to expel the Chams, and then crowned himself. The last great Khmer king, a fervent Buddhist and builder on the largest scale ever known in the empire.

Beginnings of the decline of the empire. Champa abandoned, Sukhothai independent.

Empire continued to diminish; Lopburi independent. Diplomatic relations avoided submitting to Kubla Khan. Shivaite resurgence.

Little known about the reign, but described by Chou Ta-Kuan, the visiting Chinese diplomat.

Little known about the reign.

The last king mentioned in inscriptions.

RELIGIOUS SYMBOLISM

Bronze chariot fitting showing Garuda clutching the naga.

E very surviving Khmer building had a religious purpose. The reason is simply that only temples and other religious foundations merited the use of permanent materials – brick, sandstone or laterite – and all else has decomposed over the centuries. Even the palace of the king at Angkor was timber.

To appreciate fully these monuments built by the Khmers between approximately the 7th and the 13th centuries, it is important to know something of the Hindu and Buddhist cults to which they were dedicated. The buildings and their artefacts were single-mindedly designed for worship. "Most of the objects to be met are devotional in nature, created with religious and utilitarian rather than aesthetic motives; and they were fashioned by craftsmen who worked in a tradition which dictated strict canons of iconography and manufacture, and who could never have understood the meaning of the word 'artist' as it is used today." This is Roy Craven writing about Khmer artefacts, and his comments apply equally to the architecture. None of the work of this period lends itself to being judged on modern grounds of taste, even though the results may well inspire and delight.

Over the Khmer Empire as a whole, Hinduism dominated until the end of the

12th century, when it gave way to Mahayana Buddhism, although not for long. Both came from India, and although the exact means are in doubt, it is likely that Indian traders were the first to introduce their religion to Cambodia. Hinduism over the centuries had changed its focus, with different gods in ascendancy, but by the time it reached the Khmers there were two principal cults – that of Vishnu and that of Shiva. These two gods were part of the Hindu Trinity (the third was Brahma) which commanded a pantheon of lesser gods and had inter alia a complex relationship. They were connected in many of the same myths, acted partly in concert, partly in rivalry.

Vishnu, four-armed and holding a conch, discus, mace and lotus, is the Protector. His fundamental role in cosmology is to conserve the status quo in the universe. He takes a particular interest in human affairs, so much so that on occasions he takes on an earthly form to intervene. These various forms of Vishnu are known as *avatar,* and the two most famous are Rama, eponymous hero of the Ramayana epic, and Krishna. Both of these personalities embody a kind of magical ideal; they are true heroes, physically and morally. Other *avatar* of Vishnu include a lion, wild boar, dwarf, turtle and fish. In the range of Hindu deities, Vishnu is essentially kindly and well-disposed to man, and this accounts for a large part of the god's popularity as a cult.

Small bronze statue of the 4-armed Vishnu, 12th-13th century, at the National Museum, Khon Kaen.

Shiva contrasts with Vishnu in a number of ways. His main cosmological role is as the Destroyer – he brings each *kalpa,* or world cycle, to an end with his dance of destruction. However, Shiva's force is by no means just a negative one. As in modern physics, Hindu cosmology envisaged the universe as having a cyclical nature. The end of each *kalpa* brought about by Shiva's dance is also the beginning of the next. Rebirth follows destruction. In the cosmological sense, Shiva's powers are more fundamental than Vishnu's.

The Khmers worshipped Shiva primarily in the form of a *linga* – a pillar, usually in stone, derived from a phallus and representing the essence of the god. The *linga,* mounted in a pedestal representing an equally abstract *yoni,* or female organ, occupied the shrine of a temple, and was the focus of rituals conducted by the priests. The other forms in which Shiva was represented were as the 10-armed god dancing the universe to destruction, as the supreme yogi, or ascetic, and riding with his consort Uma on his steed, the bull Nandin.

Stone linga representing the essence of Shiva from Sung Noen, Nakhon Ratchasima.

The third member of the Trinity, Brahma, despite his designation as the Creator, inspired no cult, and so appears incidentally in Khmer temples – emerging from the lotus that grows out of Vishnu's navel as he sleeps, and in small statues. Brahma is recognisable by his four heads, each facing a cardinal direction.

Other, lesser gods make appearances. The most commonly met with is Indra, formerly the principal Vedic god but by the time Hinduism reached the Khmers simply the god of the sky and rain. Like all Hindu gods he has a steed, or *vahana*. In Indra's case, this is the elephant Airavata (in Thai, Erawan), normally shown with three heads. Other gods include Ganesha (Shiva's elephant-headed son), Agni (the Vedic god of fire), Kubera (guardian of the North), Surya (Vedic god of the sun), Varuna (god of seas and rivers and guardian of the West) and Yama (god of Death and guardian of the South).

A temple marker stone with Shiva and Uma on Nandin (Phimai Museum).

In addition, a number of mythological creatures play important parts. The most ubiquitous is the *naga*, serpent inhabitant of the underworld. *Nagas* appear throughout Khmer art and architecture, and are usually multi headed. Individual *nagas* have roles in particular myths, such as the sleep of Vishnu (the *naga* Ananta supports the god's body as he floats on the cosmic ocean) and the Churning of the Sea of Milk (the *naga* Vasuki's body is used as a rope entwined around Mount Mandara and pulled alternately by the gods and the demons to rotate the mountain). In reality, the *naga* derives from ancient snake-worship pre-dating major religions such as Hinduism. Other creatures that make an appearance include the *garuda* (the man-bird steed of Vishnu and mortal enemy of the *nagas*), the *kala* (the guardian face of a demon commanded to devour itself), *simhas* (mythological form of lions), *makaras* (marine monsters with, usually, the body of a crocodile and an elephant-like snout) and *hamsas* (sacred geese).

Bronze Ganesha, 12th century (Khon Kaen Museum).

Statue of Brahma in the Baphuon style.

Buddhism was the other principal religion. Its two forms are Mahayana ('Greater Vehicle') and Theravada (also known as Hinayana – 'Lesser Vehicle' – a term not surprisingly considered derogatory by its followers). The Buddhism practised throughout Southeast Asia today is Theravada – the more traditional and conservative form – but at the time of the Khmer Empire, Buddhist worship was exclusively Mahayanist.

Mahayana Buddhism seems to have played a more important role in what is now Thailand than in Cambodia – or at least, it was important over a longer period. At Angkor, it made its major appearance at the end of the 12th century with the accession of Jayavarman VII, but on the Khorat Plateau it was established

Bronze Buddha image protected by naga, 13th century.

much earlier. The temple of Phimai, in particular, was a centre of Buddhist worship. After the 7th century, Tantric thought began to infiltrate both Buddhism and Hinduism, and makes an important appearance at Phimai. Tantra is 'the doctrine and ritual of the left hand', in which the female force, or *shakti*, plays a dominant role in the universe. This esoteric belief involved many magical and mystical rituals, and female divinities played an increasing part. Vajrayana Buddhism was a development of Tantric thought, and had elaborate iconography. It was named after *vajra*, meaning thunderbolt or diamond, thus thunderbolts appear as its symbol in the shape of arrows and tridents, while the diamond represents pure and indestructible knowledge and virtue.

One of the characteristics of Mahayana Buddhism is the number of *bodhisattvas* literally 'Buddhas-to-be', beings who had voluntarily halted their progress on the path to Buddhahood, stopping just short of Enlightenment in order to be able to assist mankind. In some ways they were the Buddhist equivalent of saints, and their proliferation (particularly under Vajrayana Buddhism) gave the religion some of the characteristics of Hinduism, with its pantheon of gods. The iconography at Phimai, for instance, is complex and varied.

Khmer temples are full of symbolism – not just in the details of lintels and pediments, but in the architecture itself, and on the largest scale. One of the pleasurable surprises in discovering Khmer architecture is to realise that the logic behind it is an attempt to recreate an entire cosmology on Earth. Jeannine Auboyer wrote that "Indian architectural symbolism, even within India itself, was never interpreted with more precision than in the Khmer Empire". The large temples, such as Phimai, Phnom Rung, Preah Vihear and Muang Tam, are nothing less than great models in stone of the universe. Both the Hindu and Buddhist universes share the same essential components: a succession of concentric mountain ranges and seas surrounding a central continent, out of the centre of which rises Mount Meru, the five-peaked home of the gods. That the gods of the Khmer universe inhabited mountain tops attracted the builders to any natural prominence, hence the hill-top temples of Khao Noi, Phnom Rung, Preah Vihear and Wat Phu (this last on the slopes of a mountain topped with an enormous natural *linga*).

Hills and mountains, of course, make their own topographical demands, and are not necessarily located conveniently for administration, trade and settlement. Temples on the level plateau, such as Phimai, Muang Singh and Muang Tam, were often designed for a closer resemblance to the concentric layout of seas and mountain ranges. Moats, ponds, enclosure walls and galleries were the means, in the large temples forming a series of nested enclosures.

The centrepiece in each case is the sanctuary tower built over the shrine. In the majority of temples there is just one shrine and tower, but in some there is a group, commonly three or five. Given the five peaks of Mount Meru, the latter number had a special significance. In what Claude Jacques calls 'State Temples' (successive principal temples at the Khmer capital), five towers were often arranged in a quincunx, in faithful imitation of Mount Meru's peaks – four smaller ones surrounding a large central tower. Unusually, there is an example of this in Northeast Thailand, at Sikhoraphum – unusual in that this is quite a small foundation and certainly no State Temple.

One further piece of symbolism that establishes the larger temples as microcosms of the universe involves the *nagas*, the serpent rulers of the underworld – the subterranean reaches of Mount Meru. *Nagas* themselves are rich in symbolism in both Hinduism and Buddhism: they play a part in a number of key events, including creation myths, and are associated with water and fertility. But their serpentine bodies can also represent the rainbow, which in Khmer cosmology is a bridge between heaven and earth. The main entrance to a number of significant Khmer temples is in the form of a causeway flanked by *nagas*, the symbolism being that, this is the bridge from the world of men to the abode of the gods. The *naga*
'bridges' at Phimai, Phnom Rung and Preah Vihear are particularly prominent.

Almost certainly, the religious symbolism which dictated the form of Khmer temples also influenced the details of the architecture. Although there is no general agreement among archaeologists and architects, the dimensions and proportions of the buildings probably followed a precise system. This may have been arithmetical or religious or both, and various attempts have been made to show how the ground plans for temples were arrived at. No contemporary Khmer architectural texts have been found – there was no Khmer equivalent of Palladio – and this has left the matter open to some ingenious explanations.

Naga antefix on the tower of Phnom Rung.

The models worked on have so far been in Cambodia, but they translate to Thailand.

American art historian Eleanor Mannika proposes numerology as the basis for temple plans, based on her studies of Angkor Wat. In this, key numbers from Hindu cosmology are used as units of measurement. Another system, after Matila Ghyka and René Dumont, uses basic geometry. Applied to the simplest type of sanctuary, a redented square cell with one doorway, a sequence of circles can give all the dimensions and angles. The type example of this is the southern sanctuary of Banteay Srei, north-east of Angkor. Starting with the doorway as the 'module', the plan can be drawn with no more than a compass and a straight line. And, as Dumont points out, circles are simply drawn with only a length of cord attached to a central point. Nevertheless, the basic dimensions are even simpler than this: the sides of the square interior of the cell are twice the width of the doorway, and the exterior sides are twice as large again, and although a succession of circles and intersections can explain the redenting, they are by no means essential.

The three most common Hindu icons found in Khmer temples in Thailand are Vishnu Reclining *(Vishnu Anantasayin)*, Shiva Dancing *(Shiva Nantaraj)* and Shiva riding with Uma on the bull Nandi *(Umamahesvara)*; these occur mainly on pediments and lintels. There is less surviving Buddhist imagery built into the architecture, despite the strong Mahayana and even Tantric tradition in the upper Mun Valley in the Northeast. There is, however, a great deal of statuary, and by far the most common image is that of the Buddha meditating while sheltered by the *naga* Muchalinda.

In addition to these representations, certain scenes and stories recur, drawn mainly from Hindu epics and texts. The Ramayana furnishes the material for many lintels and pediments; even when the episodes depicted are obscure, the presence of certain characters, such as monkey troops, is a fairly strong indication. Scenes from the life of Krishna also occur, as does the Churning of the Sea of Milk, although this last does not play the same important role in Thailand as it does in the architecture and bas-reliefs at Angkor.

The more popular motifs are:–

Vishnu Reclining, depicted at:

Ku Suan Taeng (E lintel, N tower, at the National Museum, Bangkok)
Phnom Rung (E lintel, *mandapa*)
Preah Vihear (S outer lintel, main door, *Gopura III*)
Kamphaeng Yai (Inner lintel, N library)
Narai Jaeng Waeng (N pediment)

Vishnu on Garuda, depicted at:

Phnom Wan (lintel at Phimai Museum)
Phimai (cornice level, faces of the sanctuary tower)
Wat Phu (E lintel, N door of E entrance to *mandapa*)

Vishnu Vamanavatara, depicted at:

Muang Khaek (lintel at Phimai Museum)
Ku Suan Taeng (lintel at Phimai Museum)

Shiva Dancing, depicted at:

Phimai (S pediment, *mandapa*)
Phnom Rung (E pediment, *mandapa*)
Sikhoraphum (E lintel, central tower)
Narai Jaeng Waeng (E pediment)

Shiva with Uma on Nandi, depicted at:

Muang Khaek (gable fragment at Phimai Museum)
Muang Tam (E lintel, N tower of front row)
Preah Vihear (S inner pediment, main door, *Gopura III*)
Kamphaeng Yai (S pediment, central tower; inner lintel, S library)
Wat Phu (E pediment, N 'palace')

Shiva as supreme ascetic, depicted at:

Phnom Rung (E pediment, central doorway of E *Gopura*)

Indra on Airavata, depicted at:

Muang Khaek (lintel at Phimai Museum)
Ku Suan Taeng (E lintel, S tower, at Khon Kaen Museum)
Preah Vihear (S inner pediment, *Gopura III*)
Ban Phluang (S lintel; single-headed Airavata, E lintel & N pediment)
Huei Thamo (scattered lintels and pediments)
Wat Phu (inner lintel, *mandapa*)

Ramayana, depicted at:

Phimai (both W & E lintels & pediments, *mandapa*)
Phnom Rung (W & N pediments, sanctuary tower; N pediment, *antarala*;
N pediment, mandapa; E pediment, N doorway of E *Gopura*)
Preah Vihear (possibly – S lintel, main door, *Gopura III*)
Kamphaeng Yai (possibly – S lintel, central sanctuary tower)

Shiva and Uma on the bull Nandi.

Krishna fighting a lion and elephant - lintel at Phimai.

Life of Krishna

J ust before the present era, demons threatened the order of the universe, and the Earth goddess pleaded with Vishnu for help. The principal demon was Kamsa who, though once killed by Vishnu, had returned to Earth. Vishnu plucked two hairs from his head, one fair and one dark, and these became two half-brothers, Krishna and Balarama. Kamsa learns of their presence on Earth, and for protection they are forced to spend their childhood disguised as cowherds. In one scene, Krishna uses his supernatural powers to shelter the cattle he tends from a storm unleashed by the sky god Indra, by holding aloft Mount Govardhana. In other episodes he battles the forces of evil: tearing apart the wicked *naga* Kaliya, fighting various animals sent to kill him including the bull Arishta, the horse Kesin, the elephant Kuvalayapida and the lion Simha, and ultimately killing Kamsa himself.

Krishna Govardhana, depicted at:

Muang Tam (lintel of NW tower)
Preah Vihear (N inner pediment, main door, *Gopura* III)
Ban Phluang (E pediment)
Kamphaeng Yai (N pediment, central tower)

Krishna fighting the *naga* Kaliya, depicted at:

Phnom Rung (lintel at the National Museum, Bangkok)
Muang Tam (E lintel, main door of E *Gopura* II, W lintel, E *Gopura* I)
Ban Phluang (N lintel)

Krishna fighting lions and elephants, depicted at:

Phimai (lintel over E entrance to 'library')
Phnom Rung (N lintel, *antarala*)
Preah Vihear (N outer pediment, main door, *Gopura* III)
Sikhoraphum (lintel at Phimai Museum)
Narai Jaeng Waeng (E lintel and N lintel)
Ban Rabang (lintel at Phimai Museum)
Wat Mahathat, Lopburi (S lintel, *mandapa*)

Krishna fighting horses, depicted at:

Phimai (N lintel, Prang Brahmadat)
Preah Vihear (N outer pediment, E door, *Gopura* III)
Kamphaeng Yai (Outer lintel, N library)

Krishna killing Kamsa, depicted at:

Muang Khaek (possibly – unfinished lintel at Phimai Museum)
Phimai (E lintel, sanctuary tower)
Wat Phu (inner lintel, S entrance, *mandapa*)

Churning of the Sea of Milk, depicted at:

Ku Suan Taeng (lintel at Phimai Museum)
Preah Vihear (S pediment, main door, *Gopura* IV)

Buddha under *naga*, depicted in statue form from many locations, at all museums.

T Y P E S O F T E M P L E S

Most Khmer temples derive from Indian models, and the more complex constructions owe much to those of the Chola dynasty in southern India. There was nevertheless an evolution over the centuries, as the ambitions of the builders grew. The earliest sanctuaries were single shrines, but this design was later expanded to a number of sanctuary towers on the same platform. The size and shape of the tower built over the shrine also evolved, eventually becoming, by the time of the building of Angkor Wat and Phimai, the most characteristic feature of Khmer temple architecture.

It even outlasted the Khmer empire, being taken up by the Siamese in the form of the *prang*. In Thailand, this is the term used to describe Khmer towers such as that at Phimai and at Phnom Rung, although inaccurately, as it was never used in Cambodia. Strictly speaking, it refers specifically to later towers in Khmer style (there was a 'Khmer Revival' period when Ayutthaya became the Siamese capital). More accurately, *prasat* is the usual term for a sanctuary tower, although in Thailand it is often used to refer to the entire temple. The various types of Khmer temple found in Thailand and Laos are the following:

▲
Single Sanctuary

Surrounded by a moat and often in a small enclosure. The enclosing wall typically has a single eastern *gopura*, and a single 'library' facing west, located in the south-east corner of the enclosure. There may be a small *baray* or pond to the east, often on the axis of the temple. *Examples: Ban Phluang, Muang Gao.* A similar layout was also used for the chapels for hospitals from the reign of Jayavarman VII in the 13th Century. *Examples: Prang Ku, the two Kuti Reussis, Ta Muen Toch, Kamphaeng Noi.*

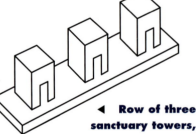

◄ **Row of three sanctuary towers,**
Normally facing east. Sometimes in an enclosure with at least an eastern *gopura*, and sometimes with one or two west-facing 'libraries' in the eastern part of the enclosure. *Examples: Khao Noi, Ku Suan Taeng, Bai Baek, Wat Si Sawai.*

◄ **Double row of sanctuary towers,**
Three in front, two behind, in an enclosure with *gopuras*, and normally with two 'libraries' in the usual position facing towards and located in front of the towers). *Examples: the central complex of Muang Tam, Kamphaeng Yai.*

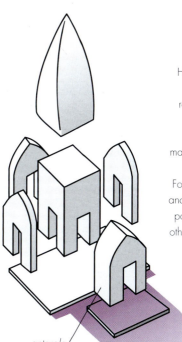

◄ Single dominant tower,

Highly developed architecturally, connected by a vestibule *(antarala)* at the front to a rectangular antechamber *(mandapa)*. These three structures together form a single architectural unit, and lie at the centre of a major temple's principal enclosure. *Examples: Phimai, Phnom Rung, Preah Vihear.*
For major temples, the plan is more complex, and the arrangement of the towers is the focal point of a larger distribution of buildings and other structures. There are two kinds of layout, both found in this northern part of the former Khmer Empire:

antarala

mandapa

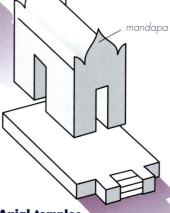

Concentric layout of enclosures and moats

The sequence of wall, galleries and moats represents the concentric mountain ranges and seas surrounding the central continent and Mount Meru. Typically, there might be an outer wall and two enclosures, with a moat or four corner ponds within the outer enclosure. *Examples: Phimai, Banteay Chhmar, Muang Tam, Muang Singh.* (not illustrated)

Axial temples,

in which the structures are laid out in line, ending with the sanctuary and its surrounding enclosure. The three most famous temples with this plan are all in this region, two in Thailand, one in Laos, and all are axial for the same reason, to take advantage of the slope of a prominent hill. *Examples: Phnom Rung, Preah Vihear, Wat Phu.*

◄ Quincunx of towers

On a central platform, the central, principal tower being the largest. The cosmological symbolism is obvious (➥ see p. 22), but such a layout is normally reserved for major temples, and in particular temple-mountains. *Example: Sikhoraphum.*

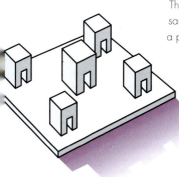

The three building materials used by the Khmers were brick, sandstone and laterite, but the importance of each changed over the centuries. The earliest temples were in brick, the easiest medium to work in. It was not, however, used exclusively because of its limitations. Door frames and windows were always in stone, with the lintels and pilasters bearing the load. At its best, Khmer brickwork was of a high order – the size of the individual bricks was small by modern standards (on average about 30 x 15 x 7cm), allowing a detailed and often delicate effect from a distance, while the bonding was made not with mortar but a vegetable compound, which was both strong and virtually without thickness. In some instances, the brick was carved directly with designs: in Thailand there are examples at Yai Ngao, Muang Tam and Khao Noi, although brick carving never reached the peaks of the bas-reliefs at Prasat Kravan at Angkor.

Sandstone was altogether more difficult to work, requiring more labour (for

Pediment in the style of Banteay Srei from Phimai Museum.

Redented brickwork at Sikhoraphum.

transporting, dressing and lifting into place), and importantly, labour that was skilled. The jointing and dressing of blocks took much longer than simply laying courses of bricks. New types of joint had to be worked out in order to hang lintels and fit various parts together; metal bars were sometimes used, clamping blocks by means of shaped holes cut into the stone. Nevertheless, once the Khmer builders had gained confidence in using sandstone, they were able to take on much larger projects. In particular, they were able to realise the ambitions of their rulers to

31

Stone window balusters at Muang Tam.

create microcosms of the universe on a grand architectural scale. Sandstone had always been used for decoration – lintels especially – but when it formed the main structure of the temple, friezes and bas-relief panels could be applied directly. Phnom Rung is an outstanding example of an entire sanctuary that is for the most part decoratively carved.

Despite their mastery of many building techniques, the Khmers never adequately solved the problem of roofing their structures. They were not heirs to any architectural traditions that included arching and vaulting, and never discovered it for themselves. Instead, roofs were closed by the technically primitive device of making each successive course project a little over the one below, until the sides finally met at the top. Known as corbelling, this prevented the Khmers from spanning large interiors; galleries and shrines remained narrow and cramped. It is argued that this was not particularly important, given that the central sanctuary was a place for rituals performed by priests and ruler alone, and there was no need to shelter a congregation. However, temples like Preah Vihear and Phimai show a love of building on a grand scale where possible, and if the Khmers had acquired the means to create large spaces by vaulting – as was happening in Europe at exactly that time – it is very likely that they would have taken full advantage. Sandstone building reached its peak during the Angkor Wat period in the early and middle 12th century. Not surprisingly, this was also the architectural peak for the Khmers.

Laterite is a type of iron-rich clay quite common in mainland Southeast Asia. It is easy to cut out of the ground, but after exposure to the air and sun dries very hard. Its pitted structure when dry makes it impossible to work finely, but it is ideal for foundations and the core of buildings faced in stone or brick. When stone was the main material used, laterite often furnished the foundations and platforms and less important structures such as outer enclosing walls. Laterite was also used decorated with stucco; this became the main construction method in Thailand during Jayavarman VII's ambitious building programme at the end of the 12th and beginning of the 13th centuries. Examples of this are Muang Singh, and the various chapels of hospitals and rest-houses.

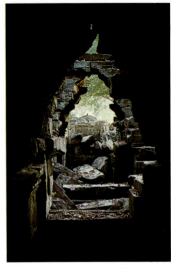
Vaulting over gallery, Angkor.

CHANGING STYLES

Angkor Wat-style 'narrative' lintel showing Krishna, at Phimai Museum.

The obvious and convenient way of visiting the Khmer temples is by location – for instance, starting with those around Khorat and working your way east – but their chronology followed no such direction. Inevitably, you will see temples out of their date order, and for this reason it helps to have an idea of the different periods of Khmer architecture and art. The table on pages 34 and 35 is a quick guide to the succession of styles which developed as building techniques improved and as tastes in decoration changed. It does, however, need to be used with a little caution, for the following reasons.

The accepted sequence, shown in the table, was devised by the French, using models that are, for the most part, at Angkor. There, the different periods make perfect sense. Throughout the rest of the empire, however, this system does not work quite so well. For example, as already mentioned, the Baphuon style from the middle of the 11th century is by far the most common in Thailand, and may well have persisted for longer than it did at the capital, while some of the key features that distinguish a particular style are not found north of the Dongreks – face-towers, for instance, during the Bayon period, or (with two small exceptions) *apsaras* decorating walls and doorways during the time of Angkor Wat.

Another complication is that some temples, especially the larger ones, underwent building and remodelling under different kings. Phimai, Preah Vihear and Wat Phu, to name just three examples, were worked on over several centuries; what you can see now tends, naturally enough, to be from the later periods.

Architectural Styles

Style	Dates	Ruler	Where found in Ankgor
PRE-ANGKOREAN			
Thala Borivat	early 7th C	Isanavarman I	
Sambor Prei Kuk	c.600-635	Bhavavarman II	
Prei Kmeng	c.635-700		
Kompong Preah	c.706-825		
TRANSITIONAL			
Kulen	c.825-875	Jayavarman II	
ANGKOREAN			
Preah Kô	c.875-893	Indravarman I	Preah Kô, Bakor
Bakheng	c.893-925	Yasovarman I	Bakheng, Phnon Krom, Phom Bc
Koh Ker	c.921-945	Jayavarman IV	Prasat Kravan (b mainly at Koh K
Pre Rup	c.947-965	Rajendravarman II	Pre Rup, East Mebon
Banteay Srei	c.967-1000	Jayavarman V	Banteay Srei
Khleang	c.965-1010	Jayavarman V, Suryavarman I	The Khleangs, T. Keo Phimeanaka
Baphuon	c.1010-1080	Udayadityavarman II	Baphuon
Angkor Wat	c.1100-1175	Suryavarman II	Angkor Wat, Banteay Samré, Thommanon
Bayon	c.1177-1230	Jayavarman VII	Bayon, Preah Kh Ta Prohm (and Banteay Chhma

Where found in Thailand & Laos	Chief Characteristics
	Brick towers, usually single, sometimes two or three in a line.
Khao Noi	
Khao Noi, Phum Phon	
	Brick with stone elements
Phnom Wan (part)	Simple plan: one or more towers on a single base. Extensive use of brick.
Phnom Wan (part), Huei Thamo	Stone used for all important temples.
Muang Khaek, Non Ku, Muang Gao, early Phnom Rung	Scale of buildings diminishes towards center.
	Transitional between Koh Ker and Banteay Srei. Long halls partly enclose sanctuary.
Preah Vihear (part)	Ornate, tiered pediments, sweeping gable ends, rich carving.
Muang Tam (part), Preah Vihear (part)	Galleries used for the first time. Cruciform first time. Cruciform gopuras. Lintels less rich than Banteay Srei.
Muang Tam (part), Sdok Kok Thom, Ta Muen Thom, Ban Phluang, Phnom Wan (part), Preah Vihear (part), Kamphaeng Yai, Narai Jaeng Waeng	A return to rich carving: floral motifs, but also lintels with Vishnuite scenes. Nagas without head-dress. At the Baphuon itself, walls carved with small enclosed scenes.
Phimai, Phnom Rung, Sikhoraphum, Ku Suan Taeng, Yai Ngao, Wat Phu (mainly) Chaosay Tevoda	The high classical style of Khmer architecture. Fully developed conical towers with curved . profile. Nagas with headdress; naga balustrades raised off the ground. Invention of cross-shaped terrace. Richly carved lintels and other decorations. Bas-reliefs. Apsaras.
Prang Ku, Kamphaeng Noi, the Kuti Reussis, Ban Bu, Muang Singh, Ta Muen, Ta Muen Toch, Prang Sam Yod (Lopburi), Prang Kheak (Lopburi)	The last great style. Hurried construction, often using laterite instead of stone, carving less elegant. Complex plans, enormous temples such as Wat Mahathat (Lopburi). In Cambodia face towers, and historical narrative bas reliefs.

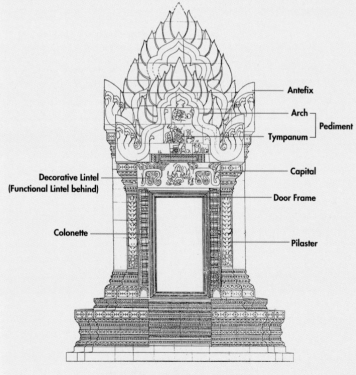

Antefix

Arch
Pediment
Tympanum

Capital

Decorative Lintel
(Functional Lintel behind)

Door Frame

Colonette

Pilaster

KHMER SANCTUARY DOOR

STYLES

OF

LINTELS

The decorative lintels over almost every doorway in a Khmer temple provided the carvers with a standard rectangular frame in which to work. Although by no means the only surfaces that were decorated with reliefs, Khmer lintels were of great importance. They often carried the most significant icons: divinities and scenes from Hindu epics in particular. From their designs and locations, lintels can often be read for information about the temple, such as the god to whom it was dedicated, and the importance of a particular cult. Even more than this, lintels are a means of dating temples. The motifs and styles changed over the centuries, and minute variations have been studied. However, all the models after which the styles were named by French art historians are in Cambodia, and the development of lintels in what is now Thailand did not follow exactly the same course. There are many cases of a style of carving appearing much later than it did in Cambodia, and elements from two styles sometimes appear in the same lintel. Muang Tam, for example, has two Khleang lintels among the other Baphuon ones, even though they were all carved at the same time.

Also, elements from local folk art often creep in to the designs, whether as a naïve treatment or as the occasional erotic gesture (as in the Reclining Vishnu lintel at Kamphaeng Yai).

The interpretation of lintels is a study in itself; for a full treatment, see the standard work by Smitthi Siribhradra and Mayurie Veraprasert (➡Bibliography). In this guide, we describe the lintels as they appear when we walk around the temples, and on the following pages show some of the key points in dating lintels found in Thailand.

Unlike Cambodia, where the style of carving appears in the period of the same name, lintel styles in Thailand sometimes lasted longer, and are found at later dates. The styles named here are from Cambodian prototypes, but these examples are from Thailand. Some of the styles are very poorly represented in Thailand – Kompong Preah, Bakheng, Pre Rup, Banteay Srei and Khleang – while Baphuon lintels are notably abundant.

STYLES OF LINTEL

Thala Borivat

(A variety of Sambor Prei Kuk). Inward-facing short-bodied *makaras*. Two arches joined by central medallion. Small figure on each *makara*.

Sambor Prei Kuk

Inward-facing *makaras* with tapering bodies. Four arches joined by three medallions. Small figure on each *makara*.

Prei Kmeng

Continuation of Sambor Prei Kuk, but *makaras* disappear, being replaced by incurving ends and figures. Arches carry a straight line, and are sometimes rectilinear.

Preah Kô

Kala appears in centre, issuing garland on either side. Distinct loops of vegetation curl down from garland. Outward-facing *makara* sometimes appear at the ends.

Kompong Preah

Arches replaced by a garland of vegetation (like a wreath) more or less segmented. Medallions disappear, central one sometimes replaced by a knot of leaves. Leafy pendants spray out above and below garland.

Bakheng

Continuation of Preah Ko. In Thailand, garland becomes a *naga* (heads facing outwards at the ends). Loops of vegetation below the *naga* form tight, circular coils.

Pre Rup

Tendency to copy earlier styles, especially Preah Ko and Bakheng. Central figures. Reappearance of lower border.

Koh Ker

Centre occupied by a prominent scene, taking up almost the entire height of the lintel. Usually no lower border. Dress of figures shows a curved line to the *sampot* tucked in below waist.

🟨 *Khleang*

Central *kala* with triangular tongue, hands holding garlands, but no other figures. Vegetation above *kala* forms a triangle. Loops of garland on either side divided by floral stalk and pendant. Vigorous treatment of vegetation.

🟨 *Banteay Srei*

Increase in complexity and detail. Garland sometimes makes pronounced loop on either side, with *kala* at top of each loop. Central figure.

🟧 *Bayon*

Most figures disappear: usually only a *kala* surmounted by small figure. Mainly Buddhist motifs. Garland cut into four or more parts – these sometimes become individual shorls of vegetation.

🟥 *Baphuon*

Kala surmounted by divinity, usually riding steed, or a scene from life of Krishna. Loops of garland no longer cut. (In Cambodia there is a second type: a scene with many figures and little vegetation).

🟧 *Angkor Wat*

Two distinct types: 1. Centred, framed and linked by garlands. 2. A scene, often narrative, filled with figures. When *nagas* appear, they are crowned. When there is vegetation, its curls are tight and prominent. *Sampots* and head-dresses on figures are in the Angkor Wat style. No empty spaces. At Phimai: Tantric Buddhist motifs.

Cock fight, bas-relief at the Bayon, Angkor.

Khmer stone inscriptions were concerned exclusively with matters of religion and state. What glimpses they give of the more ordinary basis of life – populations, harvests, produce and so on – come obliquely, such as in the endowment of a temple and the people and provisions needed for its upkeep, and in the lists of public works undertaken by Jayavarman VII. The two most vivid sources of daily life in the Khmer Empire are some of the bas-reliefs, particularly those executed in the reign of Jayavarman VII at the Bayon, and the account written by a member of the Chinese embassy to Cambodia, Chou Ta-Kuan, of his visit from 1296 to 1297. Both of these are relatively late views of Khmer life, and significantly they are accounts of Angkor itself. To what extent they correspond with provincial life is a matter of conjecture. Nevertheless, simply by comparison with life during this century in the countryside – both in Northeast Thailand and lowland Cambodia – there are scenes and descriptions which seem universal:

"Straw thatch covers the dwellings of the commoners, not one of whom would dare place the smallest bit of tile on his roof. In this class, too, wealth determines the size of the house, but no one would venture to vie with the nobility."

"Every man or woman, from the sovereign down, knots the hair and leaves the shoulders bare. Round the waist they wear a small strip of cloth, over which a larger piece is drawn when they leave their houses. Many rules, based on rank, govern the choice of materials."

"Generally speaking, the women, like the men, wear only a strip of cloth, bound round the waist, showing bare breasts of milky whiteness. Their hair is fastened up in a knot, and they go bare-foot."

"Women of the people knot their hair, but there is no sign of hairpins or comb, or any other adornment of the head. On their arms they wear gold bracelets and rings of gold on their fingers: the palace women and court ladies also observe this fashion. Men and women alike are anointed with perfumes compounded of sandalwood, musk, and other essences."

Market scene at the Bayon.

"Market is held every day from six o'clock until noon. There are no shops in which the merchants live; instead, they display their goods on a matting spread upon their ground."

"Men of the people own their houses, but possess no tables, benches, basins, or buckets. An earthenware pot serves to cook the rice, and sometimes an earthenware stove for making sauce. Three stones are buried to form a hearth; ladles are made from coconuts. They also keep beside them a bowl of tin or earthenware filled with water for rinsing the hands, since only their fingers are used in eating rice, which is sticky and could not be got rid of without this water. Wine is drunk from metal goblets; while poor people content themselves with earthenware cups." Interestingly, this is an accurate description of sticky rice (*khao niao* in Thai) which is still the staple in Northeast Thailand, but not in Cambodia.

Rice-eating bas-relief at the Bayon.

One reference to a festival at which rockets are launched sounds so similar to the Rocket Festival held annually at Yasothon and surrounding towns that it is tempting to see an event which has survived intact over the centuries, even though it no longer takes place in Cambodia. The description of the launching towers would serve equally well today.

"In Cambodia the New Year begins with the tenth Chinese moon, and is called *chia-te*. Opposite [the royal palace] rises a lofty scaffold, put

Bas-relief showing rice baskets.

together of light pieces of wood, shaped like the scaffolds used in building stupas, and towering to a height of one hundred and twenty feet. Rockets and firecrackers are placed on top of these...The rockets can be seen at a distance of thirteen kilometres."

In ceremonial life, there is one famous coincidence linking the description of the capital with Phnom Rung. Chou Ta-Kuan goes into great detail about a puberty ceremony in which the priest breaks the hymen of the girl. At the side of the entrance to the central sanctuary at Phnom

Rung is carved a scene that appears to illustrate just this event (described under the temple entry on p. 108). Then there are a number of references specifically to the provinces:

"Although certain fabrics are woven in Cambodia, many are imported from Siam and Champa, preference being given to the Indian weaving for its skill and delicacy."

"The Cambodians are not given to raising silkworms or to cultivating the mulberry tree, and their women are entirely ignorant of sewing, dress-making, and mending. Recently, much attention has been given to Siamese settlers in this country to raising silkworms and cultivating mulberries; their mulberry seed and silkworm stock all come from Siam. The Siamese use silk to weave the dark damask-like textiles with which they clothe themselves. The Siamese women can sew and mend, and when the fabrics worn by the Cambodians become torn, Siamese are called in to repair the damage." The cottage silk industry still flourishes in Thailand's Northeast.

"Dwellers in the remote fastness of the mountains bring out the elephant tusks – two for each dead elephant. It was formerly believed that the elephant grew new tusks each year, but this is not true." The annual Elephant Round-up in Surin, though now very much a tourist show, has genuine origins, for the local Suai people specialised in capturing elephants from the forests to the south, and training them. Until the 1960s, the site of the Round-Up was the Suai village of Ban Ta Klang in Amphoe Krapho; the villagers still train elephants, but no longer hunt them wild in Cambodia.

"Along the highways there are resting places like our post halts; these are called *sen-mu (samnak)*." These are the *dharmasalas*, or rest-houses – the laterite chapels of which survive at Ta Muen, Ban Bu and Banteay Chhmar (in the area covered by this guide).

Fighting with elephants - the royal terraces at Angkor.

DISCOVERY
AND
RESTORATION

Muang Singh before reconstruction (compare with page 238).

Until quite recently – the early 1960s – these monuments stood neglected, a condition that was not necessarily to their disadvantage. The questions of when to restore, to what extent and in what manner are vexed ones. The interests of those involved, which include archaeologists, provincial and national government, local inhabitants and visitors, do not all coincide. From one point of view, full restoration is the ideal, involving a full rebuilding to its original state, even if this requires new stones or bricks carved to replace lost ones. At the opposite end of the scale is the view that these monuments are at their most evocative and rewarding when left as they are, bar the minimum emergency work to prevent further collapse.

The restoration of Prasat Kamphaeng Yai.

In restoration, there are conflicting opinions, and conflicting interests also. The choices range all the way from making the least possible disturbance to a site up to a full rebuilding, using new materials and adding parts (including decorative elements) that are missing. The interested parties, who each have different needs and priorities, include archaeologists, art historians, the national government bodies under whose jurisdiction the sites fall, the tourist industry, local government and international aid agencies. In numbers, the people who make the most use of these monuments are ordinary visitors with no professional interest, but their views are rarely sought. Tourists, indeed, are often seen by government agencies principally as a source of revenue, and this naturally colours official policy towards the temples. Increasingly, development around ancient monuments is geared to attracting more visitors and encouraging those who do come to spend more.

The Khmer temples in Thailand and Laos have variously received the full range

East facade, Phnom Rung.

of attention, from neglect to over-enthusiastic remodelling. Most of the restoration work has been comparatively recent, and all of it has occurred since the early 1960s. This contrasts with the treatment of the Khmer sites in Cambodia, for historical reasons. The French colonisation of Indochina made it possible for French archaeologists, epigraphers and art historians to undertake detailed studies and extensive restoration, under the umbrella of the École Française d'Extrême Orient. Thailand's independence, however, attracted few foreign scholars, and the Northeast has traditionally been the country's neglected backwater – poor, under-developed and under-supported.

Nevertheless, the Khmer monuments beyond Cambodia did receive some attention, if no physical assistance. Two classic studies were made at the beginning of the century – the inventories of Khmer temples by Lunet de Lajonquière and Etienne Aymonier. These were later elaborated on, particularly by Henri Parmentier and Jean Boisselier, and added to by Thai historians, from Prince Damrong to, more recently, H.R.H. Princess Mahachakri Sirindhorn, M.C. Subhadradis Diskul and Smitthi

Siribhadra.

Restoration in Thailand began with the surveys carried out in the late 1950s by the Fine Arts Department, followed at many sites by a preliminary excavation. The country's two principal sites, Phimai and Phnom Rung, were the first to be fully restored (Preah Vihear, known to the Thais as Khao Phra Viharn, ceased to be a part of Thailand in 1907). At Phimai, a study by B. P. Groslier laid the groundwork for a programme under the direction of Prince Subhad, from 1964 to 1969. Phnom Rung's even more extensive restoration followed this, from 1972-1988. These two major temples, however, were considered the jewels in the crown of Khmer sites on the Khorat Plateau, and the many others were generally of less interest. Thus even important sites like Muang Tam, only a twenty-minute drive from Phnom Rung, existed until recently in a state of benign neglect, gradually subsiding into the ground.

This state of affairs began to change with the boom in Thailand's economy in the 1980s. The Northeast belatedly received government financing, under the banner of a programme called Green Isaan, and this included the restoration and development of the region's historical sites. One of the main reasons for this is that the Northeast's Khmer temples are among its very few potential tourist attractions: there are no beaches and the landscape can most charitably be described as flat and usually dusty. When a budget exists, it is usually easier to do something to an archaeological site than to leave it untouched, and the number of neglected Khmer temples is now steadily decreasing.

The restoration treatment which involves the least alteration relies on shoring up parts likely to collapse further, using concrete and iron bands. The type example of this approach is Ta Prohm in Angkor, where the French deliberately left the site in as close a condition as possible to that in which it was rediscovered in the nineteenth century. The intention was to give visitors an idea of how such temples appeared before the full restoration that was applied to most of the others.

So, for example, a collapsing door frame with a broken lintel was simply shored up with a concrete beam cast to shape. While the undergrowth was kept reasonably clear, the ficus and silk-cotton tress were left intact, their roots intertwined among the stones. Not surprisingly, this preservation of a temple in its discovered, unaltered state, has always been popular with visitors for its romantic atmosphere. It has generally been less popular, however, among archaeologists, many of whom would prefer to see a complete restoration. In Thailand, this minimum-interference approach has never been applied, and although Ta Muen Thom, in its forested location, would have been an ideal candidate, it has received a rather more vigorous treatment.

The more usual restoration methods are more far-reaching, and owe a great deal to techniques developed by the French at Angkor Wat, the Bayon, Banteay Srei and other Cambodian temples. The term *anastylosis* was coined to describe an extremely thorough method whereby the ruins are surveyed down to the last stone, all of which are numbered. Parts may even be disassembled; finally the structure is completely rebuilt using the original

Pediment from the south side of tower, Prasat Ban Phluang.

materials, adding where necessary new parts to replace those missing. It was first attempted, with great success, at Banteay Srei a little north of Angkor, building on Dutch experience in Indonesia.

This approach places considerable onus on the restorers to be careful and accurate. What should happen is that the rebuilding is preceded by a careful excavation so that no important archaeological information is lost. At Ban Phluang in Surin Province, for example, the excavations revealed the broken remains of hundreds of ceramic vessels in positions demonstrating that they were used ritually.

Equally, however, there are cases where the excavation programme was undertaken too hurriedly, and the original disposition of the site is no longer properly known. This happened at Muang Singh, for example, while at the *baray* of Muang Tam, digging by the municipality displaced the original laterite blocks that bordered the artificial basin.

At Ban Phluang, the stones recovered produced a structure that ended just above the cornice level, leaving the question of whether or not there had ever been a tower above (for one reason or another, the building of many temples was not completed), and if so, in what materials. The presence of bricks scattered around the site suggested that these may have been used in a superstructure, but in the absence of any conclusive evidence the sanctuary was completed only up to the cornice. In the contrasting case of Muang Singh, the *gopuras* have been rebuilt in a form that a number of archaeologists consider imaginative.

When new elements are added, whether stone or laterite blocks, or bricks, there is again a difference of opinion, between on the one hand trying to blend the repair in with the original materials, and on the other making it obvious which parts are new. The danger of blending in by means of a kind of architectural invisible mending is that the new parts may be mistaken in detail for the original. If they are decorative, this matters even more. One solution, which can be seen at Phimai, for example, is to use the same building material (such as stone from the inside of a tower) but to leave the blocks roughly dressed.

Another method, less elegant but honest, is to use a material such as concrete that stands out very clearly as being a part of the restoration. Brick and laterite, being easier to work and use than sandstone, offer more temptation to rebuild imaginatively rather than accurately. The recent additions to the brick sanctuaries at Kamphaeng Yai, for example, will eventually weather well enough to look old, but the plans to which they were built are open to question.

The most controversial approach is the remodelling of decorative, non-structural pieces, such as the *naga* heads on the balustrades at Phnom Rung. Although the argument for this is to give visitors an impression of the temple as it was intended by its original builders, the authenticity suffers considerably. This approach also draws attention to any shortcomings in carving ability by modern workmen. Such additions in sandstone nevertheless have more integrity than decorative repairs to stucco, which was used in late Khmer temples to cover laterite. The restoration of the stucco decoration on the towers at Wat Si Sawai in Sukhothai is particularly egregious for using cement.

Finally, alterations which essentially convert sites into tourist parks are the most objectionable of all. New pathways, flower beds, lights and so on, only serve to trivialise a site. Fortunately, they can be removed – and certainly should be.

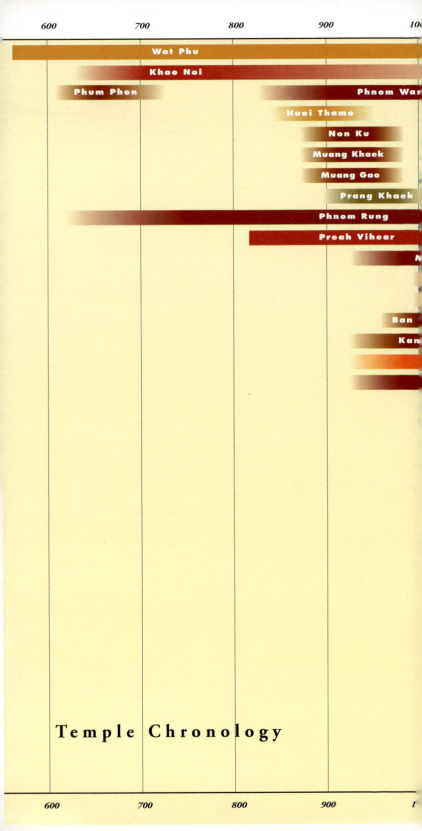

600	700	800	900	100

Wat Phu

Khao Noi

Phum Phon

Phnom War

Huei Thamo

Non Ku

Muang Khaek

Muang Gao

Prang Khaek

Phnom Rung

Preah Vihear

Ban

Kan

Temple Chronology

600	700	800	900	1

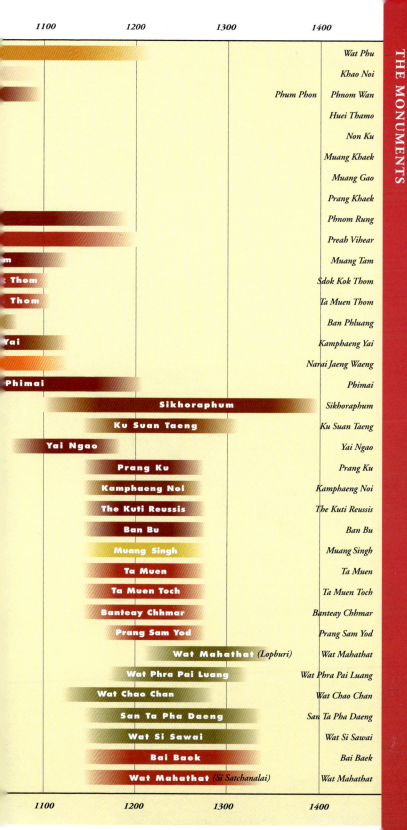

1100	1200	1300	1400	
				Wat Phu
				Khao Noi
			Phum Phon	Phnom Wan
				Huei Thamo
				Non Ku
				Muang Khaek
				Muang Gao
				Prang Khaek
				Phnom Rung
				Preah Vihear
				Muang Tam
				Sdok Kok Thom
				Ta Muen Thom
				Ban Phluang
				Kamphaeng Yai
				Narai Jaeng Waeng
				Phimai

Sikhoraphum — Sikhoraphum

Ku Suan Taeng — Ku Suan Taeng

Yai Ngao — Yai Ngao

Prang Ku — Prang Ku

Kamphaeng Noi — Kamphaeng Noi

The Kuti Reussis — The Kuti Reussis

Ban Bu — Ban Bu

Muang Singh — Muang Singh

Ta Muen — Ta Muen

Ta Muen Toch — Ta Muen Toch

Banteay Chhmar — Banteay Chhmar

Prang Sam Yod — Prang Sam Yod

Wat Mahathat *(Lopburi)* — Wat Mahathat

Wat Phra Pai Luang — Wat Phra Pai Luang

Wat Chao Chan — Wat Chao Chan

San Ta Pha Daeng — San Ta Pha Daeng

Wat Si Sawai — Wat Si Sawai

Bai Baek — Bai Baek

Wat Mahathat *(Si Satchanalai)* — Wat Mahathat

THE MONUMENTS

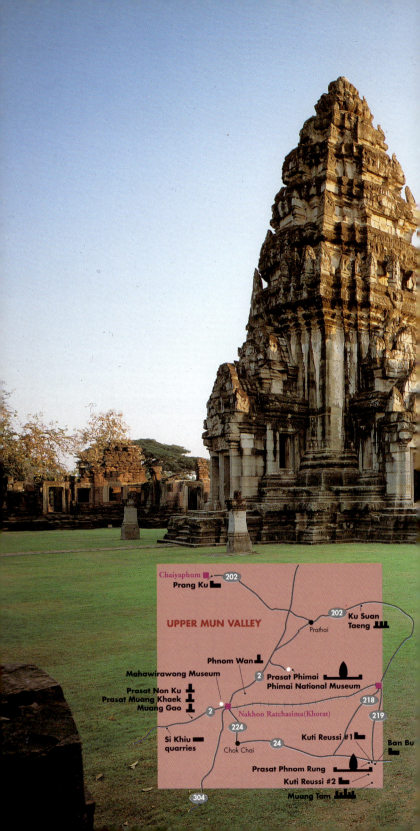

Chaiyaphum ▪
Prang Ku ◼ — 202

UPPER MUN VALLEY

202 — **Ku Suan Taeng** ◼

Prathai •

Phnom Wan ◼

Mahawirawong Museum

2 — **Prasat Phimai**
Phimai National Museum

Prasat Non Ku ◼
Prasat Muang Khaek ◼
Muang Gao ◼

2 — **Nakhon Ratchasima (Khorat)** ▪

218

219

Si Khiu quarries ◼

224

Chok Chai •

24

Kuti Reussi #1 ◼

Ban Bu ◼

Prasat Phnom Rung ◼

Kuti Reussi #2 ◼

304

Muang Tam ◼

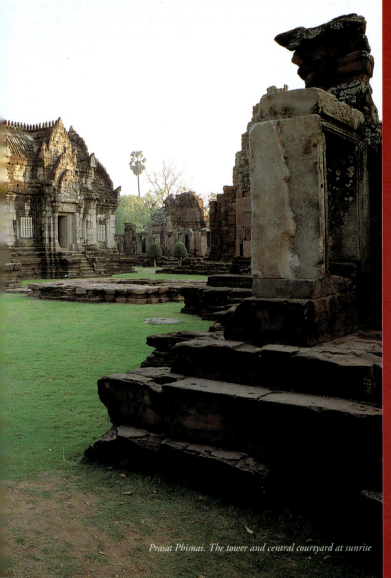

NORTHEAST
UPPER MUN VALLEY

Prasat Phimai. The tower and central courtyard at sunrise

The eastern third of Thailand, forming a great bulge on the map that borders the Mekong River in the east and Cambodia to the south, is known as Isaan. This is the country's traditionally poor region, frequently beset by drought. Recent government investment here has caused some changes, but these are more visible around the main towns such as Nakhon Ratchasima and Khon Kaen. The north and west of Isaan are generally more prosperous than the southern area – where the majority of Khmer temples were built. In the south-west of the region, which is the first part that you reach on the road or railway line from Bangkok, the land rises to around 200 m. This is the Khorat Plateau, and the hills that mark its western edge are the source of the many streams that flow eastwards in the direction of the city of Nakhon Ratchasima (Khorat). These coalesce to form the Mun River that eventually joins the Mekong above Pakxé, and it is this broad valley of the Mun that was the centre of Khmer civilisation in the region.

Si Khiu Quarry 🔴 แหล่งหินตัดสีคิ้ว

Si Khiu Quarry, Khorat.

On the road from Bangkok to the Northeast, this is the first Khmer site on the plateau, and one of only two known stone quarries of the period in the country. Conveniently, it lies right on the main road, and requires no effort to visit. The interest lies in the many partly cut blocks evidently intended to be lintels, roof finials, and so on.

The main road cuts through the quarry (*laeng hin tad* in Thai), which occupies the lower ridge of a line of hills running south-east to join the Dongrek Mountains, and what remains now lies to the south. The slope of the hill that overlooks the road is almost entirely incised with narrow vertical trenches, but most of the rectangular blocks, which need only cutting through at the base, are *in situ*. A few circular incisions were probably intended as lotus-flower finials for towers. The quarry continued on the other side of the hill, to the south, but here all the stone has been removed.

A circular incision may have yielded a lotus-flower finial for a tower.

Best times to visit Any time. **Admission** Unrestricted, no charge. **Nearby sites** Non Ku, Muang Khaek (24 km) and Muang Gao (27 km). **Location** In the Si Khiu district of Nakhon Ratchasima province, on Route 2 east of Khorat city. **By car** *From Bangkok and Saraburi:* Driving towards Khorat on Route 2, look out for the crest of hills that rise to the right of the road after passing the Lam Thakong reservoir, some 220 km from Bangkok and 105 km from Saraburi. A golden *chedi* on the lower part of the ridge identifies the hills. The quarry is at the foot of the ridge; turn right into the new car park on the right of the road, next to the quarry. 3½-4 hrs from Bangkok depending on traffic in the capital, 1½ hrs from Saraburi. *From Khorat:* Continue 2 km past the Si Khiu interchange (Route 201 to Chaiyaphum), itself 47 km east of Khorat. The quarry lies just over the crest, so that you come across it quite suddenly, without warning. 30 mins. **Nearest accommodation and food** Khorat (➻ pp. 264-67).

To Si Khiu

To Khorat

(2)

Quarries

△ chedi

The sanctuary at sunset.

Prasat Non Ku ปราสาทโนนกู่

Date: 1st half of 10th century
Style: Koh Ker
Reign: Jayavarman IV
Visit: 10 mins

Built in the early 10th century, Non Ku is believed to have been, with nearby Muang Khaek, one of the temples of the ancient city of Muang Khorakhopura, which occupied a strategic position close to the western edge of the Khorat Plateau. Apart from the two unusually old 7th-century temples of Khao Noi and Phum Phon, Non Ku and Muang Khaek are among the earliest Khmer monuments in Thailand. Together with Phnom Wan, some 60 km to the east and built around the same time, this pair of temples marks the start of the main period of Khmer building in the Northeast.

Plan

When first surveyed in 1959, Non Ku was no more than a large mound nearly 20 metres across, with the tops of two stone door frames jutting out. Since its excavation and partial restoration, the temple can be seen to have been small but substantially built. The entire enclosure, with brick walls on the northern and southern sides and stone on the eastern and western, measures 32 by 24 metres, with *gopuras* east and west. The sanctuary inside faces east, while in front and to either side are two west-facing 'libraries'.

All that now remains are the bases of these buildings and their door-frames; the tower has long since collapsed. Interestingly, a large amount of sandstone was used

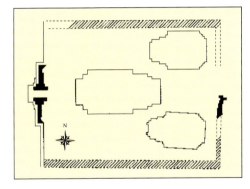

on this small site, even though the two 'libraries' were built of brick. The base of the sanctuary is particularly high – 2 metres – and the bases of the 'libraries' and gopuras are also massive. Perhaps the nearness of the Si Khiu quarries made sandstone the easiest material to use.

Artefacts

Various antefixes and statues have been found, and are now on display at the Mahawirawong Museum, Khorat (↔ p. 61). They include demon-faced guardians, a *garuda*, and small models of the tower. A pediment at the Phimai Museum,(↔ pp. 90-3), recorded as being found here, is in a later style (Banteay Srei, late 10th century), and may not actually have come from Non Ku.

Best times to visit No special time. **Admission** Unrestricted, no charge. **Nearby sites** Muang Khaek (500 m), Muang Gao (4 km), Si Khiu quarry (24 km), Phnom Wan (60 km). **Location** In the Sung Noen district of Nakhon Ratchasima Province, midway between the Lam Thakong reservoir and the city of Khorat. **By car** *From Bangkok*: This is the first Khmer temple on the road to the Northeast. On Route 2 from Bangkok and Saraburi, approaching Khorat and having passed the Lam Thakong reservoir, continue 15 km beyond the Si Khiu interchange (Route 201 to Chaiyaphum) and turn left onto Route 2161 signposted to Amphoe Sung Noen. After 2½ km, just before Sung Noen village, turn right; continue on this road, which curves left after 2 km and crosses the main Northeast railway line (unguarded crossing). From the railway line, Non Ku lies 800m ahead, immediately to the right of the road. 3½- 4 hrs from Bangkok depending on traffic in the capital, 1¾ from Saraburi. *From Khorat*: On Route 2 to Bangkok, pass through the town of Pak Thong Chai and look for the turning right onto Route 2161, 32 km from Khorat. Turn and continue as above. 20 mins. **By bus** *From Khorat*: Take a bus to Sung Noen and there negotiate a *songthaeo* for the remainder of the journey. Consider combining this with a visit to Si Khiu quarry as well as Muang Khaek and Muang Gao.

Nearest accommodation and food Khorat (↔ pp. 264-67).

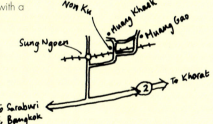

Door frames, steps and base of the central sanctuary.

Prasat Muang Khaek ♠

Date: **1st half of 10th century**
Style: **Koh Ker**
Reign: **Jayavarman IV**
Visit: **20 mins**

ปราสาทเมืองแขก

Just ½ km north of Non Ku, the remains of Muang Khaek are contemporary and related. When first surveyed, Muang Khaek appeared, like Non Ku, to be little more than a large mound with only the tops of the door frames of the sanctuary visible, though surrounded by an ill-defined moat. However, now that the full extent of this 10th century site has been uncovered in recent excavations, beginning in 1990, its considerable importance has been revealed. Because most of the construction was in brick, as at Non Ku, and this has not survived the thousand years that have passed, little remains to give a full impression of Muang Khaek's original appearance. The recent reconstruction has attempted, quite successfully, to remedy this by having a few new courses of brick laid on the sandstone bases.

Plan

Unusually, the orientation is to the north rather than the expected east. Not only is the central sanctuary aligned north-south, but the entrance is through a particularly massive *gopura* on the north side. The wall broken by this *gopura* encloses an area approximately 40m square, and within this a moat 15m wide surrounds the sanctuary and its inner enclosure almost completely – save for a broad causeway on the north. 220m north of the northern *gopura* is the Takhong stream, which might have fed the moat. In front, and on either side of the northern *gopura* are the lower parts of two brick *prasats*, each closely surrounded by brick wall.

Northern *gopura*

Although the usual approach to Muang Khaek is from the south, and the now-dry moat makes it easy to walk straight over to the sanctuary from this direction, walking around to the north side first will give you a better sense of the temple's layout. Only the sandstone base, steps and pillars of the north *gopura* remain; the upper structure, which would originally have been in brick, has long since disappeared (the few bricks are new). There were three windows on each side to the left and right of the doorway, and some of the balusters have been found and replaced.

The massive construction is apparent, but if this is one of the first Khmer temples visited on a tour of the Northeast, what might not be so obvious is the scale. Compared with most other Khmer sanctuaries in Thailand, the *gopura* is much larger than the size of Muang Khaek would seem to merit. The reason is the age and style of the temple, for most of the building work appears to have been carried out in the 10th century at the end of the Koh Ker period. The type example for this style is Prasat Thom at Koh Ker, north-east of Angkor and where the capital was briefly relocated for about 20 years from 921 AD by Jayavarman IV. One of the characteristics of this period of temple building was that the structures decrease in size from the outside towards the central

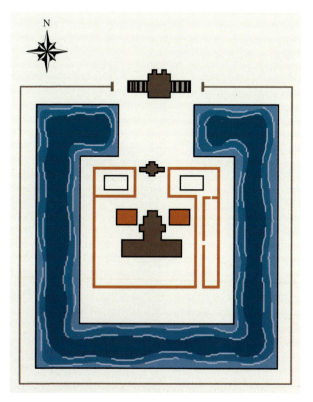

The northern gopura before restoration.

sanctuary. This style of diminishing scale came in turn from Chola temples in Southern India, such as Chidambaram, but later Khmer monuments reversed the principle, striving for an effect of increasing grandeur towards the centre.

Long hall

Within the outer enclosure wall, now only a sandstone base, it seems as if the builders intended to surround the courtyard with long halls. However, only the remains of one, on the east, have been found. Preparation appears to have been carried out for another on the west side.

Having entered through the north *gopura*, walk over to your left, to the foundations of this long hall. Although there is not a great deal to see, the architectural interest is that such long halls were the forerunners of the galleries that became such an important feature in Khmer temples – and which can be seen at Phimai, Phnom Rung and many other sites. Here is another link with Prasat Thom at Koh Ker, where a rectangle made up of closely spaced long chambers, or halls, became a *de facto* gallery surrounding the sanctuary. This was probably the intention here, but the building work was never finished, as often happened. Although there is space for a similar long hall on the other side, no construction was started.

Both the outer and inner walls here were of brick, with rectangular windows regularly spaced in the outer. The ends of the chamber were closed off by brick walls, and the whole would have been roofed with tiles on wooden rafters. A door in the inner wall gave access to the inner courtyard and the sanctuary.

Central sanctuary

At the middle of the site are the base and door-frames of the central sanctuary. The base, which is particularly high

The pedestal for a linga, in the remains of a small brick tower near the northern gopura.

(almost a metre), would have supported the main brick construction, since vanished. The door-frames that are still standing are, in fact, from the *mandapa*, on the north side of the shrine (this is now marked only by a *linga* pedestal on the platform). On either side of the shrine, to the west and east, are extensions to the platform, giving it a T-shape and suggesting that other buildings were intended to have been built – possibly two other towers. A number of bronze objects, including a mirror, palanquin hooks and rings were found in the porch on the north side of the *mandapa*.

Artefacts

There are various antefixes at the Mahawirawong Museum, Khorat, and four lintels, all important, on display at Phimai Museum.

Best times to visit No special time. **Admission** Unrestricted, no charge. **Nearby sites** Non Ku (500m), Muang Gao 3 ½ km, Si Khiu quarry (24 km), Phnom Wan (60 km). **Location** In the Sung Noen district of Nakhon Ratchasima Province, midway between the Lam Thakong reservoir and the city of Khorat. **By car** As for Non Ku; continue ½ km north, turning left at a small cross-roads and continuing for just another 50m. The temple and moat are on the right. **Nearest accommodation and food** Khorat (➡ pp. 264-67).

Muang Gao   ปราสาทเมืองเก่า

Date: *1st half of 10th century*
Style: *Koh Ker*
Reign: *Jayavarman IV*
Visit: *10 mins*

Although smaller and less interesting than Muang Khaek, it has recently been restored and is worth including in the side trip to the old temples of Muang Khorakhopura. Note in particular the strange proportions of this stone and laterite monument, in which the single eastern *gopura* is the most massive element.

Plan

Essentially this fits the pattern of the simplest Khmer temple layout, with a single sanctuary tower set in a small walled enclosure, a single eastern *gopura* and an offset 'library' facing west. Here, however, the sandstone *gopura* dwarfs the sanctuary tower, which is in laterite except for the door frames. The 'library' in the south-east corner is also in sandstone, while the enclosure walls are a mixture of sandstone and laterite blocks. Immediately to the north of the *gopura* is a small rectangular pond, or *srah*, with another, larger pond a short distance to the north-east.

Best time to visit No special time. **Admission** Unrestricted, no charge.
Nearby sites Non Ku (4 km), Muang Khaek (3½ km), Si Khiu quarry (27 km), Phnom Wan (60 km). **Location** In the Sung Noen district of Nakhon Ratchasima Province, midway between the Lam Thakong reservoir and the city of Khorat.
By car As for Non Ku and Muang Khaek as far as the railway line. Then, either turn immediately right on the road signposted to Muang Gao for 3½ km, or else visit Muang Gao after Muang Khaek – this entails going straight east without turning right to go back to Non Ku, and continuing for 3½ km as far as a small cross-roads in front of a modern *wat*. Muang Gao is in the grounds of this *wat*, at the back. Driving times: As for Non Ku.
Nearest accommodation and food Khorat (➡ pp. 264-67).

Uma's hand holding lotus.

Vishnu's hand with conch.

Mahawirawong Museum, Khorat ♣ พิพิธภัณฑ์มหาวีรวงศ์

Although the collection is limited in this small museum, there are some good Khmer pieces, including a fine statue of Brahmani from Phnom Wan, and a four-headed Brahma from Phnom Rung. Artefacts from Muang Khaek and Non Ku include a variety of antefixes (the miniature sanctuary towers are of particular interest) and recently excavated inscriptions.

Stone hands.

Stone Statue of Asura from Prasat Non Ku.

Koh Ker style garuda antefix from Prasat Non Ku.

Antefix from Muang Khaek.

Antefix with rishi from Muang Khaek.

Head of Vishnu from Phnom Wan.

*Antefix with dancing apsara
from Muang Khaek.*

Statue of Brahmani from Phnom Wan.

*Statue of female deity from
Phnom Wan.*

*Statue of seated stone Ganesh from
Phnom Rung.*

Naga head from Phnom Rung.

Buddha sheltered by naga from Phnom Wan.

Statue of Brahma from Phnom Rung.

Seated Ganesh from Phnom Rung.

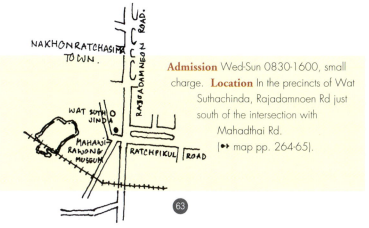

Admission Wed-Sun 0830-1600, small charge. **Location** In the precincts of Wat Suthachinda, Rajadamnoen Rd just south of the intersection with Mahadthai Rd. (➧ map pp. 264-65).

The sanctuary at sunrise from the northern corner.

Phnom Wan ปราสาทพนมวัน

Date: **Late 9th to late 11th centuries**
Styles: **Preah Kô, Bakheng, Baphuon**
Reigns: **Indravarman I, Yasovarman I,**
     Udayadityavarman II, Jayavarman VI
Visit: **30 mins**

On the route from Bangkok, Phnom Wan is the first of the large stone Khmer temples, and although considerably smaller than neighbouring Phimai, it was a religious establishment of importance. In particular, an inscription in Sanskrit and Khmer, still *in situ*, illuminates the early history of this region. As at a number of other, larger Khmer temples, building continued over an extended period (see chart pages 34-35), making it difficult to date precisely, but the inscription from 1082 shows that the major part of the construction must at least have been completed by this date. Also difficult is the history of worship; from statues and other artefacts found here, it is clear that Shiva was the principal deity for some of the time, but both a Vishnu cult and Mahayana Buddhism were practised, the latter probably in the 12th and 13th centuries.

Henri Mouhot, the French explorer credited with the 'discovery' of Angkor, appears to have been the first Westerner to visit the temple, en route to Phimai in February 1861. In a letter to his brother, he wrote "I went to see a temple nine miles east of Khorat, called Penom-Wat … the plan resembles a cross with tolerable exactness. It is composed of two pavilions, with vaulted stone roofs and elegant porticoes. The roofs are from seven to eight metres in height, the gallery three metres wide in the interior, and the walls a metre thick. At each façade of the gallery are two windows with twisted bars.

"This temple is built of red and grey sandstone, coarse in the grain, and in some places beginning to decay. On one of the doors is a long inscription… In one of the pavilions are several Buddhist idols in stone, the largest of which is 2 metres 50 centimetres high, and actually covered with rags. You might easily imagine yourself among the ruins of Ongcor. There is the same style of architecture, the same taste displayed, the same immense blocks polished like marble, and so beautifully fitted together, that I can only compare it to the jointing and planing of so many planks".

Subject to recent restoration, Phnom Wan is a well-proportioned, though incompletely decorated, temple in a pleasant rural setting. The sanctuary itself is still used for worship, though now Theravada Buddhist; the various Buddha images inside, offerings and incense sticks give an attractive sense of continuity to this 9th to 11th century religious foundation.

Plan

The symmetry of the enclosure, combined with the reasonable state of preservation, makes the layout easy to comprehend at a glance. A rectangular gallery with equal-sized *gopuras* set in the centre of each side, and four corner pavilions, surround the courtyard. In the centre, the sanctuary is aligned west-east, and comprises the expected *garbhagrha*, *antarala* and *mandapa* (shrine, vestibule and antechamber). This centred location, while seemingly straightforward, is actually unusual in Khmer temples, where more normally the north and south *gopuras* are aligned with the shrine and its tower, as at Phimai.

The only asymmetrical note is a small square structure south of the sanctuary and offset slightly to the west. There are no 'libraries', which might indicate that the building work was not completed. Originally a moat surrounded the entire enclosure and was noted by Lunet de Lajonquière in his survey, but this can hardly be made out today. Indeed, Etienne Aymonier failed to notice it at all. East of the temple is a 300 x 600m *baray*, or

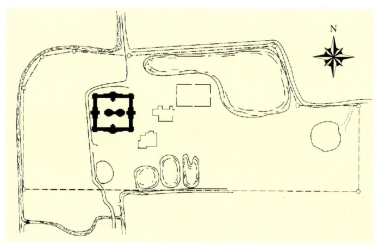

reservoir, connected to the temple by a 330m avenue, while aerial photographs reveal traces of another, even larger *baray*, 1 km in length.

Eastern *gopura* and gallery

Opposite the modern Buddhist wat is the east *gopura* which, though no larger than the other three, is nevertheless the principal entrance to this east-facing temple. To the right and left, though now ruined, galleries run to the square, redented corner pavilions, also collapsed. Closely spaced windows were set in both the inward-facing and outer walls of this gallery, giving it something of the style of a cloister.

Central sanctuary

Passing through the east gopura, walk to the right for a side view of the sanctuary, some 25m long. The tower would have been over the far (western) end – the *garbhagrha* – and although its total collapse gives a false impression of the sanctuary being simply a long low line of buildings, the layout is typical of Khmer temples built on a flat plan during this period.

View from the southern gopura.

Three structures make up the sanctuary, which is aligned west-east and stands exactly in the centre of the enclosure. The *garbhagrha*, at the far right as you face it, is square in plan with four porches. Attached to the east porch is a short narrow vestibule, the *antarala*, which connects with the *mandapa*, which has two side entrances as well as the main door from the east *gopura*.

The main building material used here and throughout the temple is a pale grey sandstone, but note the occasional use of a red sandstone. A number of blocks are just below the *mandapa* roof, while the window balustrades are all in red stone. The

Interior of the sanctuary with more recent Buddha images.

quarries for these stones are not known, but this deliberate two-tone construction is even more evident at nearby Phimai.

Note the way in which the window frames have been assembled on either side of the *mandapa's* north door. The joints are mitred at 45 degrees, a technique which makes little constructional sense in a stone building, despite the small lip at each corner. This is in imitation of wooden buildings, as is the highly distinctive form of Khmer window balusters, which look just as if they had been turned on a lathe.

The plan of the sanctuary gives six exterior doorways, and in typical Khmer fashion these were intended to carry an important sequence of decoration: pilasters, colonettes, lintel and pediment. Of these, the lintel was often the most important for carrying religious icons, but today only the one over the north entrance to the shrine remains *in situ* (others are in the Phimai Museum and the National Museum, Bangkok – see Artefacts below). This is to the right of where you stand, and worth a closer look.

Detailed comparison of the hundreds of lintels from Khmer temples has made it possible to use them for dating (although this has to be done with some caution, is needed as lintels were not always carved at the same time as the buildings were constructed, and were occasionally re-used from earlier temples). This lintel is in the Baphuon style of the 11th century – a style, incidentally, which makes a particularly strong showing in the Northeast of Thailand. The first thing to notice is that the carving is unfinished – by no means uncommon throughout Khmer art and architecture. Only the basic planes of the central *kala* face have been modelled, as has the *naga* arch over the figure. This illustrates something of the way in

Pilaster detail.

which the stone carvers worked, roughing out the volumes first, then completing the detail section by section, leaving the most important to the last.

The lintel's design is typical of the Baphuon period (➡ p. 38). A deity is seated above the head of a *kala*, whose arms grasp the ends of garlands issuing from his mouth. The lines of the foliage give a strong sense of verticality to the design. The pilasters on either side of the door are of the

same period, but the colonettes are plain, the carving not having been started.

Continue round to your right and enter the sanctuary through its rear

Baphuon-style lintel over the north entrance to the shrine.

western doorway. The several Buddha images inside are still worshipped. Close inspection reveals that some of the heads and hands have been added later to the torsos. These replacements have been locally carved to replace the originals taken by thieves. Above, notice the typical Khmer roofing technique that uses corbelled stones (↪ p. 32). The inevitably clumsy appearance of the inside of a corbelled roof was usually concealed by a false wooden ceiling.

Leave the sanctuary by the south door of the shrine, immediately to your right from the way you entered. On the inside of the door-frame is an inscription, one of several found at Phnom Wan, and of considerable historical interest for the region. This is the first mention anywhere of King Jayavarman VI, who ruled from 1080 until his death in 1107. Jayavarman was, in fact, from the local Mahidharapura dynasty, and although the circumstances of his accession are not clear (he may even have seized power), it is known that the introduction of this new line of kings was legitimized with the help of a Brahmin priest, Divakarapandita. It is not even certain that Jayavarman VI even ruled from Angkor; he may have remained here in the North. The inscription instructs priests and dignitaries to maintain this temple, referred to as Ratnapura, and also mentions, for the first time, the temple at Vimayapura (Phimai). One military commander mentioned is Rajendravarman, General of the Army of the Centre, and he is depicted in the famous procession of high dignitaries on the south wall of Angkor Wat's bas-relief galleries (see the *River Books Guide to Angkor*.

Small tower

In the south-west part of the enclosure, ahead and to your right as you leave the central sanctuary, are the remains of a small red sandstone and brick tower. Its lack of carving makes dating uncertain, but the large size of the bricks in the base are typical of building practice from the 7th to 9th centuries. Otherwise, its size, shape and location are similar to that of the small tower in Phnom Rung's courtyard (↪ p. 109).

Artefacts

Three lintels have been found; two are now in the Phimai Museum, one in the National Museum, Bangkok. They make an interesting contrast with the *in situ* lintel, being in different styles – proof that work at Phnom Wan continued over two centuries:

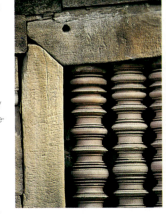

* The earliest lintel, at the National Museum, Bangkok, features a *kala*, but without arms, and foliate garlands. Here, though, in contrast to the *in situ* lintel, there is less verticality and the curls of vegetation are looser. Two triple-headed nagas emerge from the garlands and rear upwards. This Preah Kô-style lintel dates to the second half of the 9th century.

* A later lintel, from the first half of the 10th century and at the Phimai Museum, features Vishnu riding his steed *Garuda*. *Nagas* are also present, but as arch-enemies of the

Mitred stone joint, from one of the sanctuary windows.

winged *Garuda*, they are grasped firmly in his hands. Small figures of deities – two unusually with the lower bodies of lions – dance on the backs of the *nagas*. The style is that of the Bakheng period, but slight differences from the usual Cambodian lintels of the period suggest that the lintel may have been carved quite late – the small dancers in particular, full of movement and life, are similar to those of the following Koh Ker period.

• Also at the Phimai Museum is a complete Baphuon-style lintel, similar to that over the north door of the shrine. Here you can see how the finished *kala* face should look.

Apart from these lintels, a number of statues and fragments have been recovered, and can be seen at the Mahawirawong Museum, Khorat. The most interesting, and most recently found, is that of a female deity. Apart from the loss of the feet and chipped breast, she is in fine condition. Costume is often the best guide for dating statues; here, the pleated *sarong* with its aptly-named 'fish-tail' fold at the front is typical of the Baphuon style. The hand position suggests that she might be Uma, Shiva's consort. A stone *linga* and a hand of Uma holding a lotus flower confirm the Shivaite worship at Phnom Wan, but a head and hand of Vishnu have also been found. Mahayana Buddhist images are also at the museum, including a statue of Buddha under the *naga*.

Best times to visit Early morning and late afternoon have the best light. **Admission** 08.30–18.00, though in practice access is unrestricted. Small charge. **Nearby sites** Phimai (51 km), Muang Khaek and Non Ku (60 km). **Location** In the Muang district of Nakhon Ratchasima province, 20 km to the north-east of the provincial capital, Khorat. **By car** *From Khorat:* Take Route 2 north towards Khon Kaen. 2 ½ km after the bridge over the railway line, and exactly at the 15 km marker, turn right at the police box (the temple is signposted). Continue for 5 km; the road ends at the temple. 20 mins *From the north* (Phimai or Khon Kaen): Also on Route 2, the turning lies 34 km beyond Thalad Khae; again, look for the 15 km marker. 1 ¼ hrs from Khon Kaen, 30 mins. from Phimai.

By bus *From Khorat:* 3 buses a day go directly to the temple, in the morning, from the Pratu Phonsaen city gate. Check with Khorat TAT office.

Nearest accommodation and food

Khorat (•• pp 264-67).

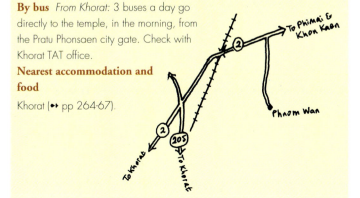

Prasat Phimai 🌺🌺🌺 ปราสาทพิมาย

Date: ***Existing buildings mainly late 11th to late 12th centuries***
Styles: **Baphuon, Bayon, Angkor Wat**
Reigns: **Jayavarman VI, Dharanindravarman I , Suryavarman II, Jayavarman VII**
Visit: **1 ½ – 2 hrs**

Phimai is unquestionably the most important Khmer monument in what is now Thailand, and its recent complete restoration makes it possible to appreciate the significance it must have had for the region at the height of the Khmer Empire. Known from inscriptions to have been the temple of the city of Vimayapura, the "city of Vimaya" (hence the modern name, with the 'V' becoming corrupted to 'Ph'), Phimai was built by the banks of the Mun River some 60 km north-east of the modern provincial capital of Nakhon Ratchasima (Khorat). It is one of the largest of all Khmer temples.

The importance of this site owes much to the local ruling dynasty, by name Mahidharapura, which furnished a succession of Angkor's kings – beginning with Jayavarman VI and including arguably the two greatest Khmer rulers, Suryavarman II and Jayavarman VII. Vimayapura and this part of the Khorat Plateau were by no

The tower, and buildings of the outer enclosure from the west.

means a backwater. The 1082 AD inscription still at Phnom Wan (↣ p. 68) mentions both the city and the king, Jayavarman VI. A century later, at Angkor itself, Phimai is mentioned in the inscription at Preah Khan as being the destination of one of the imperial roads. Two centuries after that, Chou Ta-Kuan's account of life at Angkor in 1296-7 (↣ pp. 15, 40) includes a passing reference to what might be Phimai when he mentions that Cambodia was divided into more than ninety provinces; one of them he calls P'u-mai.

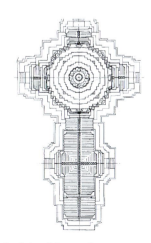

Roof plan of the central sanctuary.

Although not immediately apparent from its outward appearance, or even from some of its decorations, one of the most striking features of Phimai is that it was built as a Mahayana Buddhist rather than a Hindu temple. For anyone familiar with Angkor, this is unusual for a major temple built at the beginning of the 12th century. In Cambodia, large Khmer temples were dedicated to Shiva and Vishnu until the Buddhist king Jayavarman VII came to the throne in 1181. Here on

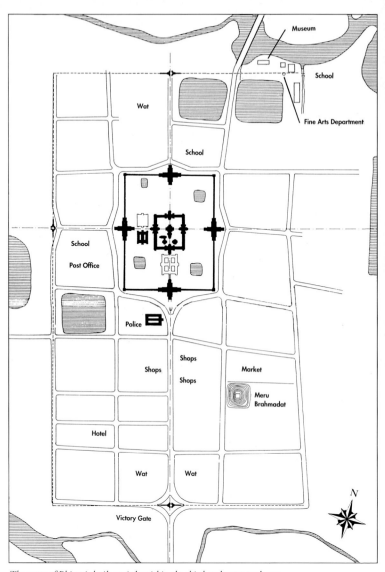

The town of Phimai, built mainly within the third and outer enclosure.

the plateau, however, there was a tradition of Mahayana Buddhism that stretched back to the 7th century. At Phimai, Tantric beliefs also played an important role, as can be seen in some of the lintels, particularly those inside the sanctuary.

The temple was built on a naturally secure site – almost a natural island – where the Mun River turns sharply south and a tributary, the Klong Chakrai, joins it. The result of this configuration is a raised strip of land bounded by water on three sides, large enough not only for the temple, but a surrounding community as well. The outer laterite enclosure of Phimai is, in fact, the outer wall of the old city, measuring one kilometre by just over half a kilometre. This wall was in turn protected by a broad moat, fed by the river. There were four entrances to the city and the temple, with the principal one known as Pratu Chai, "Victory Gate", at the south, at the end of the road from Angkor. This last was recently reconstructed; the eastern gate, as well as the east wall, has at some point in the past been destroyed by the encroaching river changing its course. East of the city, a *baray* was dug, the Sa Pleng.

This arrangement of moat and outer enclosure, with the temple proper occupying a considerably smaller area inside, is strikingly similar to that of Angkor Wat, at the capital. In fact, the dimensions are not that different. The outer enclosure of Angkor Wat, just inside its moat, measures 1025 x 800 m That of Phimai is 1020 x 580 m, no mean size for a provincial site. As today, most of the area inside was taken up with the settlement; it is possible that the modern street layout reflects the old city plan. The temple proper begins at the second enclosure.

Unusually, Phimai is oriented to the south (but not exactly), and it may be that this was in order to face in the direction of the capital, Angkor, with which it was connected by one of the most important royal roads, 225 kilometres long. Several other reasons have been suggested. One is the influence of the earlier kingdom of Funan in lower Cambodia (1st to 5th centuries), itself possibly adopting the Chinese custom of orientation to the south. Another is that the temple honours ancestors of the ruling dynasty in the traditional southerly direction. One problem in any explanation is the inexactitude of the orientation: the axis points 20 degrees east of south. Angkor lies 35 degrees east of south, and Phnom Rung, first major stop along the road, almost the same. Such inaccuracy would have been unusual for the Khmer builders, who were capable of laying highways as straight as any Roman road. Most likely, there is a combination of factors at work, with the orientation of the land between the rivers playing a major role.

Although inventoried by Aymonier in 1901, Phimai languished in ruins until the 1950s, when the Fine Arts Department began excavating and clearing the site. The technical study for the restoration was made by Bernard Philippe Groslier, the last French conservator at Angkor, and the reconstruction work carried out by the Fine Arts Department under the direction of Prince Yachai Chitrabongse from 1964-9. One peculiarity noted was that the tower, although collapsed from two levels above the cornice, was in good condition, which suggested that the superstructure might have been deliberately pulled down. Aymonier noted that this corresponded with local legends that the Burmese, or the Lao, had been responsible.

Plan

Traditionally, the approach to the temple was from the south, along the royal road from Angkor, via Phnom Rung. The approach passed a laterite landing stage on the river, and a kilometre beyond this entered the city through the Victory Gate. This and the other gates, as well as the wall, were built later than the temple proper, by Jayavarman VII. Directly ahead, north from the city gate, is the main entrance to the temple. Nowadays, however, the normal approach when travelling from Khorat skirts the eastern side of the temple.

Like Angkor Wat, Phimai is laid out concentrically, with the main

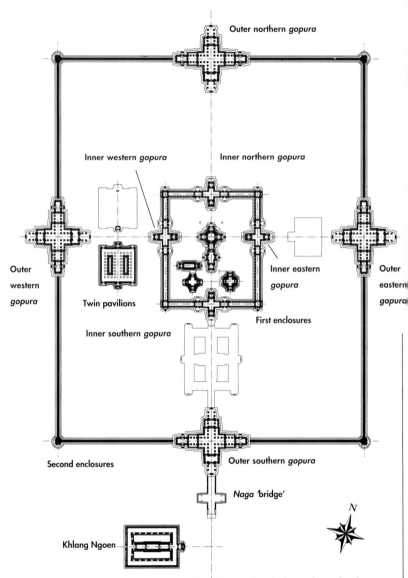

Outer northern *gopura*

Inner western *gopura*

Inner northern *gopura*

Outer
western
gopura

Outer
eastern
gopura

Inner eastern
gopura

Twin pavilions

First enclosures

Inner southern *gopura*

Second enclosures

Outer southern *gopura*

Naga 'bridge'

N

Khlang Ngoen

Plan of the temple - the first and second enclosures.

sanctuary at its heart. The first enclosure is a rectangle of 83m x 74m, offset north of the centre of the second enclosure, which measures 274m x 220m. This in turn is offset to the north within the third enclosure that makes up the old city limits. For comparison, the enclosures of Angkor Wat are also eccentrically placed away from the main entrance, although not by as much as here. When the outer city moats are included, and the four ponds in the corners of the second enclosure, the plan is clearly an ambitious model of the universe: a series of mountain ranges and oceans surrounding Mount Meru at the centre.

The naga 'bridge' at the main entrance.

Naga 'bridge'

The entrance to the temple proper begins with a cross-shaped terrace lined with *naga* balustrades, all well restored. The *nagas* with their rearing heads are a reminder right at the start that the entire temple is a model of the universe. They represent a 'bridge' from the world of men to the abode of the gods. That Phimai is a Buddhist sanctuary has not affected the layout of the temple; nor has it lessened the role of the *nagas*, which the Khmers elevated in their scheme of cosmology (➥ p. 20).

To the left of this terrace are the remains of a rectangular building, locally known as the Khlang Ngoen (Treasury). It may indeed have had some practical use, as grindstones were excavated here. They may have been used for ritual preparations.

Detail of the naga 'bridge'.

Outer southern *gopura*

The *naga* 'bridge' leads directly into the southern *gopura* of the second enclosure – the main entrance to the temple and larger than the other three *gopuras*. This entrance is a substantial building in its own right, its four wings giving it a cross-shaped plan. Here, as throughout the temple, the Khmers used two distinct kinds of sandstone, red and white. At the entrance, the red sandstone dominates the view, being used for the main structure of the *gopura* and the enclosure walls stretching left and right. A closer look shows that it is very finely textured, but soft and easy to crumble. Over the centuries it has weathered badly; a high iron content gives it its red colour, and also causes it to oxidise.

The white sandstone, on the other hand, is much tougher and very compact. In the *gopura* it has been used for the doors and windows, and for the massive pillars that divide the interior into three naves. Walking through the *gopura*, note the large wings on either side, to left and right. The windows facing out are false; those facing in toward the enclosure are real, and both types have the typical balustrades.

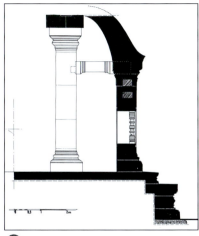

Cross-section of the northern arm of the cruciform, outer southern gopura.

Inner southern gopura.

Second enclosure

The southern *gopura* opens out onto the second enclosure, covering a little more than ten acres. Ahead, a causeway leads towards the main sanctuary, with the tower clearly visible. To the left and right are two of the enclosure's corner ponds. A short detour to see the pond at the left shows that it was originally lined with stone blocks. From its south-west corner there is a clear view of the tower and the first enclosure, reflected in the water. It is not certain when these ponds were dug.

Back on the causeway, continue towards the southern *gopura* of the inner enclosure, crossing a broad terrace that encloses four rectangular depressions, which

probably contained water for ritual use, as at Phnom Rung.

Inner southern *gopura*

Lintel over the main entrance.

This *gopura*, like the previous one, is built mainly of red sandstone, with doors, windows and lintels in white sandstone. By contrast with the newly carved red stone from the recent restoration, the original blocks show the darkening effect of weathering. The wings are much shorter than those of the outer *gopura*, but have separate doorways. Far to the left and right, beyond the rows of blind windows, the corner pavilions also have south-facing entrances. Although not obvious at first, there is an unusual asymmetry in the gallery that makes up this inner enclosure: the eastern part is shorter than the west, and there are nine windows to the left of the *gopura* but only eight to the right. In addition, there is an extra door on the left.

Lintel over side entrance.

Only a lintel tops the main entrance directly ahead. This, with a central design of a giant holding a pair of elephants aloft and standing over a *kala* head, is probably not in its original position. The style is transitional between the end of the Baphuon and the start of the Angkor Wat period, although with

Inside the second enclosure: the view from the pond in the south-west corner.

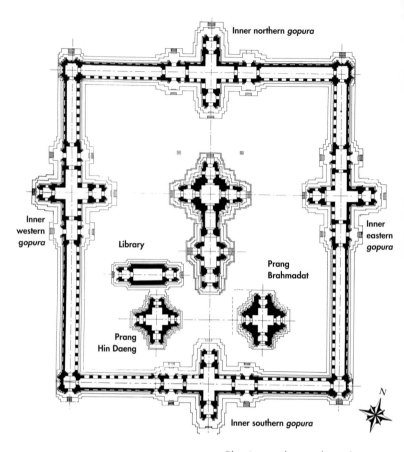

Inner northern *gopura*

Inner western *gopura*

Inner eastern *gopura*

Library

Prang Brahmadat

Prang Hin Daeng

Inner southern *gopura*

N

Plan: inner enclosure and central sanctuary.

some peculiarities, such as the very low position of the *kala*. There are no means of identifying who the giant is.

Inside the *gopura* on the right side of an inner door frame, now protected by a sheet of clear plastic, is the temple's principal inscription. The last date mentioned is 1112 AD, and among other matters, it celebrates the installation of a statue of a deity, Trailokyavijaya, by the local ruler Virendradhipativarman in 1108. This sheds some light on the temple's Buddhist cult. Trailokyavijaya was a Tantric Mahayana god who attempts to convert the Hindu god Shiva to this form of Buddhism, and in the inscription the statue is called the 'general' of the Lord of Vimaya.

Central sanctuary

Entering the central courtyard, the main sanctuary lies directly ahead, while on either side are semi-ruined towers – Prang Hin Daeng in red sandstone on the left, Prang Brahmadat in laterite on the right. The entrance facing is that of the *mandapa*, the extended antechamber to the sanctuary. This, like the ensemble of the sanctuary, is entirely of white sandstone, and richly carved.

The pediment, with an undulating frame bordered by large leaves, carries the figure of *Shiva Nantaraj* – the dancing Shiva. Although parts are missing or broken (the blank-faced stones are from the restoration), the main elements are clear. The kneeling figure on the far left is Shiva's disciple, Kareikalammeyar, who first appears in southern Indian art in the 8th century and was taken up by the Khmers in the 11th and 12th centuries. Characteristically, she is portrayed with drooping breasts. On the left, by Shiva's knee, an unidentified deity, but probably Brahma, rides what looks like a *hamsa*. On the far right, the bull Nandi kneels, with a *rishi* in attendance.

The lintel below this pediment is missing. At the base of the pilasters of this entrance are carved figures, nearly identical, and taking the role of guardians. The sheaf of arrows carried by the figure at left, however, identifies them as Vajrasattva, the Buddhist Tantric deity. In Khmer art, figurative carvings at the base of pilasters appears to have begun here at Phimai, at the end of the 11th century.

Continue through the doorway and the *mandapa*. This is connected to the cell, or *garbhagrha*, of the sanctuary by a short vestibule the *antarala*. Ahead, over the doorway to the

Vajrasattva carved on the base of one of the mandapa's pilasters.

antarala, is a Buddhist lintel. Although badly weathered, it depicts, in two registers, the unsuccessful assault on the Buddha by the army of Mara – the forces of evil. The Buddha sits above, in the centre, in the attitude of calling the earth to witness, and protected by the seven-headed *naga* Muchalinda. At his side, women tempt him, while below, four-faced warriors mounted on elephants and dragons prepare to attack. Ahead, over the entrance to the *garbhagrha*, is another two-tiered

Shiva dancing over entrance to mandapa.

Mahayana Buddhist lintel, very badly weathered, showing the Buddha meditating under the shelter of the naga's hood.

Somasutra, north-east corner of sanctuary.

Within the *garbhagrha* is a statue (a copy) of the Buddha in the same position— a popular representation that recurs often at Buddhist Khmer sites. About 1m to the right, as you face the Buddha, is a diamond-shaped hole in the floor. This is a conduit, known as a *somasutra*, leading from the base of the cell outside to the

Buddha under naga in the garbhagrha.

east; this was to drain lustral water used in rituals, and its exit can be seen in the north-east angle of the tower, just above ground level.

Continue and leave through the north door. Still inside the northern porch, turn to examine the north-facing interior lintel, which is in particularly fine condition. Again, the theme is Buddhist, and in two registers, although here the central figure breaks the two levels. As with so much Tantric Buddhist sculpture, the iconography is complex and difficult to interpret, but the three-headed and six-armed central figure is believed to be the deity Vajrasattva, although the attributes he holds are not the expected ones. Smaller identical figures flank him on either side, while dancers, accompanied by the musicians underneath Vajrasattva's pedestal, trample on human bodies. These last might represent the vanquished forces of evil and ignorance.

There are similar two-tiered interior lintels over the other entrances to the *garbhagrha*, with Mahayana Buddhist themes. In fact, there is an interesting division of themes and religions between the inside and the outside of the sanctuary. All the lintels around the shrine, and leading up to it inside, are Buddhist, while the exterior lintels, as we will see in a minute, are Hindu in inspiration. The central figure over the eastern entrance is believed to be Trailokyavijaya, the deity mentioned in the temple's main inscription, while on the western side the central figure is the Buddha, standing and in the teaching position (the way his robes are carved shows the legacy of 9th-11th century Dvaravati art that preceded the arrival of the Khmers).

Course of the somasutra conduit leading from the base of the cell.

Tower

Leave the sanctuary by the northern porch, and cross to the north-west corner of the courtyard, to the left. The tower, visible from most parts of the temple, appears at its most impressive from here in the inner courtyard. The best views are from the north-west and north-east corners, the former in the late afternoon, the latter in the early morning (➡ photograph opposite). These diagonal views show the lines of the tower at their clearest, and it is worth pausing here to see just how this landmark in Khmer architecture achieves its effect.

The importance of Phimai's tower should not be underestimated. The inscription of 1112 refers to the dedication of a deity in 1108, so that Phimai pre-dates Angkor Wat by several years. This central sanctuary and the surrounding gallery are the oldest surviving parts of Phimai, and were begun during the reign of Jayavarman VI (1080-1107). Without doubt, the ogival profile of this tower, a major architectural innovation, influenced the design of Angkor Wat's five towers.

This inward-curving silhouette is one of the most distinctive, and unique, symbols of Khmer architecture, variously likened to a pine cone, bombshell and corn-cob. Even after the collapse of the Khmer Empire (temple building other than in wood virtually ended in the 14th century, and the capital at Angkor was abandoned in 1432), this type of tower persisted. The Siamese, who conquered Angkor, revived and remodelled it as the *prang*, in brick or laterite, covered with stucco. Ayutthayan temples such as Wat Buddhaisawan are in direct lineage to Phimai.

The origin of these Khmer towers was the Indian *shikara*, in particular those of the Chola dynasty in southern India (end of the 9th to middle of the 13th centuries). The Khmers, however, developed these pyramidal designs into soaring curved towers. The view from these corners of the enclosure illustrates how. The points along the curved profile are set by the five tiers, beginning at the main cornice. Each is a reduction of the one below, both in height and diameter. There is, in fact, no mathematical progression, and the calculations must have been worked out simply by eye, probably from a model. Importantly, each of these tiers has an overhanging lip, and the space below allows enough room for a series of antefixes at each angle. These free-standing stones, in a shape that echoes that of the tower, fill in the line of the curve, and on the upper tiers even lean inwards to complete the shape. The result is a silhouette that curves to a point without being unduly massive. Far from being just decorations, the antefixes have an architectural role.

In addition, the builders have used redenting both to alter the shape of the tower and to give a vertical component. In principle, redenting means cutting back the corners of a square into a number of angles, and this helps to articulate the structure. Here, compressing the corners in a series of angles makes the section of the sanctuary more rounded. Later, at Angkor Wat, the corner angles were taken back even further, so that the towers appear virtually round. Here there is still a sense of four sides.

Finally, the tower has been made as imposing as possible by various

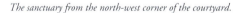

The sanctuary from the north-west corner of the courtyard.

means, and seems even taller and grander than its actual 28.15 metres above the level of the courtyard. The techniques used are the reducing height of the tiers, which gives a simple perspective effect from ground-level, the vertical lines of the redenting, the rising levels of the porches, and the outward bulge at the main cornice level, which gives an almost arrow-head profile.

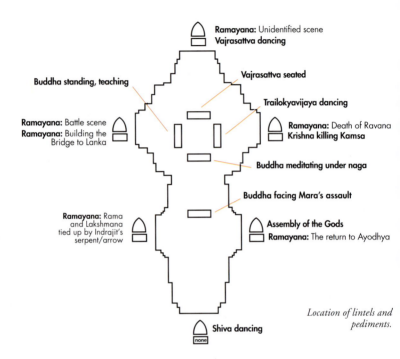

Ramayana: Unidentified scene
Vajrasattva dancing

Buddha standing, teaching

Vajrasattva seated

Trailokyavijaya dancing

Ramayana: Battle scene
Ramayana: Building the Bridge to Lanka

Ramayana: Death of Ravana
Krishna killing Kamsa

Buddha meditating under naga

Buddha facing Mara's assault

Ramayana: Rama and Lakshmana tied up by Indrajit's serpent/arrow

Assembly of the Gods
Ramayana: The return to Ayodhya

Shiva dancing
none

Location of lintels and pediments.

Lintels, pediments and decorations

Locally, the tower invites comparison with that of Phnom Rung to the south-east, built a little later but quite different in its impression, being more definitely pointed and squatter. The comparisons are made under the entry for Phnom Rung on p.107. It is also worth noting that each part of the sanctuary starts at a different level, related to its importance. The sanctuary tower has the highest base, followed by the *mandapa*, and then the porches.

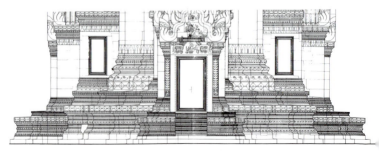

Carved friezes along the multi-level base of the sanctuary.

Giant garuda on the tower's west face, surmounted by Varuna.

The entrances to the sanctuary, the faces and tiers of the tower, all allow room for the carving of scenes and figures, and all have been used to the full. The resulting iconography is rich and complex. The lintels and pediments provide standard spaces for the most important carvings, which on the outside of the sanctuary mainly show scenes from Hindu epics like the Ramayana. This mixture of religious motifs – Buddhist and Hindu – is a reminder of how easily they co-existed for most of Khmer history.

A series of two or three superimposed pediments rises over each entrance. Above these on each of the four faces of the tower, giant figures of

Scene from the Ramayana: the west lintel of the mandapa.

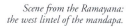

garudas support the cornices with outstretched arms and wings. From here in the north-west corner of the enclosure, the west face of the tower can be seen at its best. Directly above the *garuda* an antefix stands on the cornice. This represents one of the deities of direction: Varuna, who guards the west, supported by *hamsas*. On the same level, all the way round the tower, are other antefixes: gods of direction in the centre, *nagas* at the corners, and a mixture of guardians and female divinities at the other angles formed by the redenting.

Antefixes on the tower.

We start a clockwise circuit of the sanctuary at the west side door of the *mandapa*. Unusually, both the lintel here and what is left of the pediment show the same scene, and the action crosses between them. This is the scene in the Ramayana epic in which Rama and his brother Lakshmana have been entrapped in the coils of a *naga*. This happens when Indrajit, Ravana's son, fires at them with an arrow, which magically turns into a serpent. In the top left corner you can see Indrajit aiming the arrow, while some of the monkey troops on the lower register point at him to warn Rama. Others show their anguish in various ways, and Sita cradles Rama's head. Above, on the pediment, however, help is about to arrive in the form of a *garuda* and monkey reinforcements flying down.

Further along, the west entrance below the tower also has scenes from the Ramayana on both the lintel and the pediment. The lintel shows Rama's troops building the causeway across the ocean to Lanka in preparation for their invasion. The monkey warriors carry boulders to throw in the sea, which is represented by various denizens on the lower right, including fish and dragons. The pediment above is a battle scene from the same epic.

Over the north entrance to the sanctuary, the lintel shows a 4-armed Vajrasattva dancing, while the incomplete pediment carries an as-yet uninterpreted scene, probably from the Ramayana.

Around the corner, the lintel over the eastern entrance to the shrine has had different interpretations applied to it. Originally it was thought to be a scene from the Ramayana, in which Lakshmana cuts off the ear and nose of the demon Ravana's

Lintel over northern entrance to shrine.

younger sister Surpanakha, while Rama and Sita look on. That the victim looks distinctly unfeminine seems not to have been noticed until more recently. A second interpretation had Rama killing Viradha, but then Rama would have appeared twice in the same scene. More likely is the suggestion by Bruno Dagens that this is a scene from the life of Krishna (one of the earthly manifestations of the god Vishnu). In this, Krishna is killing Kamsa with his parents watching. The clue is the half-hidden figure of a bull, up-ended with its legs tied. This could represent the bull Arishta which, with a *simha* (also shown), unsuccessfully tried to kill Krishna under instruction from Kamsa. In all,

an interesting example of the problems of finding the meaning in Khmer carvings.

The pediment probably shows the death of Ravana, near the end of the Ramayana epic. Until recently, however, it was thought that this was the judgement of Ravana's uncle, the Brahma

Pediment over east entrance to mandapa.

Malivaraja (also from the Ramayana), shown in the middle descending from heaven on a *hamsa*. Heaven here is represented by no less than the temple of Phimai itself! Below, on chariots, are Rama (left) and Ravana (right). So far so good, but if you look carefully under the horses' hooves, you can see an

inverted head. Khmer lintel carvers were quite fond of including the various parts of a story in a single narrative lintel, and this head is now thought to be Ravana's, as he is killed.

Over the east side door to the *mandapa* is a lintel that may show yet another episode from the Ramayana, possibly the return of Rama to Ayodhya, having finally conquered Ravana in the battle of Lanka. The pediment shows a gathering of the major gods: Shiva above and, from left to right, Brahma, Indra and Vishnu. Possibly, they are conferring blessing on the victorious Rama in the lintel below.

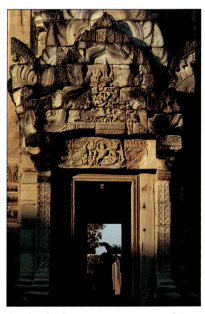

Lintel and pediment over east entrance to shrine.

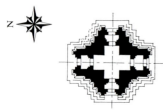

Prang Brahmadat

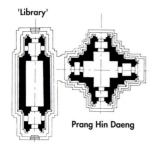

'Library'

Prang Hin Daeng

Other buildings in the inner enclosure.

Other buildings in the inner enclosure

This point in the circuit around the courtyard brings us to the so-called Prang Brahmadat. Square in plan and 16m high, this laterite tower is in generally poor condition. It was built later than the main sanctuary, around the beginning of the 13th century during the reign of Jayavarman VII. Inside is a reproduction of an important statue discovered here – a portrait of Jayavarman VII himself in the posture of the Buddha. The original is in the National Museum in Bangkok (•• p.8). This is one of a few lifelike statues of the king that have been discovered. Another, almost identical, but carved when Jayavarman was younger, was found in the capital at Angkor, and is now on display at the National Museum in Phnom Penh; this museum also has another head from a similar statue. There are lintels over the north, east and south entrances, all weathered to black – on the east and south are Buddhist scenes, while the north carries an image of Krishna fighting a horse. The western lintel remains uncarved.

On the other side of the courtyard is another partly-ruined square tower, almost as high at 15m but built in red sandstone. This is locally called Prang Hin Daeng,

Tantric lintel, interior, north side of shrine.

'Red Stone Tower', and was also built at the start of the 13th century. Adjoining it to the north is a 'library', aligned east-west and facing in towards the *mandapa*; its entrance has a lintel apparently showing Krishna battling animals. A number of *lingas* were found here during restoration.

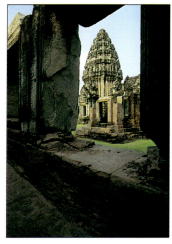

Inner galleries

The galleries that surround the inner enclosure form a continuous walkway broken only by the four *gopuras*. Re-enter the main southern *gopura* and turn either right and continue to the west *gopura*, or left to make a longer

The sanctuary from inside the galleries.

anti-clockwise circuit that takes in various Tantric Buddhist lintels around the galleries. The windows open onto the courtyard.

At the west *gopura*, turn to look through to the tower. Note that the west and east doorways of the tower are aligned with those of this *gopura* and the east *gopura* beyond. However, as it is the ensemble of the sanctuary rather than the tower that is centred within the courtyard, this alignment of doorways is offset to the north. This is the reason for the west and east *gopuras* being north of the centre – not only here in the inner enclosure, but in the outer enclosure as well.

Lintel, north-eastern corner of the galleries.

The twin pavilions

Leave the west *gopura* through its west doorway. Directly ahead is the corresponding *gopura* of the outer enclosure. In the space between, on either side, are the remains of two large rectangular buildings, of uncertain purpose. They have identical plans, although the northern of the pair is almost completely ruined. The entrances to the southern building are on the north and south sides. Inside, rows of metre-square holes cover the surface of the laterite floor.

Outer gopura.

The eastern outer gopura with acaciea.

The remaining outer *gopuras*

Walk around the north side of the inner enclosure to the east outer *gopura,* which is in reasonably good condition and has an attractive setting, particularly at the start of the hot season when the acacia trees around it are in flower. The massive square columns that divide the interior into three naves are especially impressive, buttressed by angled beams just below the capitals.

Artefacts

The most famous is the statue of Jayavarman VII already mentioned and now at the National Museum. In addition, a number of unplaced lintels, statues and *lingas* are kept at the Phimai National Museum nearby (➜ pp. 90-93).

Best times to visit Early morning and late afternoon, although access is restricted by the temple opening hours below. **Admission** 0600-1800, small charge. **Nearby sites** Phnom Wan (29 km), Ku Suan Taeng (75 km). **Location** In the Phimai district of Nakhon Ratchasima province, the temple is in the centre of the town, as originally built. It occupies a bend in the upper Mun River some 60 km north-east of Khorat city. **By car** *From Khorat:* Take Route 2 in the direction of Khon Kaen for 49 km, and at Thalad Khae take 206 right for 12 km to the town of Phimai. In the town, the road curves to the left around the sanctuary and runs down by the eastern wall of the second enclosure. At the sanctuary's south-east corner, turn right; the entrance is just ahead on the right. 45 mins. *From Khon Kaen:* Take Route 2 and make the same turning at Thalad Khae as above. 2 hrs. *From Surin and Buriram:* This route is less obvious: take 2074 north from Buriram in the direction of Putthaisong. After 36 km turn left onto 2226. After another 30 km, continue south-west through Chum Phuang on 2175 for 34 km, and at the junction with 2163 turn right into Phimai (another 4 km). This last road (2163) is part of the original royal road *from* Angkor, entering Phimai through the Victory Gate. 1½ hrs. **By bus** Regular service from Khorat's Old Bus Station (Terminal 1). The last bus back to Khorat leaves at 1800. Phimai's bus station is close to the Victory Gate. 1-1½ hrs. **Nearest accommodation and food** In Phimai itself (➦pp. 272-73). Otherwise, more comfortable accommodation and a wider choice of restaurants is at Khorat (➦ pp. 264-67).

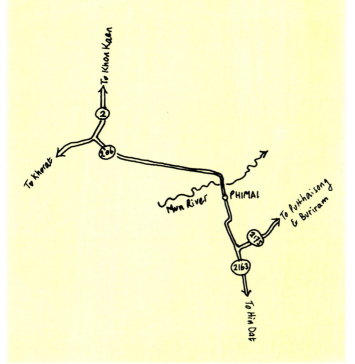

Phimai National Museum

Visit: 45 mins พิพิธภัณฑ์พิมาย

Avisit to the recently enlarged museum is an essential part of the trip to Phimai. In addition to pieces from Phimai itself, it has lintels and pediments from several other sites. These are described under the temples, and include Non Ku (↦ p. 54), Muang Khaek (↦ p. 56), Phnom Wan (↦ p. 64) and Ku Suan Taeng (↦ p. 96). Other new additions include red sandstone pediments and columns from Prang Pako, Amphoe Chokchai. The following lintels found at Phimai itself are of particular note:

Narrative Mahayanist lintel.

Mahayanist divinities in heaven

A narrative lintel of the type that started to become popular towards the end of the 11th century shows a compartmented scene (the right part is missing). The row of *hamsas* and *garudas* along the bottom are holding the main panels – a clear sign that the scene is celestial. The various divinities are carved in sizes according to their importance, from the principal male figure to the praying *rishis* on the upper left.

Lintel with row of standing Buddhas.

Row of standing Buddhas

There are a few such lintels featuring a line of Buddhas, each in a niche, with the hands raised in the preaching attitude – the Vitarka Mudra. The interest of these lintels lies in the garments, for while the figures are clearly Buddhas and male, they are wearing women's dress of the period. This is hard to explain under any circumstances, but the most convincing hypothesis (by Jean Boisselier) is that this was a tradition of a local Tantric sect.

Fragment of lintel with giant *simha*

This incomplete lintel (the right third is missing) is carved with great flair and vigour. It has an unusual design for its period (that of Angkor Wat), with a fully-formed *simha* taking the role of the *kala*. The garland and vegetation is particularly deep.

Angkor Wat style lintel with Simha.

Ashvamedha ceremony

This lintel also uses the narrative technique which, when it is possible to identify the scene, can be of great interest. This ceremony, with a horse's head in the middle, and one priest pouring water onto the hands of another, comes from India and is known as the Ashvamedha. It occurs at the end of a year in which the King releases a favourite horse to roam wherever it will, in order to test the loyalty of his subjects. A troop of soldiers

Lintel showing the Ashvamedha ceremony .

follow the horse to observe how it is treated – and if it is harmed in any way, to mete out punishment.

Kala surmounted by a divinity

This recently excavated lintel has many features from the Preah Kô style of the previous century – the *kala* head disgorging the garland and the strong loops of leaves trailing down from the garland. This is one of many examples in Thailand of styles lingering beyond the normal dates in Cambodia.

Kala lintel showing the continuing inference of the Preah Kô style.

Lintel with Indra on Airavata.

Indra on Airavata

Very similar to the previous lintel, this features the god Indra on his three-headed elephant Airavata.

As well as the carving style, the dress is typical of the mid-10th century. One anomaly in both is the detail of Ganesh at each end riding on his own trunk. Elsewhere, this is found earlier or later than this period.

Vishnu lintel in Koh Ker style.

Vishnu stepping over the ocean

This beautifully carved lintel, with a prominent scene in the centre standing in high relief out from the rest of the design, is typical of the Koh Ker style

(➥ p. 38). The episode in the central panel is part of the Three Steps of Vishnu, in which Vishnu steps over the ocean onto a lotus held by the Earth goddess Bhumidevi. Note the two figures of Ganesh on either side, and the row of *hamsas* worked into the foliage above the garland. A row of *rishis* sit in meditation above.

Unfinished Lintel.

Krishna killing Kamsa?

Another lintel from the most recent round of excavations is incompletely carved: the most important central scene, left until the last, has only been outlined. The episode seems on the face of it to be that of Krishna killing Kamsa by tearing him apart; a fully finished version of this scene is at Wat Phu (➥ pp. 200). However, the figure's hair ought to be tied up, but here is loose. Also, if you look closely, you can see what might be the outline of a fang on the side of his cheek. If so, he might be Vishnu transformed into a lion, and killing Hiranya.

Shiva, Uma on Nandi from Muang Khaek.

Churning of the Sea of Milk

This is one of the few known examples from Thailand of one of the favourite Khmer cosmological stories. The magnificent bas-relief at Angkor Wat – one of the finest and best-

Lintel showing the churning of the sea of milk from Ku Suan Taeng.

known of all Khmer works – gives this subject a special importance. The removal of the heads by thieves underlines the sad necessity of removing valuable artefacts from the sites. The composition is more typical of the earlier Baphuon period than of Angkor Wat, but details, such as of dress, belong firmly in the mid-12th century.

Mount Mandara is here shown as a pole (as at Preah Vihear ↦ pp 162); Vishnu wraps himself around it to command the proceedings, but is also incarnated as the turtle to stop the mountain sinking. The *naga* Vasuki is held by the two teams – gods and demons. Other characters in the story to look for are Brahma sitting on top of the pole (unusually, we see his multiple heads in a three-quarter rather than a full profile) and Lakshmi and the horse Ucchaisaravas peering over the top of the turtle. The flying maidens are the *apsaras*, just created by the churning. Various small animals and flowers add the provincial touch.

Vishnu stepping over the ocean

In another of Vishnu's exploits, less often treated, he appears as a dwarf, crossing the ocean and subduing King Bali. This version of the Vamanavatara, as the incarnation is known, is Angkor Wat in style, as evidence by the

Lintel showing Vishnu stepping over the ocean from Ku Suan Taeng.

clothing and ornaments of the period. Vishnu takes both the central position, as he steps over the sea, and at the right, where he subdues Bali.

Vishnu on Garuda, Bakheng style, 10th century from Phnom Wan.

Admission Wed-Sun 0830-1630, small charge. **Directions** A short walk north of the temple along Route 206, immediately before the bridge over the river (↦ map, pp 272-73).

Remains of the laterite tower.

Prang Ku ปรางค์กู่

Date: *Late 12th to early 13th century*
Style: *Bayon*
Reign: *Jayavarman VII*
Visit: *15 mins*

A laterite tower 5m high, surrounded by a rectangular walled enclosure with a *gopura* on the east side, marks the chapel of one of Jayavarman VII's many hospitals. As a fervent Buddhist, Jayavarman VII appears to have felt a duty to undertake public works that would benefit his subjects, and the 102 hospitals that he had built throughout the empire were part of that programme. The inscription at Ta Prohm in Angkor mentions that they were dedicated to the god of healing, Bhaisajyaguru. It also eulogises the king in the usual fashion: "He suffered from the maladies of his subjects more than from his own; for it is the public grief which makes the grief of kings, and not their own grief." In itself, the site is quite interesting, although probably not worth a special visit, as essentially the same type of chapel can be seen at Kamphaeng Noi and Ta Muen Toch (➻ pp 186 and 151 respectively). Nevertheless, it can be fitted in to a journey from Phimai or Ku Suan Taeng to Muang Khaek etc., or into a journey from Khorat to Phitsanulok. Prang Ku is one of the more northerly Khmer remains.

Plan

In the rectangular enclosure, the tower is offset slightly to the west, while in the south-eastern corner is a typical 'library'. Compare this with Kamphaeng Noi. As in other such sites, the actual hospital buildings were in light materials, and all traces have long since disappeared.

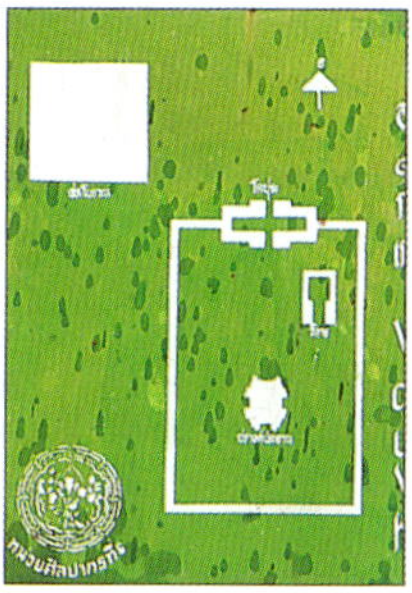

Prang Ku temple plan.

Best times to visit Any time. **Admission** Unrestricted, no charge. **Nearby sites** Ku Suan Taeng (100 km), Phimai (110 km), Muang Khaek etc. (124 km) **Location** At Nong Bua village, 1½ km east of the town of Chaiyaphum, in Chaiyaphum province. **By car** ➻ pp 254 for directions to Chaiyaphum. At the town, take the road that goes east from the roundabout at the town's southern entrance, passing the provincial administrative offices (Tessabaan), for 1½ km. ***Driving times:*** 1½ hrs from Khorat, 1¼ hrs from Phimai, 2½ hrs from Khon Kaen. **Nearest accommodation and food** There is a small choice of accommodation in Chaiyaphum; otherwise stay in Khorat (➻ pp 264-67) or Khon Kaen (➻ see pp 258-261).

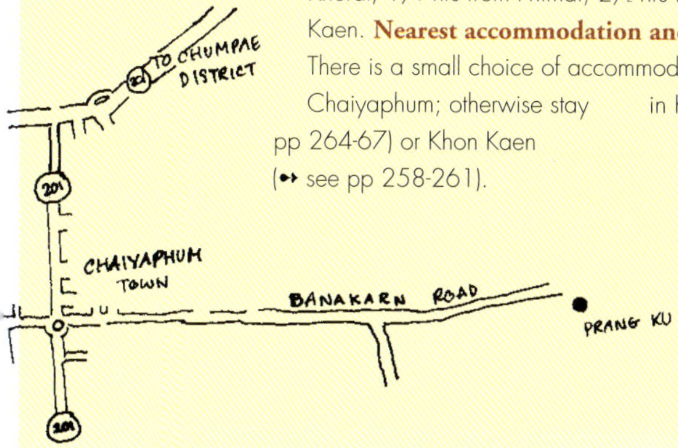
TO CHUMPAE DISTRICT
201
201
CHAIYAPHUM
TOWN
BANAKARN ROAD
PRANG KU
201

The central tower from the east.

Ku Suan Taeng   กู่สวนแตง

Date: Mid-12th to second half of 12th century
Style: late Angkor Wat, early Bayon
Reigns: Suryavarman II, Jayavarman VII
Visit: 15 mins

SUAN
TANG
SCHOOL

KU

This fairly late temple, dating from the end of the Angkor Wat period and the start of Jayavarman VII's hurried building programme, features the common arrangement of three brick towers in a row on the same base. At Angkor, by this time, brick was hardly used, having long been superseded by stone. Here in the north, however, brick still played an important part – Sikhoraphum and Yai Ngao, both a little to the east of Surin (▸▸ pp. 178 and 176), were almost contemporary and also in brick. The site has a small modern wat adjacent.

Plan

The three towers face east, in a row, on the same platform, and are surrounded by a moat, which is partly filled in the rainy season. De Lajonquière was here on his 1904-05 survey, and found two other buildings to the east, in the positions usual for 'libraries', and the laterite foundations are still

The central and northern towers.

visible. There was originally a large *baray*, also to the east.

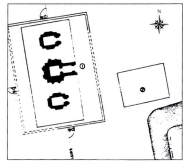

All three towers have a single door on the eastern side; in addition, the central tower has a porch at the front, and three false doors. These false doors are of some specialised interest architecturally, because of the massive projecting stone slab above them. These are the functional lintels and supported the pediment above. The decorative lintels, however, was not hooked onto it (the usual technique up to this time – see Building techniques, pp. 30-32), but would have rested entirely on the colonettes. Ku Suan Taeng is the first temple in the region to feature this.

Artefacts

Some interesting lintels were discovered here, but for the usual reasons of safe-keeping are now in museums (↠ pp 93).

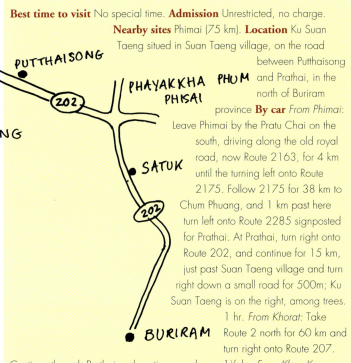

Best time to visit No special time. **Admission** Unrestricted, no charge. **Nearby sites** Phimai (75 km). **Location** Ku Suan Taeng situed in Suan Taeng village, on the road between Putthaisong and Prathai, in the north of Buriram province **By car** From Phimai: Leave Phimai by the Pratu Chai on the south, driving along the old royal road, now Route 2163, for 4 km until the turning left onto Route 2175. Follow 2175 for 38 km to Chum Phuang, and 1 km past here turn left onto Route 2285 signposted for Prathai. At Prathai, turn right onto Route 202, and continue for 15 km, just past Suan Taeng village and turn right down a small road for 500m; Ku Suan Taeng is on the right, among trees. 1 hr. *From Khorat:* Take Route 2 north for 60 km and turn right onto Route 207. Continue through Prathai and continue as above. 1½ hrs. *From Khon Kaen:* Take Route 2 south for and turn left onto Route 207. Continue as above 1¾ hrs. **Nearest accommodation and food** Khorat (↠ pp 264-267), Buriram (↠ pp 252-54) and Phimai (↠ pp 272-73).

Naga balustrade and pond, entrance.

The tower from the north-west corner.

ปราสาทพนมรุ้ง

Prasat Phnom Rung 🌺🌺🌺🍃

Date: Existing buildings from the early 10th to the late 12th century
Styles: Koh Ker, Baphuon, mainly early Angkor Wat
Reigns: Jayavarman IV, Udayadityavarman II, mainly Suryavarman II
Visit: 1 $1/2$ – 2 hrs

This major temple, built mainly in a high-quality pinkish sandstone, combines an impressive hill-top site that commands the surrounding plain, and an extraordinary amount of architectural decoration of the highest order. The restoration programme from 1972 to 1988 has enhanced this, and despite inevitable development of the site for visitors, which has robbed it somewhat of what Lawrence Palmer Briggs called "its lonely grandeur", Phnom Rung is one of the most rewarding of all Khmer temples to visit.

Added interest is given by its intensely local associations, for much of Phnom Rung's iconography and decoration is a celebration of this region's most powerful family – that of Narendraditya, a member of the Mahidharapura dynasty (➤ p. 70). Throughout Phnom Rung there is evidence of the autonomy of local rule. The builders certainly owed allegiance to Angkor, but they were much more than mere vassals.

Eleven inscriptions have been found at Phnom Rung, and together give a patchy account of its history. The most important is the last, a stele erected in 1150 by Hiranya, son of Narendraditya. In it, Narendraditya is described as claiming suzerainty over this region as a result of having defeated many of King Suryavarman II's enemies. Suryavarman II, builder of Angkor Wat and one of the greatest Khmer rulers, was indeed a relative and a contemporary of Narendraditya, and the campaigns that led to the king's rule at Angkor from 1112 to 1152 may well have involved Narendraditya and his troops. The tone here is that of a powerful regional ruler supporting the king. There is a battle scene carved on one of the upper pediments above the south entrance to the sanctuary, with war elephants, one of which crushes an enemy soldier with its trunk. If this is from Narendraditya's campaigns, it may be the earliest historical scene in the country. Inside the south doorway is a lintel showing a king performing a ritual, aided by a *rishi*, and this also may be an image of Narendraditya.

Battle scene over the southern entrance to the shrine.

Soon after the campaigns, probably at the beginning of the century, Narendraditya turned his back on war and entered monastic life as a *yogi* and *guru*. Hiranya, his son, claims for himself to have completed his Brahmanic education by the age of 16, became a great elephant hunter by the age of 18, and at 20 had a golden image of his father erected. Stating his lineage and accomplishments in this way, Hiranya was using the inscription to legitimize his claims to rule – standard practice at the time.

This inscription begins with a hymn to Shiva, and the god appears in important locations in the temple: dancing over the main entrance to the *mandapa*, and as the supreme *yogi* over the main entrance to the east *gopura*. There is no doubt that Shivaite worship was well established at Phnom Rung, but Vishnuite images have also been found, and are referred to in another inscription.

Looking back in time from Narendraditya and Hiranya, there are 10th century accounts (in inscriptions) of land being purchased to build the sanctuary and its neighbouring community, with slaves assigned to its upkeep, and of a feudal-style land distribution system known as *Kalpana*, in which land was allocated to servants of the temple who would then return a proportion of the produce to the monastery. The earliest inscription of all was carved in the 7th or 8th century, at least a century before the earliest buildings that can be seen today.

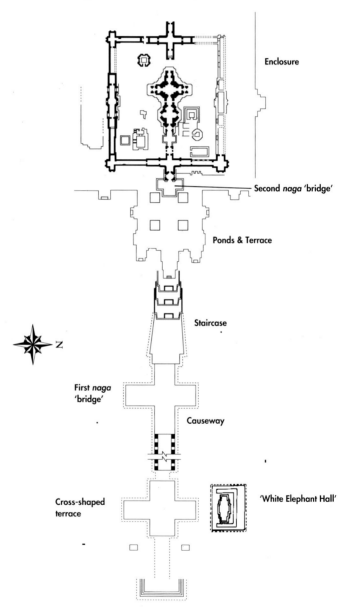

Enclosure

Second *naga* 'bridge'

Ponds & Terrace

Staircase

First *naga* 'bridge'

Causeway

Cross-shaped terrace

'White Elephant Hall'

N

Plan

The 383m inactive volcano that rises over the flat farmland that stretches 30 km south to the visible Dongrek Mountains provides the setting for one of the Khmer empire's few, but spectacular, axial temples. The Khmer concern with architectural symbolism, increasingly focused on the recreation of Mount Meru and the surrounding elements of the Hindu universe, made mountains particularly compelling and special sites.

The Khmer word 'phnom', meaning hill, describes the location. Like Preah Vihear, the cliff-top temple 190 km to the east, and Wat Phu even further east in Laos on a mountainside overlooking the Mekong River, Phnom Rung was built to take advantage of its naturally commanding site, and a sequence of causeway, steps and terraces make a long, impressive approach to the sanctuary at the top. The entire complex is strung out on an east-west axis, a little over ½ km from the first laterite terrace on the eastern slope of the hill to the western *gopura*.

Although the modern approach to the temple is by roads from the east and west that converge on the entrance gate close to the top of the hill, the real start is another ½ km to the east, at the foot of the eastern slope. Now partly covered in vegetation, its laterite steps lead up to the first of a series of cross-shaped platforms. Continuing west, a long causeway, second platform, succession of staircases and final platform lead to the enclosure. This, surrounded by a gallery with a *gopura* in each face and corner pavilions, contains the central sanctuary and several other buildings of different periods.

'White Elephant Hall'

From the visitor centre near the entrance, walk back down the slope and to the left in the direction of the first cross-shaped terrace. The large laterite and sandstone structure that you come to first is known locally as the 'White Elephant Hall'. This is a rectangular building with porches on its east and west walls, surrounded on three sides (west, north and east) by galleries and walls. The name is no more than imaginative folklore: there is no reason for believing that this building had anything to do with white elephants and the term 'white' is in any case a popular but erroneous term. Before restoration, Phnom Rung was locally thought to have been a king's palace, and as a king would have been expected to possess white elephants, they would have had to be kept somewhere. The real function of the building is not known.

Causeway

 The cross-shaped terrace just south of the 'White Elephant Hall' marks the beginning of the principal approach to the temple. From the middle of this platform, which measures 40m north-south and 30m east-west, face east – the view is directly towards the staircase and the tower. 67 lotus-bud-tipped boundary stones line each side of the 160m causeway; their shape is the first indication on the visit of Phnom Rung's architectural style, which is of the Angkor Wat period from the first few decades of the 12th century.

Naga balustrade outside the eastern gopura.

First *naga* 'bridge'

Walk along the laterite-paved causeway towards the next cross-shaped stone terrace in the distance. This terrace, with five-headed *naga* balustrades, is one of the special inventions of the later periods of Khmer architecture. Found also at Phimai, and at Angkor Wat itself, it is known as a *naga* 'bridge'. The bridge in question is less of a physical one, even though the platform is raised on pillars, than a cosmological one. The *nagas* lining it in the form of balustrades here perform the function of a rainbow, with which they are sometimes compared in Khmer inscriptions, and are a bridge between this world and the divine. The hill beyond, and the sanctuary at its top, are a recreation of the centre of the Hindu universe. This platform, fully restored, is particularly fine. It rises 1½m on carved pillars, and can be ascended from the east, north and south. In its centre, a large lotus leaf is very lightly carved – unfinished, in fact. The balustrade of rearing five-headed *nagas* is in the style of Angkor Wat, and carved in great detail; note the scales and backbones.

Staircase and second *naga* 'bridge'

From here a broad staircase rises in five sections to the sanctuary. At the top is another large terrace just before the entrance, set with four artificial ponds. These, intended for ritual use now once more contain water since the restoration has been completed.

Between the western two ponds is the eastern projection of a second *naga* 'bridge'. Similar, though smaller than the first at the foot of the staircase, it features *naga* balustrades facing in three directions: east, north and south. In fact, there is a subtle difference in the balustrades. Look carefully at the point where the *naga* heads rear up and notice that they are being disgorged by another creature.

This is a *makara* (➡ p. 20), and its body, rather than the snakes', lines the cross-shaped platform. Post-holes indicate that this terrace had, or was intended to have, a wooden roof.

Eastern *gopura*

The level of this terrace broadens and extends west as a platform for the entire sanctuary. The enclosure is marked by a rectangle of galleries, with *gopuras* in the middle of each of the four sides. Facing the sunrise over the distant plains, the eastern *gopura* is the principal entrance. A succession of doorways lies ahead on the line of the temple's axis – through the *mandapa* (or entrance pavilion), the *antarala* that connects it to the garbhagrha, and out again through the western *gopura*.

This eastern *gopura* is an elaborate building in its own right, with diminishing chambers on either side that give it a 'telescoped' appearance. The main doorway has a double-sectioned projecting porch, with a double pediment at the front, and a slightly higher one behind. Note that the rear pediment has not been finished: the 5-headed *nagas* that should project at the base of the arch are merely undressed blocks.

Pediment showing Shiva as ascetic.

The pediment at the front features a Hindu *yogi,* surrounded by female attendants and celestial dancers. In such a key location for an east-facing temple, this almost certainly represents Shiva as the supreme ascetic. One clue is the hairstyle, the same as that on the dancing Shiva on the *mandapa* inside. Another is the posture, known as *lalitasana,* or 'royal ease' – a relaxed position with the right leg extended. Not only this, the carving may also be an image of Narendraditya, the local ruler who became a *yogi*. Identifying a king with a god was a practice common at Angkor; this may be a regional version. Unusually for the 12th century, the area around the figure of the yogi is blank; perhaps the carvers intended to add another lightly-incised garland, or perhaps this area symbolises the ascetic life of a yogi. The lintel below shows a divinity seated over a *kala,* who grips the hind legs of a pair of lions.

Lintel over main entrance to eastern gopura.

The *gopura* also has two smaller entrances. The northern of these, to your right as you stand facing the main door, carries a small pediment with a scene that must be from the Ramayana – one of the battles between the monkeys troops and the demons.

The view from the top, with the help of a map, gives a clue to Phnom Rung's importance during a long period from the 8th to the 13th centuries. From the platform in front of the east *gopura* there is a good view to the south and east. Just 6 km to the south-east, hidden by trees, lies the other important

The view from the summit – rice-fields on the plateau.

temple in the area – Muang Tam (the 'Lower City', so-called because of its relation to Phnom Rung) – and the *baray* just to its north of it can be seen glistening from here. Muang Tam was connected to Phnom Rung by a road – one of the most important of the royal roads that spanned the empire. It continued on to Angkor, via the Ta Muen Pass in the Dongrek Mountains (too far to be made out from here). Resting houses and hospitals lined this route (•• p. 151-53), and with binoculars, you should be able to spot the laterite tower of Kuti Reussi, the chapel of a hospital, just to the right of the nearest corner of the *baray* (•• also p. 113). Beyond this, another hospital, and resting house, was located at the Ta Muen Pass, close to the important temple of Ta Muen Thom (•• pp. 145-49). To the north and west, the view is obscured by trees and the slope of the hill, but the royal road continued north-west to Phimai. Khao Phnom Rung, as the hill is called, is clearly strategic, while the fertile plain that surrounds it, aided by a water management programme of *barays* and canals, provided the local rulers with a powerful economic base. The view today of rice-fields and trees, at its best in the rainy season, gives a sense of continuity with this past.

Enclosure

Enter the main doorway of the *gopura* and continue through to the enclosure. As you emerge on the other side of the *gopura,* the *mandapa* lies directly ahead, so close to the doorway that it blocks the view of the tower beyond. This restricted view makes the pediment and lintel of the *mandapa* the first things that you can see, and both are masterpieces.

The pediment depicts a 10-armed dancing Shiva – *Shiva Nantaraj* – and while it resembles the one in a similar position at Phimai, it is more complete, the god has a more benign expression, and there is great suppleness to the posture. The figures at Shiva's feet are badly damaged, but are Ganesh, the elephant-headed son of Shiva, and two female disciples, one of whom (with the drooping breasts) is almost certainly be Kareikalammeyar (•• p. 79).

South fronton of antechamber.

Below the pediment is the lintel, which in recent years has become the most famous in Thailand. In counterpoint to the dancing Shiva, the image here is of Vishnu reclining – *Vishnu Anantasayin* – and despite the missing left edge and being broken in two pieces, it is one of the finest representations of this well-known Hindu scene. Its recent history has been dramatic. Before restoration work began, the lintel rested on the ground, but at some time in the early 1960s, it was found to be missing, presumed stolen. Later, it was discovered to have been acquired by an American art foundation and on loan to the Art Institute of Chicago. As the restoration of the temple neared completion in the 1980s, public outcry grew in Thailand for its return, which was successfully negotiated in exchange for a payment made to the American foundation from private sources in the United States and an agreement to allow temporary loans of artefacts to the Art Institute of Chicago. The lintel was replaced in 1988, the year that the Phnom Rung restoration was finished.

Vishnu reclining over the mandapa entrance.

Vishnu reclines on his right side on the back of the *naga* – the world-serpent Ananta or Sesha. However, in the development of this famous scene over the centuries, by the 12th century when this was carved, the body of the *naga* has diminished, and the most prominent creature is a long-bodied dragon with a lion's head. The few dragons that have entered Khmer iconography seem to have come from China and Vietnam. Possibly, this was inspired through contact – direct or indirect – with the Chams of the central Annam coast. Brahma rises from Vishnu on a lotus flower, while Lakshmi as usual

Enclosure

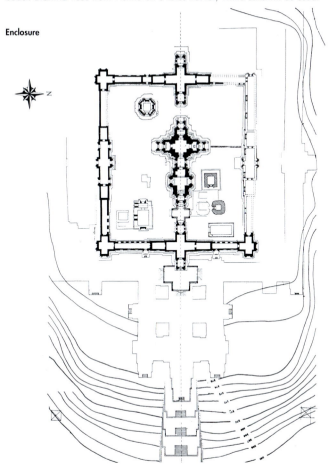

cradles Vishnu's legs; the tail plumage of two *hamsas* makes an arch for the scene. The motifs on either side (though the left is missing) are a *kala* face issuing garlands and two elegantly carved parrots below, with other figures, such as a female monkey with young fitting precisely into the tightly-knit design.

Cross over the small platform (the third and final *'naga* bridge') and enter the *mandapa*. Steps lead down into the room, which is about a metre below the level of the *antarala* and shrine. The steps are recent additions, and there is no agreement as to why the floor should be so low. Perhaps there might have been a raised wooden floor; the ceiling was certainly of wood to conceal the corbelled construction of the roof. The *mandapa* contained cubic blocks of sandstone carved with the guardians of

Interior of the mandapa.

direction, which are now in the National Museum Phimai. Six of what would originally have been eight were found, and are:-
Indra on the elephant Airavata (God of the Sky and the East)
Agni on a rhinoceros (God of Fire and the South-East)
Brahma on a *hamsa* (unusually here, as not a guardian of direction)
Varuna on a *naga* (though elsewhere normally on a hamsa – God of water and of the West)
Kubera on an *gajasimha* – an elephant-headed lion (God of wealth and of the North)
Isana on a bull (God of Air and Wind and of the North-East)

Indra.

Kubera.

In the *antarala* beyond, an interior lintel carrying five *rishis* or *yogis* reaffirms the importance of Shivaite worship. Continue through into the shrine, where the *linga* would have been situated. To your left, inside the porch that opens to the south, are two lintels. One shows a row of figures, the central one bearded, and this is believed to show the ceremony in which Narendraditya became a *rishi*. The other lintel shows Shiva as an ascetic surrounded by other *rishis*. On the opposite side, in the porch opening north, one of the lintels is too badly damaged to be identifiable, while the other shows Arjuna firing an arrow. Leave the sanctuary through the west door, pausing inside the porch to look at the lintel in which Krishna kills Kamsa (the other interior lintel is missing). As you emerge from this western porch, the west *gopura* lies directly ahead; to your left is the small square

Ceremony with Narendraditya.

building known as the Prang Noi. Walk over to the right instead, for a general view of the tower.

Tower

Compare this view with the same one at Phimai. From the decorative details, Phnom Rung's tower was built in the early 12th century, after that at Phimai but still before Angkor Wat. Unusually, however, while you might expect to see some progression – an intermediate stage between the towers of Phimai and Angkor Wat – in some important ways it is actually further from Angkor Wat and closer to Chola Indian *shikaras*, such as that at Rajarajesvara.

The redenting of Phimai's tower, with 6 interior angles at each corner, gives it a rounded section, and those at Angkor Wat even more so. Here, however, the corners have been redented to only 4 interior angles, and the tower is distinctly pyramidal. You can see also that the cornice is much less prominent than at Phimai, so that there is none of the waisted arrow-head impression that

Sanctuary and laterite 'library'.

helps make Phimai so imposing. If you step closer for a moment to the west door below the tower, you will see that the scene carved on the pediment includes a model of this very tower, with its slightly squat, pyramidal shape. Two tiers of pediment above this, roughly at cornice level, is another representation of the tower

None of this implies that Phnom Rung's tower is in any way less than that of Phimai. It has its own unique character, and the quantity and standard of carving that decorates it is exceptional. As at Phimai, there are 5 levels, including the cornice, each smaller than the one below, and the pyramid is topped with the vase of plenty. Originally, this might have been surmounted with Shiva's trident, where the lightning rod now is; some justification for thinking this is the image of the tower in the west pediment, which carries this symbol.

The north entrance to the mandapa.

Lintels, pediments and decorations

The *antarala* at Phnom Rung has a door on each side, giving a total of eight entrances in the sanctuary, each of them the opportunity for placing a lintel and pediment. These locations, together with the interior lintels, give Phnom Rung a wealth of imagery, all of it Hindu. We start at the western end.

Pediment over the west door of the sanctuary.

The badly damaged lintel over the west door of the sanctuary carries the same scene as over the west door of Phimai's *mandapa* – that of Rama and Lakshmana caught in the coils of a serpent. The pediment is related to it, and shows Sita being taken under Ravana's orders to the battlefield to see them. She is carried in a flying chariot, rendered as a miniature of this very temple, while the air all around is filled with Rama's monkey warriors.

Pediment over the north door of the sanctuary.

Continue clockwise around the sanctuary. Note the pilasters and colonettes that frame the north door – the former carved with rampant lions at the base, the latter with praying *rishis*. The lintel above is damaged, but originally showed Vishnu riding *garuda*. Above, monkey troops fill most of the pediment in an unidentified scene from the Ramayana.

Lintel over the north door of antarala.

A little further along, the lintel over the *antarala* shows Krishna despatching an elephant and lion in a carving that, despite the loss of Krishna's face, has a fine sense of movement. In the pediment, Sita is being abducted by Ravana. Appearing twice, she is taken prisoner in the lower part, and carried away at the top in Ravana's chariot. The gravity of the occasion appears not to concern two monkeys copulating with abandon in a tree.

The next doorway along is the north entrance to the *mandapa,* showing the battle of Lanka, with airborne monkey troops swooping down from above. Continue around the corner to the east entrance of the *mandapa,* where you first entered the enclosure. It has a false half roof on either side, and under the east gables of these are two half-pediments. That on the left as you face the entrance is of special interest, because it seems to show a rite described in the 13th century at Angkor by Chou Ta-Kuan (◆ p. 41). Although the carving is damaged, it

Deflowering ceremony.

appears to show a puberty ceremony in which a priests breaks the hymen of a girl with a miniature *linga*. Chou Ta-Kuan's account goes: "Daughters of rich parents, from seven to nine years of age (or eleven, in the case of poor people) are handed over to a Buddhist or Taoist [but Chou Ta-Kuan defines Taoists as "worshipping nothing but a block of stone (*linga*)"] priest for deflowering – a ceremony known as *chen-t'an*. Each year the proper authorities choose a day of the month corresponding to the fourth Chinese moon and let this be known throughout the country…I have been told that at a given moment the priest enters the maiden's pavilion and deflowers her with

his hand, dropping the first-fruits into a vessel of wine. It is said that the father and mother, the relations and neighbours, stain their foreheads with this wine, or even taste it."

Along the south side of the sanctuary, the pediment over the *mandapa* shows a fine carving of the bull Nandi, but the images of Shiva with Uma on his back have been unscrupulously hacked away. The lintel is missing.

Doorway at the South entrance.

Other buildings

In the south-west corner of the enclosure is a tower known as the Prang Noi ('small prang'), that rises no higher than cornice level. The styles of the eastern and southern lintels date it to between the late 10th and early 11th centuries – pre-dating the main sanctuary complex. Unusually, it is lined with laterite, and as no trace was ever found of a superstructure, it may have been unfinished.

In the south-east corner is a laterite 'library', and on the north side of the

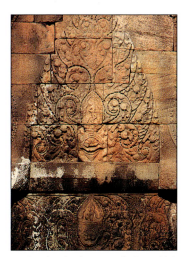

central sanctuary are the remains of two brick buildings, one facing south, the other east. The colonettes still standing are stylistically from the Koh Ker period, so that these brick structures must date to around the early 10th century.

Lintel and pediment on the Prang Noi.

109

Western *gopura*

On April 13th each year, as the sun rises, it shines directly through the succession of 15 doorways and halls, from the east gopura, through the sanctuary, to the west where you now stand. This is the day chosen for the Phnom Rung Festival. Given the importance attached by the Khmers to auspicious dates, the dedication of the temple may well have been made on this day, when the plane of the ecliptic is aligned with the axis of the temple.

Artefacts

The Mahawirawong Museum in Khorat has a few interesting pieces, notably a statue of the elephant-headed Ganesh in 8th-century Prei Kmeng style that is the oldest artefact recovered from Phnom Rung, a statue of Brahmani in early 10th-century Koh Ker style, and another of a four-headed Brahma.

There is also a lintel showing Krishna killing the serpent Kaliya at the National Museum, Bangkok.

Best times to visit Early morning in particular, for sunrise at the east *gopura* (and especially in April for the solar alignment – see above). Late afternoon is also a pleasant time. **Admission** 0600-1800, small charge. **Nearby sites** Muang Tam (8 km), Ban Bu (4½ km), the two Kuti Reussis (2½ km and 8 km), Ta Muen Thom (58 km). **Location** On the summit of Phnom Rung Hill, south of Route 24 between Nang Rong and Prakhon Chai, in Buriram Province. The hill, an extinct volcano, overlooks the plain that stretches north from the Dongrek Mountains. **Directions** There are two approaches from Route 24: from the west and from the east: **By car** *From Khorat and the west:* Driving east on Route 24, turn south on Route 2117 at the village of Ban Ta Ko (112 km from Chok Chai). After 6 km, turn left on Route 222 and continue 7 km up the hill, past the army post, to the temple entrance. 2 hrs. *From Surin:* Drive south on Route 214 to Route 24 and turn right. After 37 km, turn south from Route 24 onto Route 2075 at the town cross-roads of Prakhon Chai. Watch out for the fork in the road after 1 km; take the road to the right, signposted to Phnom Rung and Muang Tam. Phnom Rung is another 19 km from the fork. Note the signposted turning to Meuang Tam just before the road starts to ascend the hill. 1½ hrs. *From Ubon:* Take Route 24 west to Prakhon Chai and continue as above. 4 hrs. *From Buriram:* Drive south on Route 218 to Prakhon Chai, and follow the directions above. Alternatively, take Route 219 and turn right onto Route 24; continue for 10 km to Ban Ta Ko and follow the directions above. 1 hr. *From Muang Tam:* Follow the road north towards Prakhon Chai, but at the T-junction, after 5 km, turn left instead of right. This leads up the hill to the temple entrance, 3 km further on. 10 min. *From Aranyaprathet:* Drive north on Route 348 (the road turns sharp left after 55 km at a cross-roads just north of Ta Phraya). After crossing a low pass in the mountains, 112 km from Aranyaprathet, leave Route 348, which veers left, and continue on Route 2075 straight ahead. Lahan Sai is 16 km further on; turn right at the T-junction in town (still Route 2075), and after 1 km turn left onto a road signposted to Phnom Rung and Muang Tam. After 24 km (the road winds about the countryside), turn right onto Route 2221, which leads 7 km up the hill to the temple. 2 ¼ hrs. **By bus** *From Khorat:* Take a bus travelling to Surin as far as Ban Ta Ko; then either hire a *songthaeo* or motorcycle taxi to Phnom Rung, or take a cheaper regular *songthaeo* to the foot of Phnom Rung hill and another to the summit. *From Ubon and Surin:* Take a bus travelling in the direction of Khorat as far as either Prakhon Chai or Ban Ta Ko, and then hire either a *songthaeo* of motorcycle taxi. *From Buriram:* Take a bus as far as Ban Ta Ko, and continue as above. **Nearest accommodation and food** Buriram (↦ pp. 252-54), Surin (↦ pp. 283-84), Khorat (↦ pp. 64-67).

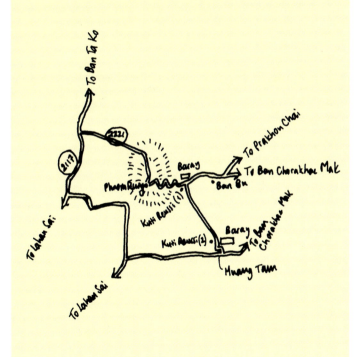

The laterite tower.

Kuti Reussi #1 ꕤ ꕥ កុដិឫសី ១

Date: Late 12th to early 13th centuries
Style: Bayon
Reign: Jayavarman VII
Visit: 10 mins

Close to the foot of Phnom Rung Hill, this redented laterite tower with 3x2.6m porch on its east side was one of Jayavarman VII's hospital chapels (♦♦ also pp. 115, 151, 153, 182). Confusingly, it shares the same name with the nearby laterite chapel close by the *baray* of Muang Tam (♦♦ p. 115) – the name, however, means nothing more than 'hermit's cell' and is a local description. Although not worth a special trip, it is a short stop on the way between Phnom Rung and Muang Tam.

Plan

Like other similar chapels of the period (e.g. the other Kuti Reussi, Prang Ku and Kamphaeng Noi), the layout is very simple – a small tower with east-facing porch, set in a small rectangular enclosure with a single eastern *gopura*.

Best times to visit No particular time. **Admission** Unrestricted, no charge. **Nearby sites** Phnom Rung (2½km), Muang Tam (5½km), Ban Bu (2 km), the other Kuti Reussi (5 km). **Location** At the foot of Phnom Rung Hill, on the west side, in Buriram province, surrounded by a small hamlet. On the other side of the road, to the north, is a rectangular *baray* known as Nong Bua Rai or Sa Pleng, and still in use. **By car** *From Phnom Rung:* Leave Phnom Rung to the east, in the direction of Prakhon Chai. After 2½ km – about 500m from the foot of the hill – look for the laterite tower behind some small houses. You need to cross the garden of one of these houses to reach the chapel. 5 min. *From Muang Tam:* Leave on the road north that skirts around the *baray*, signposted to Phnom Rung. After 5 km, turn left at the T-junction, still heading for Phnom Rung. The chapel is on the left after 500m. 10 min. For thumbnail map, see Phnom Rung. **Nearest accommodation and food** Buriram (♦♦ pp. 252-54), Surin (♦♦ pp. 283-84).

The laterite remains of the dharmasala.

Carved rosette detail..

BanBu บ้านบุ

Date: *Late 12th to early 13th centuries*
Style: *Bayon*
Reign: *Jayavarman VII*
Visit: *10 mins*

Though more collapsed than Ta Muen, and in a location lacking atmosphere (the grounds of a school), this laterite chapel is another of the eight *dharmasalas,* or rest-houses, so far found on the road to Phimai. They were usually between 4 and 5 metres wide by 14 to 15 metres long. Spaced approximately 12 to 15 kilometres apart, they were an easy day's walk from one to the next. Although the rest-houses on the longer eastern road from Angkor to Champa were built in sandstone, these on the Phimai road were laterite.

This was originally a laterite tower with a long entrance hall, measuring 11.5 x 5.1m. Only the walls of this chapel remain, and it is really worth a stop only if you are driving this route to or from Phnom Rung. The only *in situ* carving is a rosette-shaped sandstone panel, which must have been brought here from another temple of an earlier period.

Best times to visit No special time. **Admission** Unrestricted, no charge.
Nearby sites Phnom Rung (4½ km), Muang Tam (6 ½ km) and the two Kuti Reussis (2 km and 4½ km). **Location** In the grounds of Ban Bu High School (Rongrian Ban Bu Witthiasan), between Phnom Rung and Prakhon Chai. **By car** *From Prakhon Chai:* Follow the directions to Phnom Rung (•► p. 98). After 14 km the road enters the village of Ban Bu; the high school is on the left after another 1½ km (immediately after the primary school). 20 min. *From Phnom Rung:* Take the road east down the hill towards Prakhon Chai. Continue 1½ km after the turn-off to Muang Tam; the high school is on the right. 5-10 min. *From Muang Tam:* Follow the directions for Phnom Rung, but turn right instead of left at the T-junction after 5 km. The high school is on the right after 1½ km. 10 min. **Nearest accommodation and food** Surin (•► pp. 283-84), Buriram (•► pp. 252-54).

Kuti Reussi #2 🌿🔖 កុដិឬសី ២

Date: Late 12th to early 13th centuries
Style: Bayon
Reign: Jayavarman VII
Visit: 10 mins

The laterite tower in the enclosure.

Very similar in appearance to the other Kuti Reussi at the foot of Phnom Rung Hill (➟ p. 112), this redented laterite tower in its small enclosure was built during the reign of Jayavarman VII as the chapel for another hospital. Set among rice fields with picturesque rural views all around, this compact site is little visited but worth stopping for on the way between Phnom Rung and Muang Tam.

Plan

The small enclosure, bounded by laterite walls, contains an east-facing laterite tower 7 x 7m in plan, with a 3.2 x 2.2m porch. The other building in the enclosure is a 4 x 7.5m 'library' in the south-east corner. The single entrance *gopura* is on the east, facing towards the *baray* of Muang Tam 300m away. Formerly, there was a large pond between the chapel and the *baray*.

Best times to visit Early morning and late afternoon. **Admission** Unrestricted, no charge **Nearby sites** Muang Tam (1 km), Phnom Rung (8 km), the other Kuti Reussi (5 km), Ban Bu (4/₂ km) **Location** 300m west of the north-west corner of the large baray north of Muang Tam (➟ p. 116). **By Car** *From Muang Tam*: Take the road leading north and signposted to Phnom Rung. It first skirts the *baray* around the west side. Just before reaching the north-west corner of the *baray*, turn left onto a track (driveable if dry). The chapel, which you can see easily from the road, is ahead. 5 min. *From Phnom Rung*: Follow the directions to Muang Tam (➟ p. 116). Just after reaching the north-west corner of the *baray*, turn right onto the track. 10-15 min. **Nearest accommodation and food** Buriram (➟ pp. 252-54), Surin (➟ pp. 283-84).

Muang Tam

ปราสาทเมืองต่ำ

Date: 11th century
Style: combination of Khleang and Baphuon
Reigns: Jayavarman V, Suryavarman I, Udayadityavarman II
Visit: 1 hr

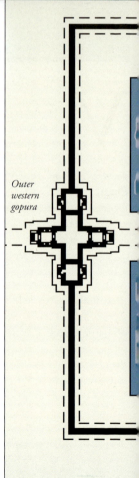

Outer western gopura

Overlooked by Phnom Rung, and so now known as the 'Lower City', Muang Tam has a particular charm from its tranquil setting and its ponds. It was formerly in deep forest, but gradual settlement in the area has turned it into a pleasant rural landscape, still partly wooded. In the early 1950s a village was built here by about 50 families from Ubon Ratchathani to the east, and the addition of a fairly traditional farming community to the 11th century temple enhances the site, as, when it was still active, Muang Tam, like other Khmer temples, would have been supported by attendant villages.

The temple has recently been restored by the Fine Arts Department. Its former air of neglect and dilapidation had a certain charm, but some preservation work was clearly necessary to prevent further collapse, particularly the effects of subsidence. During the course of the restoration work, excavations uncovered some important finds, including two statues

(⟶ Artefacts p.122).

So far, however, no inscriptions have been found, which makes it difficult to place Muang Tam in the history of the region. The styles of carving, particularly in the lintels, are the best guide to the temple's dates. Most are a combination of Khleang and Baphuon styles, and so were probably carved between the end of the 10th century and the end of the 11th. The temple was dedicated to Shiva – a large *linga* was found in the central shrine, and a prominent lintel from the north-east tower features Shiva and Uma riding the bull Nandi – but fragments of a statue of Vishnu have also been uncovered. Worship of the two gods in the same temple was by no means uncommon.

The outer northern gopura from the pond.

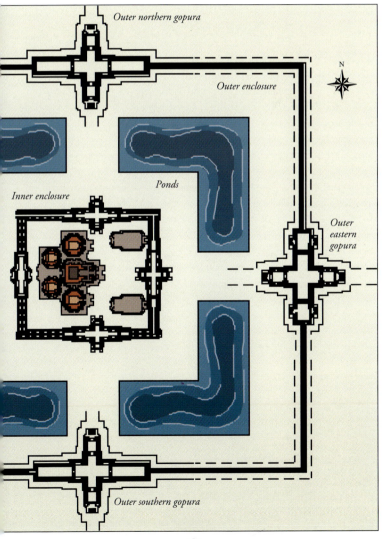

Muang Tam is a substantial 'flat' temple built to a concentric plan, but with two unusual features. It is flat in the sense that there was no attempt at physically elevating the central sanctuary, either by raising the platform or by building a dominant tower. At the same time, the five central towers and the dedication to Shiva make it clear that the central sanctuary was supposed to represent Mount Meru (and the larger main tower probably Mount Kailasa, where Shiva lives). The five brick towers are one of Muang Tam's peculiarities, being built as a front row of three and a back row of two rather than as a quincunx.

The other special feature of the temple is the importance given to the four corner ponds that surround the inner enclosure, each L-shaped so that they appear as a continuous square moat intersected by four broad causeways. Each of the ponds is surrounded by an embankment in the form of ground-hugging *nagas;* their tails meet to form low gates leading down into the water, and these would have had a ritual role. It is likely that these ponds represent the four oceans surrounding Mount Meru, but this layout is unique among Khmer temples.

The five brick towers, together with two 'libraries', occupied the inner enclosure. Its wall, broken at the four cardinal points by *gopuras,* is surrounded by the four ponds. These are themselves surrounded by the wall that bounds the outer enclosure, also with *gopuras* on the east, south, west and north. The main entrance is, as usual, on the eastern side. East of this, and beyond the courtyard of the modern wat (Wat Prasat Burapharam), are the remains of a small *baray,* now dried up. It is aligned exactly with the axis of the temple, and so may have built at the same time. Further north is a much larger *baray* – 1150m x 400m – which you skirt round in the usual approach to the temple from Phnom Rung or Surin. This *baray* is one of very few that have remained full since they were built – although it was dug after the temple, this means close to 900 years of continuous use. Very possibly, it was contemporary with the great West Baray at Angkor, also still in use. It is fed by streams flowing from the Dongrek Mountains to the south while openings on the *baray's* northern side were intended to regulate the flow of water into the artificial Khlong Pun ('Lime Canal') to the north. This canal, dug in the lowest part of the plain between the Dongreks and Phnom Rung Hill, stretches 20 km to the north-east, and was a major part of a Khmer irrigation system designed to cope with the region's notoriously unreliable rainfall.

The baray.

The outer eastern gopura.

Outer eastern *gopura*

From the small village road that leads south from the *baray* by the modern *wat*, a short path leads to the main eastern entrance. The lintel over the main doorway in the centre features Krishna fighting the five-headed *naga* Kaliya.

The pediment above is carved around a central *kala* face, as are both the lintels and the pediments of the two side entrances. The *kala* plays a particularly important role in the decoration at Muang Tam, and occurs frequently in the lintels and pediments. More than this, there are two different styles of *kala* carved at Muang Tam – most, such as those here over the outer doorways, are Baphuon style, but a few, such as over the inner south door of this *gopura*, are in the

Kala lintel over the entrance to the outer eastern gopura.

'earlier' Khleang style. This is one of several clues in the Northeast that the styles known from Angkor do not always coincide neatly with the periods.

Above, on the corners, are *naga* antefixes marking the ends of arches. The strange-looking projection held in front of the *naga* like a saxophone, is a garland that issues from the creature's mouth – very typical of the Baphuon style and a common treatment of garlands in lintels. Pass through into a cross-shaped room with connecting chambers on either side, where the two side entrances are located.

Naga antefix, outer eastern gopura.

To the left and right, laterite walls, topped with a curved coping (and a smaller sandstone coping on top of this), form the outer enclosure. These, as well as some of the other structures at Muang Tam, have suffered from subsidence – the relatively low-lying land here is close to the water- table and often waterlogged, as evidenced by the survival of the ponds and the large *baray* to the north. These walls, and other structures, have been the subject of a lengthy restoration.

Close to this *gopura*, the statue mentioned on page 122 was discovered.

Outer enclosure

Pass through the *gopura* into the temple's outer enclosure. Ahead is the inner enclosure with the restored brick towers, and on either side are two of Muang Tam's L-shaped ponds, effectively making a broad moat. They are dotted with lotus plants, which flower in the morning. On either side, note the low stone gateways with a few steps leading down into the water. The door frames are in fact formed by the tails of *nagas*, whose bodies make up the pond's embankment. A ceremony of some form would have been performed here by priests.

To the north and south are other *gopuras*, smaller than the eastern and western entrances, each with attractive views back over the ponds. This outer enclosure of Muang Tam is worth spending time walking around, particularly when there are few other people (by comparison with Phnom Rung and Phimai, Muang Tam is little visited).

Inner enclosure

Return to the central walkway leading between the ponds from the main entrance, and enter the inner eastern *gopura* that leads to the central sanctuary. Above the doorway is yet another *kala* lintel in the Baphuon style – the *kala* grasps the garlands that issue from his mouth, and a row of *rishis* forms the top border. Pass through, and turn to see the lintel that faces in towards the towers. This is a scene from the life of Krishna, in which he battles the *naga* Kaliya, and wins. The pediment above features a *simha* above the ubiquitous *kala*.

Southern gopura to inner enclosure.

Kala pediment, eastern gopura to the inner enclosure.

On either side is the gallery wall that surrounds the enclosure, sandstone on a laterite base, extensively restored. Like Phnom Wan and Sdok Kok Thom, the gallery has windows facing both in and out. There are no corner pavilions. In the south-east and north-east corners, recent excavations have uncovered the foundations of two 'library'-like buildings.

Central towers

At the heart of the temple are the five brick towers, four of them restored. The arrangement, in two unequal rows, is unusual; the main shrine, which was larger than the others, is in the middle of the front row. It had completely collapsed by the time restoration work was begun, and there were insufficient bricks found to allow

The central towers from the southeast.

reconstruction. As it stands, it has the just the lower dozen courses, on a massive stepped laterite platform.

Although the restoration with new bricks makes it a little more difficult to appreciate the quality of the original workmanship, there is still evidence of brick carving to quite a high standard. On the south side of the front row's northern tower, the pediment arch has been carved in outline only, but the nagas at each corner can be made out. During restoration work, traces of stucco were found on these towers, and it is likely that the decoration was never intended to be completed only in brickwork.

Lintel of the north tower of the front row showing Shiva and Uma on Nandi.

The lintels are of high quality. The main east-facing lintel of the northern tower on the front row is in the Baphuon style, but in other ways stands apart from Muang Tam's other lintels. Particularly deep, and in a red sandstone that has weathered to black in parts, it shows Shiva with Uma riding the bull Nandi, executed in an unusually naïve manner. Another good example of provincial folk art is the treatment of the lintel on the tower directly behind – this features a small scene of Krishna lifting Mount Govardhana, rather nonchalantly, with one of the sheltering cattle behind. Krishna stands above a *kala*, which appears on all the tower lintels. Those on the south-west and south-east towers feature divinities sitting over the *kalas*, and a row of *rishis* at the top.

Outer western gopura

Leave the inner enclosure to the west. The inner western *gopura*, unlike the others, was built of sandstone for some reason, and has long since collapsed. Continue past the ponds on either side to the outer western *gopura*. On the inner and outer entrances of this structure, note the unfinished lintels with a raised central area of stone in the shape of a diamond. For various reasons, incomplete works appear at temples throughout the Khmer empire. Quite often, it was simply a matter of the death of the king or dignitary who commissioned the building – his successor might have little interest in finishing it,

Outer eastern gopura.

Lintel of the north tower of the back row showing Krishna.

particularly when compared with the need to begin a new temple. At any rate, being able to see lintels at various stages of carving on a tour of these temples helps to visualise the way in which the stone carvers approached them. The northern lintel of Phnom Wan's shrine, for example, shows the stage between the modelling of the basic features and the detailing (•→ see p. 67). Here is a much earlier stage, in which the surrounds have been cut back to leave a plain diamond shape in the centre. This would then have been carved into the main motif – probably a *kala* face as in the other *gopuras*. The pilasters on either side of the door are also at different stages – on one the design has only been roughed out, while the other is partially carved.

Artefacts

Two stone figures were uncovered during recent excavations, both significant, and now at the National Museum, Bangkok. One figure, found near the base of the outer eastern *gopura,* was broken into three pieces, and although unfinished, is in a posture that suggests he was holding a club. If so, he would be a guardian figure known as Nandikesvara. The other statue, carved from the same sandstone, was found, unusually, in the large *baray* to the north. This figure has small fangs at the corners of the mouth, and so was almost certainly a guardian of the kind known as a Mahakala. It would originally have stood as a pair with the statue of Nandikesvara. Why it should have been moved is not known, although one obvious suspicion is that it was thrown into the *baray* by iconoclasts.

A five-headed naga emerging from one of the ponds.

Best times to visit Early mornings and late afternoons in fine weather have the most attractive lighting, and given Muang Tam's pleasant setting, it is definitely worth making the effort to be here at either of these times. The morning has an additional advantage in that the lotus flowers in the ponds are open.

Admission 0730-1800, small charge. **Nearby sites** Phnom Rung (8 km), Ban Bu (6½ km), the two Kuti Reussis (1 km and 5 km), Ban Phluang (59 km), Ta Muen Thom (57 km). **Location** A short distance south of Phnom Rung, in the village of Ban Khok Muang, in the Prakhon Chai district of Buriram province.

By car There are no buses to Muang Tam, which is rather off the beaten track. Hiring a car is the ideal choice. Otherwise, use public transport as far as Prakhon Chai (see Directions to Phnom Rung, page 108) and negotiate the hire of a *songthaeo* or motorbike-taxi *(motusai rab chang)*. In any case, a visit to Muang Tam is best combined with one to Phnom Rung, so consider hiring a *songthaeo* at Prakhon Chai or Ta Ko for the double visit (a half-day). *From Surin*: Drive south on Route 214 to the junction with Route 24 and turn right. Continue as far as Prakhon Chai and turn left (south) at the cross-roads onto Route 2075. Watch out for the fork in the road after 1 km; take the signposted road to the right. After 16 km and just before the road starts to climb Phnom Rung hill, turn left down a road signposted to Muang Tam. About 4 km after this, the road skirts the west side of a large baray; follow the road around the south side, and then left into the village of Ban Khok Muang. The temple is on the right, opposite the modern wat on the left. 1½ hrs.

From Buriram: Drive south on Route 219 to Prakhon Chai and cross over Route 24. Continue as above. 1 hr.

From Phnom Rung: Leave the temple to the east on the road down to Prakhon Chai. After 3 km turn right on the road signposted to Muang Tam; Muang Tam lies 5 km further on, immediately south of the large baray which the road skirts. 10 min.

From Aranyaprathet: Drive north on Route 348 (the road turns sharp left after 55 km at a cross-roads just north of Ta Phraya). After crossing a low pass in the mountains, 112 km from Aranyaprathet, leave Route 348, which veers left, and continue on Route 2075 straight ahead. Lahan Sai is 16 km further on; turn right at the T-junction in town (still Route 2075), and after 1 km turn left onto the road signposted to Phnom Rung and Muang Tam. After 12 km, at the village of Ban Yai Yaem Watthana, turn right – Muang Tam and the village of Ban Khok Muang lie 6 km ahead. 2 hrs.**Nearest accommodation and food**
Buriram (• pp. 252-54), Surin (• pp.283-84), Khorat (• pp.264-67).

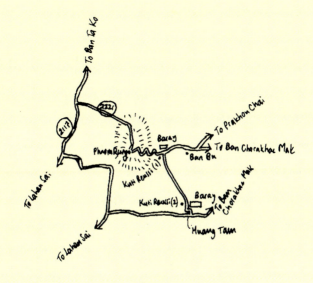

NORTHEAST –
THE BORDER
TEMPLES

*Above: Preah Vihear, Gopura III
looking east along the Dongrek
Mountains.*

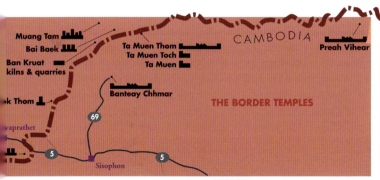

Muang Tam

Bai Baek

Ban Kruat
kilns & quarries

Ta Muen Thom
Ta Muen Toch
Ta Muen

CAMBODIA

Preah Vihear

k Thom

Banteay Chhmar

THE BORDER TEMPLES

69

vaprathet

5

Sisophon

5

ANGKOR

From a little north of Ta Phraya in Prachinburi province the border between modern Thailand and Cambodia follows the line of the Dongrek Mountains, which run almost due east towards Laos and the lower Mekong River. Seen from the north – the Thai side – they are not particularly distinguished in appearance; from Route 24 they typically seem no more than a range of low hills in the haze some 30-40 km distant. From the Cambodian side, however, they are an impressive wall rearing up over the plains – the leading edge of the Khorat Plateau, and a natural frontier. Several formerly important passes (*chong* in Thai) such as Chong Saeng, Chong Sai Taku, Chong Ta Muen, Chong Samet and Chong Chom cut through the range. Close to a number of these ancient routes, temples and resting places were built in different reigns.

Of all the Khmer sites in Thailand, these border temples are the most atmospheric, but unfortunately some are a little dangerous to visit because of mines scattered around the area. That the Dongrek range is a natural frontier has not contributed to its political stability; rather it has been for many years a sensitive area. The mountains and forests of Cambodia's north and north-west have been a refuge for insurgents during and since the Indo-Chinese wars. In the most recent chapter in Cambodia's troubled history, this border has been the base for the Khmer Rouge, and there has been sporadic fighting in some parts. Banditry is not uncommon.

As a result, access to some of the border temples is difficult to predict. At certain times it may be straightforward, at others impossible. Military and Border Patrol Police checkpoints are normal on all access roads, and will allow visitors through depending on the current political situation. Moreover, while this may ease in the future, a lasting legacy for which there is no complete solution is the land mines scattered around some areas. Modern anti-personnel mines use plastic and are difficult to detect, and although the army has given priority to clearing some temples, any overgrown area or forest is suspect, and will probably always remain so. Visitors to temples situated very close to the border should under no circumstances stray off paths.

Prachinburi National Museum   พิพิธภัณฑ์ปราจีนบุรี 🔸

Visit: 30 mins

A small museum, but well laid out. The best part of its Khmer collection is the Khao Noi exhibit, for which one entire room has been allocated. The centre-pieces are the five 7th century lintels, described in the following entry. If you intend to visit Khao Noi, it is essential to see the museum also. Otherwise, it is probably not worth a special trip, being quite far from other sites.

North lintel from the northern tower of Prasat Khao Noi.

West lintel from the northern towers of Prasat Khao Noi.

South lintel from the northern towers of Prasat Khao Noi.

East lintel from the northern tower of Khao Noi.

Lintel from the central tower of Khao Noi.

Admission Wed-Fri. 0900-1600, small charge. Phone: 037 211586 **By car**
From Bangkok: Prachinburi lies en route to Aranyaprathet – a short detour off
Route 33, 135 km from Bangkok and 29 km from Nakhon Nayok. See directions
to Aranyaprathet, page 250, and 10 km after Nakhon Nayok take Route 319 to
the town of Prachinburi. *From Aranyaprathet:* Take Route 33 west for 140 km,
and turn south onto Route 320 to Prachinburi. **By bus** frequent services from north-
east bus terminal. **By train** Phone 223 7010

Restored central tower. The lintels on site are copies.

ปราสาทเขาน้อย

Prasat Khao Noi 🍂 🌿

Date: **Mid-7th century, Reconstructed 11th century**
Styles: **late Sambor Prei Kuk – early Prei Kmeng**
Reigns: **Isanavarman I, Bhavavarman II**
Visit: **30 mins**

Close to the Cambodian border, and a short drive from the town of Aranyaprathet, the site of Prasat Khao Noi ('Small Hill') consists of the common arrangement of three small towers in a row on a common base. The location, a lightly wooded, isolated hill, gives a fine view over the Cambodian plains to the east, the direction in which the towers face. The temple dates to the middle of the 7th century, although the middle tower at least was reconstructed in the 11th century. This tower has recently been rebuilt by the Fine Arts Department in a fairly sensitive restoration, the two towers on either side having been left in their ruined state. The chief interest of Khao Noi, and the means by which it has been dated as the earliest significant Khmer monument in Thailand, lies in its lintels. Quite good copies of these have been placed *in situ,* while the originals have been removed for safety to the museum at Prachinburi, 164 km (2 hrs) to the west. For this reason, any visit to Khao Noi should be combined with one to the museum (•• p. 127).

Five lintels, all in very good condition, survive: one from the central tower and all four from the northern tower. Stylistically, the lintel that was re-used on the 11th century central tower (and may not necessarily have been

129

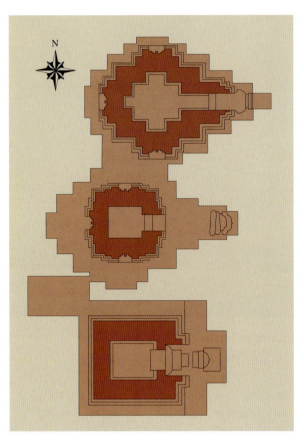

placed there originally) is one of the earliest. The inward-facing *makaras* disgorge a series of arches connected by medallions. These small medallions contain rather crudely modelled figures of divine steeds – an elephant and horses. The northern and southern lintels from the northern tower are in the same style, known as Sambor Prei Kuk, although narrower.

The eastern and western lintels of the northern tower are considerably deeper, and in the slightly later Prei Kmeng style. In this, the *makaras* have disappeared, and the series of small arches have fused into one large arch, with incurved ends. The medallions remain. Kneeling and praying figures flank the arch of the eastern lintel, *simhas* the western lintel.

Artefacts

In addition to the lintels, *lingas* and pedestals were recovered from the site, indicating the worship of Shiva. These also are now on display at the Prachinburi Museum. Interestingly, they were found shattered – in so many pieces as to suggest that they may have been destroyed intentionally. This might have been as a result of war or a change in worship. Although there was remarkable tolerance between religions in the Khmer areas, there have been other instances of desecration – for instance, at the Bayon after the death of the Buddhist king Jayavarman VII.

Best times to visit Early morning and late afternoon give rewarding views over the surrounding countryside, although the site itself, surrounded by trees, suggests no special time of day. **Admission** Unrestricted, no charge. **Nearby sites** Sdok Kok Thom is 36 km to the north-east as the crow flies (52 km by the shortest route), Prachinburi Museum is 164 km, and Banteay Chhmar 114 km into Cambodia from Aranyaprathet. A little out of the way in relation to most of the other Khmer sites, Khao Noi is probably best visited on a route that takes in Sdok Kok Thom and Ban Kruat, then approaching Muang Tam and surrounding sites from the south. **Location** South-east of Aranyaprathet, in the Prachinburi province, on the Cambodian border. **By car** Approaching Aranyaprathet from the west on Route 33, turn right at the clock tower, passing the local government offices (Amphoe). After 500m turn left onto Ratuthit Rd and continue for about 1 km to the traffic lights. There turn right onto Route 3067 and follow the winding road for 1 km; where it bends right, take the small road on the left, which runs straight as far as you can see to the south-south-east. After 12 km you reach the prominent wooded hill on which the temple is built. The road bends left; park shortly after on the right. Steps lead up to the temple – a steep walk. Near the top, where the steps finish, take the right fork, not the left. 15-20 mins. A longer alternative approach, 21 km, follows the border: turn left at the clock tower on the road signposted to the frontier. The road runs by the railway line; after 5 km, just before the border crossing to Paoy Pet, turn right on the road signposted to Ban Nong Lan. After 7 km turn right again; the road reaches the hill after another 9 km. 30 mins. For directions to Aranyaprathet, ➡ pp. 250-52. If you arrive by train or bus, hire a motorised three-wheeler motor-cycle *(samlor khreuang)* in town for the short journey to the temple. **Nearest accommodation and food** Aranyaprathet (➡ pp 250-52).

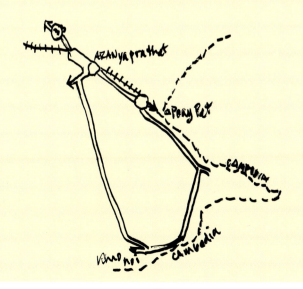

Remains of the tower from the northern corner of the enclosure.

Sdok Kok Thom ❦ ปราสาทสะด๊อกก๊อ

Date: **11th century (linga consecrated 1052)**
Style: **Baphuon**
Reign: **Udayadityavarman II**
Visit: **30 mins**

This small and little-visited temple, on the Cambodian border, lies 30 km in a direct line north-east of Aranyaprathet. Sdok Kok Thom was for a number of years in the 1980s occupied as a military post by KPNLF troops, and unvisitable. It was 'opened' – meaning that the Thai army pushed the Cambodian rebels back and began clearing the mines – in 1990 for a royal visit. A relatively compact site, Sdok Kok Thom retains a fairly complete *gopura* at the main east entrance, enclosing wall and 'libraries'. Its tower, however, has collapsed, though in an unusual way, and it now tapers to a thin spire. The rubble of fallen sandstone blocks surrounds the tower.

Sdok Kok Thom is best known, for its inscription, one of the most important in Khmer epigraphy. No longer *in situ* (it has been removed for safe-keeping to the National Museum, Bangkok), it dates to 1052 AD and chronicles the history of the Shivakaivalya dynasty of priests. More important is its summary of the reign of the Khmer kings over the preceding two centuries, from 802, for this includes the foundation of the Khmer Empire itself. It relates how Jayavarman II arrived from Java, became king of Indrapura (probably east and across the Mekong River from present-day Phnom Penh), and later moved his capital to Hariharalaya, close to Angkor on the northern shore of the Tonlé Sap. This is the first documentary evidence of the beginnings of the Angkorean era.

Sdok Kok Thom's name is in modern Khmer (it was originally known as Bhadraniketana), and although there is some disagreement, Aymonier believed that it meant '(the temple by) The Great Reed Lake', referring to the former *baray* to the east. Sdok means 'crumpled, compressed' and, according to Aymonier often turned up in Khmer inscriptions as the equivalent of the Sanskrit *hrada*, meaning a 'large body of water'; *kok* is a type of reed used for matting, and *thom* means 'large'. A prominent, isolated hill 24 km east-south-east of here is also called Phnom Sdok Kok.

The inscription carries the usual fulsome praise of the king, and describes how the land here was granted to the Brahman priest Vagindrapandita. From his title, he was clearly highly placed: "In 1052 the *dhuli jeng vrah kamrateng añ* ['dust of the feet of my lord' – the highest title ever given to a Brahman] founded the *kamrateng jagat* ['lord of the universe'] at Bhadraniketana". He informed His Majesty Udayadityavarman of it, soliciting that this establishment and these slaves"…should still constitute a gracious benevolence in favour of the *kamrateng jagat Shivalinga* of Bhadraniketana, conferring on him the exclusive right to this establishment and this land." The king went further than granting the title, and made a donation "of gold, of precious stones, of elephants, of horses, etc.," also making a vow for the *linga* to "dissipate the fogs and to project a constant splendour all around, with honour and success, up to the extinction of being".

In other words, in 1052 a *linga* of some importance was consecrated in the relatively small sanctuary, and the stele found in the gallery of the enclosure was inscribed to commemorate the event.

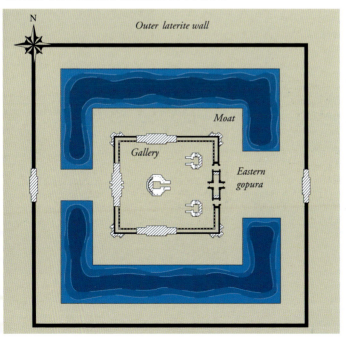

Plan

The layout is simple and compact: a central sanctuary that consisted of a shrine with tower, *antarala* and *mandapa*, set in a single enclosure closely surrounded by a moat. Two 'libraries' occupy the usual positions north-east and south-east of the tower, the main *gopura* is one the east side, with a smaller *gopura* on the west. Causeways leading from each of these *gopuras* divide the moat into two, while an outer laterite wall encloses the moat. The temple is oriented to the east, and a 300m dyke was noted by Aymonier, leading to a *baray* measuring 400-500m on each side.

Gallery and gopuras

The main eastern *gopura*, which would originally have been roofed in wood or tile rather than stone, is distinctive for Thailand in that its superstructure is stepped. Although this was normal in Cambodia for an 11th century temple, it is the only such example from its period known in Thailand – others simply have vaulted roofs. Only Muang Singh and Wat Kamphaeng Laeng (➻ pp. 238 and 241 respectively) have

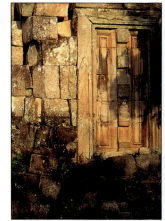

the same stepped profile, and they are from much later. The gallery is in laterite and sandstone (the stone providing the base and coping). From what is left of it, and in the north-western and north-eastern corners in particular, you can see that there were windows both on the inside and the outside – less common than windows facing inwards only.

Central sanctuary

The tower has almost completely collapsed on the eastern side so that only a thin spire remains, reaching to just above the original cornice. Carved stone blocks lie scattered around; the false door on the west side is the only architectural feature that remains intact. No doubt looting during the period when it was a military post in the 1980s added to the present state.

False door on the west side of the tower.

'Libraries'

These face west, as usual, and their most notable feature is the large side windows.

Artefacts

The inscription for which Sdok Kok Thom is best known (➻ pp. 132-33) is in the National Museum, Bangkok, but at the time of writing not on display.

The eastern gopura and northeastern 'library'.

Best times to visit Early morning and late afternoon. **Admission** Unrestricted (though there may be military checkpoints on several of the roads; ask permission to continue when within a few km of the site). No charge. **Nearby sites** Khao Noi lies 36 km south-west as the crow flies (52 km by the shortest route), near the town of Aranyaprathet. In addition, one of the largest, yet least-visited, of all Khmer temples lies a short distance across the border in Cambodia. This is Banteay Chhmar, 'Citadel of the Cat', and is worth every effort to see, although access depends on border regulations, and these of course depend on the political situation (see the following entry). **Location** Between 38 km and 53 km north-east of Aranyaprathet (depending on the route), in the Ta Phraya district of Prachinburi province. **By car** *From Aranyaprathet:* The less complicated approach is to take Route 348 north in the direction of Ta Phraya. After 39 km, turn right onto Route 3397. The roads after this point deteriorate, at the time of writing. After 12 km turn left onto an unmarked road. 1 km further on there is a kind of cross-roads, although the way is little more than a track at this point, but still driveable – take the track that heads due east. The temple appears ahead after a little more than 1 km. 53 km, 45 min.-1 hr. With slightly more chance of getting lost, leave Route 348 after 22 km, turning right onto Route 3381. 9 km further on, at Ban Khok Sung, turn left (the road is still Route 3381) and continue for 4 km, where Route 3397 leads off to the right. Take this for about 1 km and turn right onto the unmarked road mentioned above. 38 km, 45 min. *From Khorat:* Drive south on Route 224 and then east on Route 24 as far as Nang Rong (98 km). Turn right and head south through Pa Kham (another 25 km), continuing south on Route 348 which continues south over the hills to Ta Phraya. From Ta Phraya, continue south in the direction of Aranyaprathet, but after 11 km, turn left onto Route 3397 and continue as the directions from Aranyaprathet (above). 3 ½- 4 hrs. *From Phnom Rung* and *Muang Tam:* From both of these neighbouring temples, make first for Lahan Sai. *From Phnom Rung,* drive west down the hill on Route 2221 for 7 km to the T-junction with Route 2117. Turn left and follow the road (which winds) for 19 km to the T-junction with Route 2075. Turn right and reach Lahan Sai after 1 km. *From Muang Tam,* drive west out of the village for 6 km until the T-junction; turn left and drive for another 12 km until the T-junction with Route 2075. Turn right, Lahan Sai is 1 km further on. From Lahan Sai, continue as above. 2 ¼ hrs from Phnom Rung, 2 hrs from Muang Tam.
Nearest accommodation and food Aranyaprathet (➤ pp. 250-52).

Face-tower, central sanctuary.

Banteay Chhmar

Date: Late 12th (probably after 1190) to early 13th century
Style: Bayon (mainly the second period)
Reign: Jayavarman VII
Visit: 2-3 hrs

ปราสาทบันทายฉมาร์

This enormous, complex temple-city is one of the most intriguing in the Khmer empire, both for its scale and its remote location – in what was at the time a frontier region. Never excavated, Banteay Chhmar, with its ruined face-towers, carvings, forest and bird-life is the quintessence of the lost Khmer city, an extremely evocative and romantic site. The bas-reliefs, which cover the outer face of the enclosing gallery, are comparable with those of the Bayon, and include a unique and extraordinarily fine sequence of Lokesvaras. From the inscription found there, George Coedès believed that Banteay Chhmar was built as the funerary temple of Jayavarman VII's son, the Crown Prince Indravarman. It seems that the prince died early in Jayavarman VII's reign, although this is by no means certain. There is an intriguing clue in the mystery of the king's son in one of the most unusual of Banteay Chhmar's bas-reliefs, on the west wall of the gallery described below.

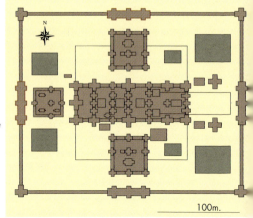

100m.

136

Plan

Like Phimai, Angkor Thom, Angkor Wat and Preah Khan, the site originally enclosed a city, with the temple proper at the heart. The entire area covers 2 km by 2 ½ km (by comparison, Angkor Thom is 3 km square, Angkor Wat 1 km by 800m., and Phimai 1 km by just over ½ km). This contained the main temple, a number of other religious structures, and a *baray* (700 x 1500m), in the middle of which was an artificial island with a small sanctuary (similar in situation to the West Mebon and East Mebon at Angkor).

The rectangular outer enclosure, now difficult to discern, was an earthen rampart 2 km north-south by 2 ½ km east-west; this was surrounded by an outer city moat, now just flat ground. On the east, the rampart cut the *baray* about 200 m from its western end. The *baray*, as usual, was built on the main axis of the temple and immediately to its east. In the centre of the entire site, the temple of Banteay Chhmar is enclosed by a moat, still filled with water in which the local villagers fish and water buffalo bathe. This is the first obvious sign of the temple as you approach it on Route 69. On its inner bank are the remains of a wall enclosing an area 600 x 800 m, while the main complex of the temple lies at the centre – an area of 5 hectares (2 acres) bounded by a rectangular gallery 200 x 250 m. What is particularly unusual about Banteay Chhmar's layout is the long and narrow central sanctuary inside this– an almost continuous succession of galleried buildings.

No traces of the city that surrounded the temple remain, but a small village bounds the east and south-east of the moat, and one may wonder whether there has been continuous habitation here since the founding of the temple, as also at Phimai. The temple dates mainly from the second of the three periods of the Bayon style; evidence for this is the dress of the carved *devatas*, and the face-towers. The date of the rest-house (see below) supports this.

The dharmasala, at dawn.

Rest-house chapel

As the track skirts the ruined entrance on the inner bank of the moat, the first building that you see is an isolated chapel in relatively good condition. This is one of the *dharmasalas*, or chapels of the rest-houses built under Jayavarman VII along the main roads (➤ p 153 and the entries for Ta Muen and Ban Bu). Banteay Chhmar's size alone shows that it would have been on a major road, and the rest-house confirms this. Unlike the similar chapels that survive in Thailand, which are in laterite, this is a completely stone structure (as are the rest-houses in Preah Khan and Ta Prohm at Angkor). However, as it is not mentioned specifically in the inscription dated 1191 (at Preah Khan) that lists the rest-houses, its construction must have started later.

Bas-relief gallery

Bas-relief multi-armed Lokesvara, west side.

The temple proper is contained by a wall measuring about 200 x 250 m, with a three-chambered *gopura* in the middle of each side, and the remains of corner towers. Its outer face carries bas-reliefs that for much of their length recall those of the outer gallery at the Bayon at Angkor. On those parts that have not collapsed, you can see that the scenes run in different registers, and show mainly military and historical events. The quality of the carving is on a par with the average at the Bayon – it does not quite reach the best (on the south and east galleries of the Bayon), but is better than most of the Bayon's north gallery. What seem to be missing – at least from what can be judged in its present state – are the scenes from everyday life that are notable at the Bayon. Against this, however, there is a magnificent sequence of multi-armed Lokesvaras on the west wall just south of the *gopura*.

A driveable track runs around the gallery wall. Having passed the rest-house

Rahu devouring ox, man and cart.

chapel at the eastern entrance, turn right to make a counter-clockwise circuit of the gallery. The entire surface has carvings, and all sections reward study. However, collapsed stones and undergrowth make this a little difficult, and most visitors drive around the circuit, stopping at key points. Because they receive no sunlight, the bas-reliefs on the north wall do not appear so clearly, and the first stop is usually by the west wall, on the north side of the three-chambered *gopura* (afternoon is best for the sunlight that throws the carvings into stronger relief).

Here is a procession, a dignitary riding a chariot, and a curious scene, featuring a monster with a *kala*-like face. The monster appears twice, in an upper and lower register. In the lower, the giant is devouring a cart and the animal attached to it. In the upper register, a man battles the same (or another) monster. The head of the monster is clearly modelled on the demon Rahu, and nothing like this scene is known from anywhere else. The explanation appears to lie in an inscription

Bas relief with Lokesvasa.

found at the site, translated by Coedès, as follows: "When Bharata Rahu manifested his spirit of treason against the King Sri Yasovarmadeva to take possession of the holy palace, all the troops of the capital fled. The Prince engaged the combat. The *anak* Sanjak Arjuna and the *anak* Sanjak Sri Dharadevapura fought to defend the Samtac. They fell before (him). The Prince struck the nose of Bharata Rahu and upset him." This is the battle illustrated here on the upper register, and the monster probably symbolises the leader of a revolt. The Samtac referred to seems to be Jayavarman VII's son Indravarman, mentioned later in the inscription as Sri

Bas-relief offering decapitated heads, south side.

Srindrakumrararajaputra *(kumara* = Crown Prince). Banteay Chhmar was dedicated to him. Continue south to the other side of the *gopura*. Here are some of Banteay Chhmar's most important bas-reliefs – a series of standing, multi-armed Lokesvaras, facing west.

Drive on around the corner to the south wall, which receives the sun throughout the day and so is the easiest place to appreciate the historical scenes. There are armies on the march and battles in abundance. Despite the lack of everyday scenes mentioned above there are some surprising coincidences with the subject matter of the Bayon. Just before the *gopura* is an intact area of wall on which

Two scenes from the battle with the Chams, south side.

is one interesting incident: the heads of two decapitated men are held aloft. This same event is carved on the west wall of the Bayon's outer gallery, and is generally supposed to be an historical event of the execution of two traitors or rebels. Another similarity with the Bayon is a battle scene featuring the Chams (with their distinctive headdresses like inverted flowers) on the eastern section of the south wall, beyond the *gopura* as you drive around. Continue to the starting point of the eastern *gopura*.

The central complex

For once, the term 'complex' is apt in both senses. Building continued here over many years, so that the structure has additions, while the collapsed state of much of it gives the appearance of a confused jumble. The central sanctuary is very complicated, consisting of three rectangular enclosures strung together on an east-west axis and covering 40 x 140 m. The galleries and *gopuras* are interconnected, so that it has the appearance of one long, narrow structure. There are three other small galleried enclosures with *gopuras*, on the north, south and west of the central sanctuary. Another building is joined to the eastern end of the central sanctuary, making it even longer and connecting it to the eastern *gopura* of the bas-relief gallery. This building, described below, is of a special type known only from this period and called a "salle aux danseuses".

Throughout this central complex there is no obvious route or path, but because of the tangled vegetation the easiest way of moving around is usually on gallery roofs and over the larger piles of collapsed stones. Beware in particular of young acacias trailing over the rocks – their small, sharp thorns easily snag clothing and tear skin!

Salle aux danseuses: frieze and doorway.

Enter the eastern *gopura* of the bas-relief gallery through its southern door as shown on the plan on page 136; some scrambling is needed from here on. Climb over and through the next doorway immediately ahead. This building – or at least, what remains – corresponds to those known as "salles aux danseuses" at Preah Khan and Ta Prohm at Angkor. Their function is not known; they are unique to this period of building, and the reason for their French name is immediately obvious from the surviving friezes. A series of dancers with arms raised fills the section of the wall just below cornice level. Their stance is reminiscent of the *garudas* and lions which support the celestial realm with their upraised arms, such as on the walls of Preah Khan and on the Royal Terraces at Angkor. In fact, if you look south from here, you can see a ruined building some 30 m away with one of these exact friezes of *garudas*. The role of the dancers, however, is uncertain. The main central east-facing lintel in the "salle aux danseuses" is both unusual and in excellent condition: a four-headed Brahma at the centre is flanked by *rishis* on the left (as you face it), one of them playing a harp, and *hamsas* on the right.

Continue westward, taking whatever route is free of vegetation. Towers surmounted the corners and crossing-points of galleries, and also the *gopuras*, as usual, but many have collapsed. The plan on page 136 shows the locations. What is not clear now is how many of the towers originally had carved faces – as no work has been done, it is not known how many parts of faces lie in the collapsed masonry. This is not just a casual observation. Even Georges Groslier, who spent a considerable time investigating Banteay Chhmar, could not in the majority of cases tell whether or not the towers had faces. Nevertheless, three face-towers still stand in recogniseable condition near the centre, and these, of course, add much to the romanticism of the site. They compare with the face-towers at the Bayon, and the entrances to Ta Prohm and Ta Som at Angkor, but here alone, at Banteay Chhmar, they stand in the centre of a large, ruined and overgrown temple. Some of the other towers at the centre are definitely without faces, and this suggests that Banteay Chhmar was built over a period of time, with some of the work starting before face-towers became a feature of the Bayon style.

Artefacts

To date, there has been no official excavation at the site. From the evidence of broken stone, some sculptures have been stolen (along with bas-relief images, particularly heads of *devatas*).

Best times to visit Early morning and late afternoon (the latter particularly for the Lokesvara bas-reliefs on the west wall). **Admission** Unrestricted (though there may be military checkpoints on several of the roads). **Nearby sites** Sdok Kok Thom lies 50 km south-west and Khao Noi 86 km south-west, both as the crow flies. **Location** In Cambodia, 60 km north of Sisophon on Route 69. **By car** From

Aranyaprathet: Should it be possible to visit from this section of the border, there are three ways of reaching the temple from Thailand. One is to cross into Cambodia from Aranyaprathet to Paoy Pet, continuing east on Cambodian Route 5 for 54 km to Sisophon. Here, turn north onto Route 69 for 43 km to the village of Thma Pok. Continue for another 17 km, where the road makes a sharp bend to the right at the southwest corner of the moat of Banteay Chhmar. The road follows the circumference of the moat. The entrance is a broad causeway in the middle of the east side, opposite some houses. Another approach, closer to Sdok Kok Thom, is to take Route 348 north from Aranyaprathet and turn right after 50 km, just100m before the road splits to encircle Amphoe Ta Phraya (the entrance to a wat is visible directly ahead). The unmarked track heads east, crossing into Cambodia after several km, where it connects with Cambodian Route 696. This leads to Cambodian Route 69; turn sharp left here and continue north16 km to the corner of the moat, as above. The third approach is from the old Site 2 refugee camp, northeast of Amphoe Ta Phraya. Just north of Ta Phraya on Route 348, turn right at the crossroads and drive for 16 km to Site 2. The road into Cambodia continues east, reaching Banteay Chhmar after 20 km. Access depends on the political conditions. Essentially, the straightforward approach is from Sisophon in Cambodia (to reach this town, cross into Cambodia from Aranyaprathet to Paoy Pet, continuing east on Cambodian Route 5 for 54 km. Banteay Chhmar lies on Cambodian Route 69, due north of Sisophon. Times depend on road conditions, which in Cambodia are in the process of change. None of the road surfaces, however, are really bad. **Nearest accommodation and food** At the time of writing there are no hotels or guest houses nearby, but it should be possible to find some form of ad hoc accommodation in Thma Pok. A restaurant was started in 1992 for UNTAC troops and police and may or may not continue in operation. Otherwise, the nearest organised accommodation and food is in Sisophon.

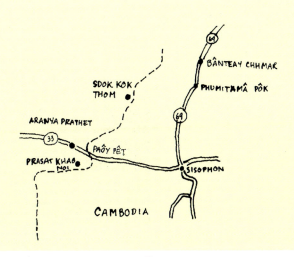

Excavated kiln site.

Ban Kruat kilns & quarries
แหล่งหินตัดและเตาบ้านกรวด

Dates **unknown**
Visit: **45 mins**

The most extensive Khmer stone quarries known in Thailand lie a little to the south-west of Ban Kruat, a few km from the ridge of the Dongreks. Also in the vicinity are the collapsed remains of many kilns, and although there is little left to see of these, pottery is constantly being turned up by the local farmers. Local archaeologists from Buriram recently excavated one of the earthen kilns, but had insufficient funds to protect it from erosion during the rainy season. It is worth asking at Ban Kruat in case other kilns have been more recently restored.

The sandstone quarries (*laeng hin tad* in Thai) offer more to see, although clearly this is of specialised interest. The area covers several acres. Look for the various techniques used to cut the stone into rough blocks – all the different stages are represented. Light incisions show where the stone was intended to be cut; at other places all four vertical cuts have been made, in preparation for cutting through at the base. Elsewhere, rows of vertical holes were a method of making deep vertical breaks by drilling.

Perhaps surprisingly, as at Si Khiu quarry (↦ p 52), no analysis has to date been carried out to find where the stone from here was used. Phnom Rung is only 24 km as the crow flies, and Muang Tam 18 km, and it is a fair guess that Ban Kruat was an important source.

Incised rock before cutting.

Artefacts

No doubt many ceramic pieces in various museums came from this area, but pottery, like votive bronzes, was highly portable, and would have left the area as soon as it was made. Unfortunately, the majority of recent excavation here has been illegal, and so the origins are never declared.

Above and right: Incisions in rock made prior to cutting.

Best times to visit No special time. **Admission** Unrestricted, no charge. **Nearby sites** Phnom Rung (32 km), Muang Tam (31 km), Ta Muen Thom etc. (38 km). **Location** In the Ban Kruat district of Buriram province, south of Phnom Rung and Muang Tam. *By car From Buriram*: Drive south on Route 219 to Prakhon Chai, and cross over Route 24. Continue south on Route 2075 for 26 km to the village of Ban Thalad Nikhom with a police box and sign showing Route 2121 to the left and Route 2075 to the right. Take the right turn, in the direction of Lahan Sai, and after 3 km turn left onto a small road leading south called Saitree 3 in Thai (but not signposted in English). The quarries, spread over several acres, lie to the left of the road after a short distance, and the access is by a track signposted 'Longhintat' after 2½ km. 75 km, 1¼ hrs. *From Surin*: Follow the directions for Ta Muen Thom (➻ p 150), but continue straight on Route 2121 at Ta Miang village for another 20 km. Turn right and then immediately left onto Route 2075 and continue as above. 1¼ hrs. **Nearest accommodation and food** Buriram (➻ pp. 252-54), Surin (➻ pp. 283-84).

Bai Baek

Date: 11th century
Style: Baphuon
Reign: Udayadityavarman II
Visit: 10 mins
ปราสาทไบเบ็ก

The small tower is two-toned brick.

This small brick temple, consisting of just three towers, was until recently hidden in the forest just north of the border, and was difficult to find without local assistance. Since 1990, however, the surrounding land has been cleared for agriculture, leaving the miniature towers visible but in a setting that is not particularly attractive. The most notable feature of Bai Baek is the unusual use of two-tone brickwork – the only instance known in Thailand. The arrangement of red and white bricks – the former used above the doorways – shows that this was deliberate and not just because two different kilns were used haphazardly. The significance, however, is lost.

Another feature that sets Bai Baek apart is that the entrances to the towers face west. This is extremely rare (the best-known example is Angkor Wat); the vast majority of Khmer temples are oriented to the east. Again, the reason is unknown. In the case of Angkor Wat, the fact that it was dedicated to Vishnu appears to be significant, although there is no complete agreement about even this the most thoroughly researched of all Khmer temples. Perhaps Bai Baek also was Vishnuite.

Plan

The three towers, built very close together in a north-south row, face west. The other three sides of each tower have false doorways, as is usual.

Best times to visit No special time. **Admission** Unrestricted, no charge. **Nearby sites** Ban Kruat quarries (17 km), Ta Muen Thom, etc. (25 km). **Location** In Ban Kruat district of Buriram province. **Directions** *From Buriram:* Follow the directions to Ta Muen Thom on page 148, but after driving 11 km east on Route 2121, turn right down a small road heading south; after 4 km the towers are 100m to the left of the road, and clearly visible. (Note: there have been several new small roads built here recently, and there is some danger of taking the wrong one. Ask locally for the *'prasat'*). 1½ hrs. *From Ban Kruat* quarries: Retrace your steps to Ban Thalad Nikhom and continue as above. 20-30 mins. *From Surin:* Follow the directions to Ta Muen Thom as above but at the village of Ta Miang continue straight west on Route 2121. After 9 km, turn left down a small road heading south; the towers are 4 km ahead (see above). 1¾ hrs. *From Ta Muen Thom*, etc.: Retrace the road to Ta Miang, and continue as above. 45 mins.
Nearest accommodation and food Surin (↦ pp 283-84).

The sanctuary and exposed rock platform of the enclosure.

Ta Muen Thom

Date: **Late 11th century**
Style: **Late Baphuon**
Reigns: **Udayadityavarman II**
Visit: **1 hr**

This important and substantial border temple, situated by one of the principal passes over the Dongrek Mountains, is one of Thailand's most evocative and atmospheric, due to its location, unique in the country, in the middle of tall, dense forest. Its recent history, however, is one of the saddest. For several years during the 1980s it was held by the Khmer Rouge who, with the connivance of unscrupulous dealers, abused it badly. All carvings of substantial value were removed, or damaged in crude attempts at removal, including the use of dynamite. Of the three towers, the central and north-eastern ones were virtually levelled. The experience of a visit is, nevertheless, very rewarding, and should be combined with visits to the nearby Ta Muen Toch and Ta Muen.

Like several other of the temples very close to the Cambodian border, the name is Khmer, but given locally long after the sanctuary's abandonment, and simply refers to the nearest village, Ta Miang. It means nothing more significant than "The big Ta Miang" temple, with even the village name having been corrupted. Ta Muen Toch nearby (↪ p. 151) is "The small Ta Miang" temple. Similarly inappropriate names are common throughout Cambodia also, and highlight the decline into obscurity of the monuments following the end of the Khmer empire – most are nothing more than vernacular descriptions given by local villagers, and very few names echo the original.

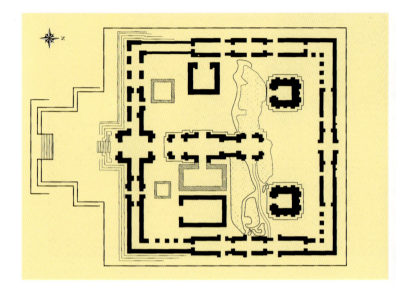

Plan

Although the location is a little difficult to appreciate in the forested setting, the sanctuary was built on a crest overlooking the small valley of a stream which runs in front of the temple. It is in the form of a rectangular enclosure 46m north-south and 38 km east-west, containing a principal central shrine with *mandapa* and *antarala*, two secondary towers on the northern side, and two other laterite buildings still standing (there are also the foundations of three other buildings). Unusually for Khmer temples, Ta Muen Thom faces south: the main *gopura*, much larger than the others, is on the southern side, and a laterite staircase leads down the hill from here. The other significant south-facing temple in Thailand is Phimai, where the orientation is probably due at least partly to the geography. Here, too, the location may have had a big influence – the pass continues south down onto the plains.

Ta Muen Thom was always considered to be quite important from its size and location (both Aymonier and de Lajonquière visited it), but recent excavations have revealed something that casts a new light on the temple. The shrine, which for centuries was choked with the collapsed tower, contains a natural rock *linga*, on a pedestal carved directly out of the bed-rock. The existence of a natural *linga* would have been extremely significant for the Shivaite Khmers (the prime example is Wat Phu in Laos, where the natural *linga* on the summit of the mountain made it the oldest site of Khmer worship) and Ta Muen Thom was clearly built around it. The later building of a hospital and resting-house nearby (Ta Muen Toch and Ta Muen) add to the evidence that this was where the principal royal road between Angkor and Phimai crossed the mountains (•► p. 154).

The natural rock linga and pedestal in the shrine.

The laterite steps up to the main gopura.

The approach from the south

Now that the immediate vicinity of the temple has been cleared, it is possible to start the visit from the lower slope – the principal approach for travellers from the plains of lower Cambodia. Walk down the slope with the temple on your right, and turn right at the bottom. Exercise caution here: at the time of writing, land-mines in the surrounding forest are a very real danger, though the warning signs are in Thai. Although the danger may diminish, any forested area will probably always remain suspect. Under no circumstances tread in any uncleared area.

The beginning of the trees marks the national border. Walk just as far as this point and turn to face up towards the temple. The steep staircase amid massive sloping ramparts, all in laterite, give Ta Muen Thom a very impressive appearance from here. At the top of the steps is the main southern *gopura*. There was obviously considerable work involved in extending the southern part of the temple out this far, when it would have been more convenient to site it 20m or so further back. The reason must have been the existence of the rock *linga* and its pedestal – this would have determined where the *garbhagrha* and its tower had to be built, and in turn, that would have controlled the rest of the layout.

Rishi on the base of a pilaster, southern door to the mandapa.

The enclosure

Climb the steps to the southern *gopura*, which is considerably larger than the others and cross-shaped. Walk through – there are chambers on either side with secondary doorways. As you enter the enclosure, the *mandapa* of the central sanctuary is straight ahead, with beyond it the collapsed remains of the tower, connected to the *mandapa* by a short *antarala*. All are in pink sandstone. The view from here takes in the southern part of the enclosure, encircled by

Unfinished Kala lintel over southern inner door to the shrine.

Southwest corner of gallery.

Carvings on the north side of the central sanctuary.

massive galleries just over 4 feet (1.40m) wide. To either side are laterite buildings, but their function is unknown, as neither conform to the usual 'library'. The building on the left is square, and its entrance faces west, away from the central sanctuary. That on the right is larger and rectangular, aligned north-south with a southern entrance. Between this and the *mandapa* are laterite foundations that are similar in plan, connected with the west side door of the *mandapa*. Two other smaller rectangular foundations are to your left and right. Next to the porch where you stand was found one of several inscriptions.

Before the Fine Arts Department began restoration work in 1991, the appearance of this enclosure was quite different, with not only a large amount of rubble, but also a number of silk-cotton trees (*Ceiba pentandra*) and strangler figs (*Ficus religiosa*) having taken root in the walls. The effect was reminiscent of Ta Prohm at Angkor, which the French conservators had deliberately left almost as it was found. Here, however, the trees have been cut in order to rebuild – a loss of romantic atmosphere, perhaps, but necessary as the trees themselves eventually die and rot.

The long somasutra leading across the enclosure.

Enter the *mandapa* directly ahead; immediately inside note the carved grooves in the stones underneath – these were originally secured by metal clamps to strengthen the joints. Continue through to the shrine. The carving on the lintel that you can see in front of you at the shrine's entrance has only just been begun, but in a peculiar way. The mouth of a *kala* face has been started, with no other preparation. Contrast this with the uncarved lintels of Muang Tam's western outer *gopura* (↪ p 121), where the stone has been prepared with a diamond blank in the centre, and with the northern lintel of Phnom Wan's shrine, where the design has been roughed out before detailing.

The shrine is of the greatest interest. Note how the circular pedestal, in two steps, has been hewn out of the rock, replacing the more usual square stone pedestal with a spout for the lustral water. The natural *linga* on top was known as a *savayambhu*, and would have been considered to have considerable power.

The second surprise of Ta Muen Thom lies outside the shrine on the east side. Walk out of the door to your right. The entire centre of the temple, underlying the shrine and its former tower and stretching out to the east and west *gopuras* on either side, is a natural rock platform, and leading north-east from the shrine right up to and through the gallery is an undulating rock channel. Set inside this is a constructed *somasutra* for draining the lustral waters that the priest would have poured over the *linga*. The entire bed-rock has had holes of various shapes and sizes cut into it, but was the channel natural or carved? If natural, the coincidence would have been remarkable, as *somasutras* were normally designed to exit from this corner of a shrine. But if carved, why in this snaking form instead of straight? There is no obvious answer.

A few metres to the north, abutting the bed-rock, is one of two isolated towers. This one was dynamited during the Khmer Rouge occupancy in the 1980s in a crude attempt to extract carvings, but the other tower, on the north-west of the enclosure, remained largely intact. Walk over to this one, noting on the way the sad destruction of carvings on the outside wall of the shrine and base of the tower (one guardian figure has had the entire head chiselled away, and there are, of course, no remaining lintels or pediments). The north-western tower, also in the local pink sandstone, has a base in the form of a redented square. Its solid, chunky appearance is very reminiscent of the towers on the summit of the Ta Keo temple-mountain at Angkor, and for the same reason: no carving was begun. The false doors on the east, north and west are unique in Thailand for having been carved out of single blocks of stone. The entrance is on the south – note how the inner walls are of laterite up to a height of several metres, and brick above. This inner brickwork may explain why Aymonier noted, strangely, that these towers were of brick.

Pond

Leave the enclosure through the northern *gopura*. Just outside and to the left is a square pool lined with stone blocks and still filled with water; this would have had ceremonial uses and been a source of lustral water.

Artefacts

Systematic plundering has removed most of the temple's carvings.

Silk cotton tree on the north enclosure wall.

Best times to visit The trees surrounding Ta Muen Thom cut the temple off from actual sunrise and sunset, but it still receives early morning and late afternoon sunlight if the weather is good. Nevertheless, Ta Muen Thom's unique forested location means that it can be appreciated in most lighting and weather conditions. **Admission** Unrestricted. No charge, but note that military permission is needed on the approach road. **Nearby sites** Ta Muen Toch (1½ km), Ta Muen (2 km), Bai Baek (25 km), Ban Kruat quarries (38 km), Ban Phluang (58 km), Muang Tam (57 km), Phnom Rung (58 km). **Location** On the banks of a stream that cuts through the Dongrek

Mountains, forming the route for an ancient Khmer road. In the Kab Choeng district of Surin province. **By car** There are no buses to the temple; you will need to hire a car or *songthaeo*. *From Surin:* Drive south on Route 214, and cross Route 24 at Prasat. Continue past the small road leading to Ban Phluang (↦ p 170) for 15 km from Prasat, and turn right onto Route 2121. After 35 km, at the village of Ta Miang, turn right (south). Note that there are two turnings at Ta Miang, both unmade roads, 1 km apart – take the second one (ask to be certain). After ½ km there is a fork in the road – take the right, not the one that appears to go straight on. Continue heading south on this road for 6 km until you reach an army post, where it may be necessary to ask for permission to continue. The road curves westward from here, with several bends, becoming narrower as it enters the forest. Just over 4 km from the army post the small laterite chapel of Ta Muen appears on the left, and 300m beyond this, Ta Muen Toch on the right. After about another 1 km the road forks – take the right. Ta Muen Thom appears ahead after another 300m, 5 km from the army post. 90 km, 1½ hrs. *From Buriram:* Drive south on Route 219 as for Ban Kruat (↦ p. 142). *From Ban Kruat,* at the cross-roads by the police box at Ban Thalad Nikhom, turn left onto Route 2121 instead of turning right onto Route 2075 for the quarries. After 20 km, turn right at Ta Miang (the first of the two unmade roads from this direction- see above). Continue as above. 100 km, 1¾ hrs. *From Ban Kruat:* See immediately above. 45 min. *From Muang Tam:* Take the road north-east out of the village to Ban Chorakhae Mak ('Village of Many Crocodiles' – no longer true since the Siamese crocodile is now almost extinct in the wild, but a sign of former times), 2 km away. There, turn right and head east for nearly 10 km to the T-junction with Route 2075. Turn right and continue to Ban Thalad Nikhom, and follow the directions above. 57 km, 1 hr. *From Phnom Rung:* Head east in the direction of Ban Bu (↦ p. 114 above), but in the village of Ban Bu, go straight east instead of following the Prakhon Chai road as it bends to the left – drive 4 km on to Ban Chorakhae Mak, then continue as above. 58 km, 1 hr. **Nearest accommodation and food** Surin (↦pp. 283-84), Buriram (↦ pp. 252-254).

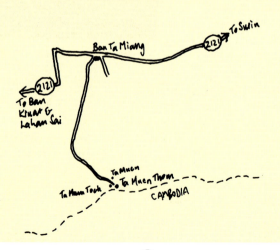

The tower, surmounted by a strangler fig.

Ta Muen Toch 🔺 ꧁ ปราสาทตาเมือนโต๊ด

Date: **Late 12th to early 13th centuries**
Style: **Bayon**
Reign: **Jayavarman VII**
Visit: **15 mins**

Given that this small temple was one of the many hurriedly built during the reign of Jayavarman VII, it stands in quite good condition. Many others of the period collapsed through poor construction. This was originally the chapel for an *arogayasala*, or hospital (↦ also pp. 113, 115, 152, 186), of which there were more than a hundred constructed throughout the empire. Although obviously associated with nearby Ta Muen Thom, this chapel, like that of the rest-house at Ta Muen, was built at least a century later. The road through the pass would already have been an established route passing a major temple.

Plan

This is one of the best examples of a hospital chapel, and a little unusual in being built partly in sandstone (an all-laterite construction was much more common). There is a central tower with a small porch and a small 'library', set in a small enclosure with one east entrance *gopura*. A 30m-long laterite platform leads up to the *gopura*, and another laterite platform inside the enclosure gives access to the shrine. The hospital buildings would have been of light material, such as wood. There is a 20m-square pond with laterite embankments at the north-east corner, no doubt for ritual use.

The enclosure

From where you park, on the west, walk around the side of the enclosure and on to the beginning of the laterite platform on the east. From here, you face the *gopura* and the east wall of the enclosure. The laterite walls form a rectangle 32m by just over 23m; the *gopura* is also in laterite, and consists of a main entrance and two side passages, a prominent outer porch, and a smaller porch on the inside. A small doorway has been cut on in the wall next to the *gopura* on its south side (to your right). As you pass through this *gopura* note the ribbed carved capitals of the laterite pillars. Laterite is very difficult to work in any detail, and the finish is inevitably pitted and rough; it is likely that stucco was added for decoration.

Inside, a laterite platform joins the *gopura* and the tower of the chapel. The tower, on a laterite base, is in pink sandstone (the same as at Ta Muen Thom) up to the cornice level, and laterite above that. The particularly large lotus-shaped finial is also carved in sandstone. The porch, roofed in sandstone and laterite, faces east, and has a single south-facing window. As usual, the other three sides of the tower have false doors.

The other building in the enclosure is a 'library', in the south-east corner to your left as you enter the enclosure. Typically, it faces west, while a false laterite door fills the wall of the east end.

Best times to visit No particular time, although, as at Ta Muen Thom, the late afternoon sun filters through the trees, and if there are no pressing demands on the itinerary, this is a pleasant time to see this group of border temples.
Admission Unrestricted, no charge, but military permission needed on the approach. **Nearby sites** Ta Muen Thom is 1500m south-east, Ta Muen 300m north-west. **Location** As for Ta Muen Thom. **By car** As for Ta Muen Thom. **Nearest accommodation and food** Surin (↦ pp. 283-84), Buriram (↦ pp. 252-54).

Ta Muen   ปราสาทตาเมือน

Date: **Late 12th to early 13th centuries**
Style: **Bayon**
Reign: **Jayavarman VII**
Visit: **10 mins**

The 'house of fire' of Ta Muen, 100 metres north of Ta Muen Toch.

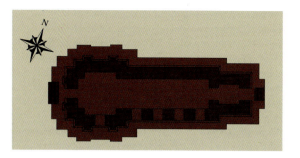

This long laterite building, nearly 1 km before Ta Muen Thom on the approach road, is of considerable historical interest, but in itself merits only a very quick visit. Its all-laterite construction places it in the Bayon period during the reign of Jayavarman VII, when rapid and often crude building techniques were the norm. This building was the chapel for one of the resting places described on page 112. Chou Ta-Kuàn referred to these *dharmasalas*, as they were known, in his late-13th century account: "On the great routes there are places of rest like our post relays." The pass through the mountains made this an inevitable location on the royal road, and we know from inscriptions at Angkor that this was one of 17 such halts between the capital and Phimai.

The chapel consists of a tower and adjoining long porch, essentially making one long hall. The tower, now 13m high, is partially collapsed; its base is 6.3m square. The 12m-long entrance is a little narrower at 5m. Five square sandstone windows line the south side only – one in the base of the tower, the other along the wall of the porch. The chapel faces nearly east, with a door at each end. There is no surrounding enclosure. Pilgrims and travellers stopping here would have sheltered in wooden buildings around the site, not in the chapel itself. The layout is very similar to the *dharmasalas* built within the outer enclosures of Preah Khan and Ta Prohm at Angkor. These, built in sandstone rather than laterite, have a long entrance hall extending east from the tower, and windows along the southern side only. The reason for this, more obvious at the Angkor sites, is that the *dharmasalas* were sited a few metres north of the road – the windows, therefore, face out onto the pilgrims' way.

Artefacts

Carvings of seated Buddha figures on a stone slab were found inside the porch, and may have been an antefix for the tower.

Best times to visit No particular time; the surroundings are quite heavily wooded. **Admission** Unrestricted, no charge, but military permission needed on the approach. As with Ta Muen Thom, beware of mines and keep to the cleared grounds of the chapel. **Nearby sites** Ta Muen Toch is 300m to the south-east, and Ta Muen Thom 1500m beyond this. **Location** As for Ta Muen Thom. **By car** As for Ta Muen Thom.
Nearest accommodation and food Surin (➧ pp. 283-84), Buriram (➧ pp. 252-54).

The Khmer rulers placed great priority on communications within the empire, and one of the great accomplishments was the network of roads fanning out from the capital. These are mentioned in several inscriptions, and although over much of their length the actual highway has disappeared, the routes can be traced by means of various constructions – bridges, rest-house chapels and hospital chapels, particularly from the reign of Jayavarman VII. In addition, maps and aerial photography reveal some stretches. One of the most important of the royal roads was that connecting Angkor to Phimai, about 225 km in length. Others ran from the capital to Beng Mealea and Preah Khan of Kompong Svai (to the east), to Koh Ker and probably on to Champa (to the north-east), to Kompong Thom and Sambor Prei Kuk (to the south-east), and towards present-day Sisophon (to the west). Although the bridges and chapels, and much of the highway construction, belong to the reign of Jayavarman VII, some of these roads must have been in use long before, simply because of the dates of the cities and temples they connected.

The royal road to Phimai almost certainly existed at the time that Suryavarman II came to power at the beginning of the 12th century, and probably considerably earlier. Phimai was then a major centre, and the road had both military and trade importance, although whether its route was the same as later is not known. However, by the early 13th century, it certainly left the capital through the north gate of Angkor Thom, and headed north-west to cross the Dongreks close by Ta Muen Thom.

Along the plateau section of the road, from the Dongrek Mountains to Phimai, there are enough buildings known to make this an interesting, and unusual, itinerary. The only part of the original road that is still driveable is Route 2163 that enters the town of Phimai. Elsewhere, maps and aerial photographs show sections that were almost certainly part of the highway but are now in poor condition. So, there is little point in trying to stick to the actual route; instead, this itinerary goes from temple to temple – from the Ta Muen Pass to the final destination, Phimai. With a short time spent at each site, you should be able to cover it in one day. For detailed information, see each individual temple entry.

Ta Muen Thom Of the several passes across the mountains, the Ta Muen Pass was pre-eminent. We know this not only because of the importance of the temple of Ta Muen Thom, built around the natural rock linga and pedestal at the heart of the sanctuary, but because Jayavarman VII had a rest-house and hospital built nearby.

Ta Muen Toch 2 ½ km to the north-west, the trail leads to the chapel of a hospital.

Ta Muen Another 300m brings you to the *dharmasala* – the chapel of a rest-house where pilgrims and other travellers would have spent the night. Its windows are on the south side only, and would have faced out onto the road.

Bai Baek There is no evidence that the three small brick towers of Bai Baek, now in farmland, were actually on the road, but the temple does lie on a direct line from the pass to Muang Tam and Phnom Rung – and we know that the Khmers built these roads straight if at all possible. You can reach Bai Baek by driving north from Ta Muen to Ta Miang village, turning left along Route 2121, and then south after 9 km.

The remains of the royal road near Nang Rong

The Royal Road
to Phimai 🏵🏵

Various styles and reigns, ending with Jayavarman VII.
Visit: 1-2 days.

Ban Kruat Around the town of Ban Kruat, which lies on the way to Muang Tam (Route 2121 west, then Route 2075 north), were many kilns. If you like, take a detour away from the former royal road to the quarries a little to the south-west.

Muang Tam Reach Muang Tam and its important *baray* via the village of Ban Chorakhae Mak.

Kuti Reussi #2 Continuing on towards Phnom Rung, clearly visible to the north-west, skirt the west side of the *baray*, and stop at this chapel of a hospital.

Ban Bu At the T-junction with the road from Prakhon Chai to Phnom Rung, make a short detour right for 1½ km to see the remains of this chapel of a rest-house.

Kuti Reussi #1 Return in the direction of Phnom Rung. After 2 km, just past the road to Muang Tam, stop at this chapel of another hospital (why there were two so close together is not known).

Phnom Rung Continue up the hill to Phnom Rung, the major stop on the road between Angkor and Phimai.

Phimai There is no completely easy and direct modern road from Phnom Rung, and in order to enter Phimai along the surviving section of the original road, you will have to negotiate some winding country roads. Go first to Nang Rong (the road down the hill, Route 2221, is in exactly the right alignment to have been part of the royal road). Then take Route 24 west in the direction of Chok Chai and Khorat. If you have time, and enough sustained interest, there is a surviving straight section of the road that covers more than 15 km – as a cattle trail among the fields. To see part of it, turn right from Route 24 onto an un-numbered road 11 km west of Nang Rong (the nearest km marker shows 87 km to Khorat), signposted to Ban Nong Thanon. After nearly 4 km the road bends left; the straight section ahead probably follows the original route. After another 3 km, where the road bends right, the trail directly ahead is a path that continues straight for more than 15 km – the original route (ignore the track that veers off the left). There is of course, nothing to see, and though fascinating as a piece of amateur archaeology, it is an enthusiast's detour. Continue to Phimai by re-joining Route 24, driving another 17 km to Nong Ki, turning right and follow the winding roads to the village of Hin Dat on the main of North-Eastern Railway line. From Hin Dat continue north on Route 2163, entering Phimai by the Victory Gate on the south.

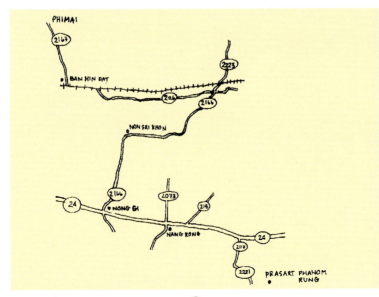

Gopura V at sunrise.

Preah Vihear เขาพระวิหาร (Khao Phra Viharn)

Date: *Late 9th to mid-12th centuries*
Styles: *Surviving buildings mainly Baphuon and early Angkor Wat, with some Koh Ker influence, and Banteay Srei and Khleang elements*
Reigns: *Yasovarman I, Suryavarman I, Jayavarman V, Jayavarman VI, Suryavarman II*
Visit: *2-3 hrs*

O ccupying probably the most magnificent site of any Khmer temple, and containing some of the finest *in situ* carvings, political events have rendered Preah Vihear (Khao Phra Viharn to the Thais) all but inaccessible to ordinary visitors for most of its recent history. When the border was surveyed in preparation for the Franco-Siamese treaty of 1907, Preah Vihear was anomalously left on the Cambodian side, whereas if the line of the frontier had followed the watershed, the temple would have been unquestionably in Thailand. The resulting dispute between the two countries over Preah Vihear was officially settled in 1962 by the International Court of Justice at The Hague in favour of

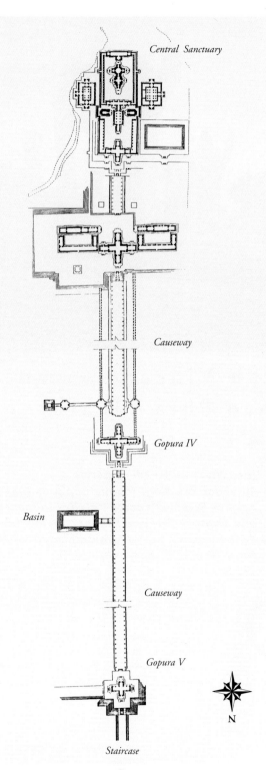

Central Sanctuary

Causeway

Gopura IV

Basin

Causeway

Gopura V

Staircase

N

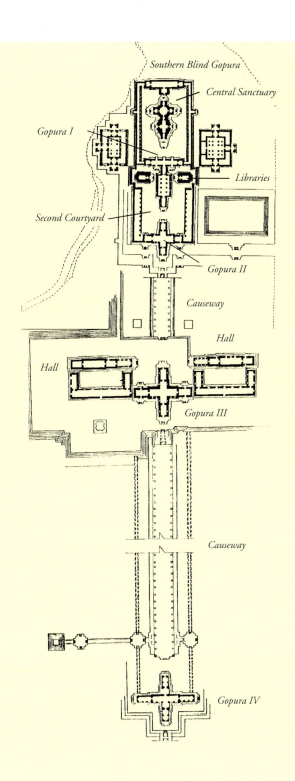

Southern Blind Gopura

Central Sanctuary

Gopura I

Libraries

Second Courtyard

Gopura II

Causeway

Hall

Hall

Gopura III

Causeway

Gopura IV

Cambodia, but most Thais still feel that this decision was unjust.

Ironically, the only practical access is from the Thai side. Preah Vihear's commanding location has given it some strategic importance in recent history, and it has intermittently been a Cambodian military post. Indeed, the difficulty of reaching it from the Cambodian plains helped to make it the last place in the country to fall to the Khmer Rouge in 1975 – Lon Nol troops and their families held on here for two days after April 17, when Phnom Penh was taken. Access from the Thai side depends on the current political situation, which is not likely to become completely stable in the near future.

For most of their length, the Dongrek Mountains form a 300 metre-high wall along the northern edge of the Cambodian plain; a difficult enough obstacle to movement between the lowlands and the plateau. Slightly east of the middle of the range, however, a triangular promontory juts out southward, rising to 525 metres in a great overhanging cliff. If ever there was a location for a temple, this is it. In about 813, Yasovarman I's builders began work here on a sanctuary dedicated to Shiva as Sikharesvara, 'Lord of the Summit'.

Building continued in later reigns. From about 921 to 945 the Khmer capital was moved from the Angkor region to Koh Ker, considerably closer to the Dongrek Mountains. This move, by Jayavarman IV, was accompanied by a new architectural style (which also affected Muang Khaek – page 56). Here, the influence of the Koh Ker style from the new capital can be seen in the way that the lower corners of the pediments sweep upwards.

During the reign of Jayavarman V (968-1001), something of the Banteay Srei style – contemporary with that of the Khleangs – appears also, in the gallery and *gopuras* surrounding Courtyard I, and in the two 'libraries'. The sweeping, sharply peaked gables introduced in the Koh Ker period, arranged in tiers, were developed further at this time.

In more than 300 years of construction at Preah Vihear, there was inevitably a great deal of remodelling, particularly under Suryavarman I in the early 11th century. Indeed, most of the surviving structures date from his reign, notably a large part of the third courtyard, where inscriptions from the period have been found. In the 12th century, Suryavarman II and his priest Divakarapandita made more alterations and additions, particularly in the second courtyard and the staircases and causeways. What was originally a small sanctuary under Yasovarman I developed into one of the greatest Khmer temples.

Plan

The site dictated at least the main elements of Preah Vihear's layout, for while concentric enclosures were typical of temples being built elsewhere around this time, Preah Vihear is laid out on a north-south axis, stretching some 800m. From the entrance up through five *gopuras*, the connecting causeways and steps rise about 120m.

The compactness of most Khmer temples gives the visitor some measure of choice in approaching them. Indeed, in larger temples like Phimai, it is necessary to retrace steps in order to see everything and include the axes and the concentric galleries and enclosures. Preah Vihear, however, was designed to be approached and entered in just one way. The succession of stages has been built so as to create the maximum impression, and the impression striven for is the major theme of Khmer architecture on its biggest scale. Most of the large monuments were built as microcosms of the Hindu universe, a magical recreation on Earth of the home of the gods and, often, the surrounding seas and continents. Entering such a temple was to experience the ascent of Mount Meru (⇢ p. 21).

The means of creating this version of the cosmos varied architecturally, and indeed evolved over time. Temple-mountains, whether on naturally elevated sites or on artificial pyramids, were an obvious expression. Of all the natural sites, Preah Vihear has no equal, and the builders have made full use of it. The approach to the final sanctuary from the entrance north of *Gopura V* takes time and some effort. That it is broken into stages by stairways, *gopuras* and causeways emphasises the scale rather than makes the walk easier. The symbolism of climbing up through a succession of levels, each cut off visually from the next, and with only the sky as a backdrop, would have been lost on no-one. By the time that pilgrims reached the shrine almost at the cliff edge, they would have found themselves at as convincing a reproduction of the mountain abode of the gods as existed anywhere in the empire.

Staircase

Having crossed the stream that marks the national border, the first staircase lies ahead, 78m long and comprising 162 steps, some cut directly into the bed-rock. It was originally flanked by a row of stone *simhas* on each side, although now only one remains. As it rises it becomes steeper and narrower. At the top, two large *nagas*, one on either side, dominate a platform 30m long. In contrast to the more refined and developed *nagas* at Phimai and Phnom Rung, raised on short pillars, these two earlier serpents are massive, ground-hugging and very powerful in appearance. Like those at Muang Tam, they are Baphuon in style, uncrowned, from the 11th century.

Naga guarding the top of the steps, below Gopura V.

Gopura V

Ahead, up a short flight of steps, is the skeletal form of *Gopura V*, which you can walk around on either side. Despite its numerical designation (by convention, *gopuras* are numbered outwards from the centre of the sanctuary), this is the first entrance pavilion to the temple – a beautiful, open structure with sweeping lines. Cross-shaped in plan, it carries sharply-pointed pediments with ends that turn up and outwards. To anyone who has visited the miniaturist red sandstone temple of Banteay Srei some 20 km north-east of Angkor, these flamboyant, up-swept gables arranged in tiers are immediately familiar, although the origins are a little earlier, at Koh Ker. Much of the light, airy impression is because the roof, long since disappeared, was originally in tile, with pike-head finials lining the crest.

Note the distinct traces of red, particularly on

Red-tinted capitals and naga arch of Gopura V.

the capitals. Although not easy to imagine, as we are accustomed to seeing ancient monuments in bare stone or brick, much of a Khmer temple would have been painted or in some way decorated. This red paint (prepared from the iron ore haematite) was probably a base for applying gold leaf.

There is another approach to the temple from the plains of Stung Sen below, by way of a steep path to the east leading up to here.

Causeway

From *Gopura V*, a broad causeway lined with 65 stone boundary stones on either side inclines north to *Gopura IV*, 270 metres away. The posts, tipped with the stylised form of a lotus bud, compare with those lining the approaches to the region's other two axial temples, Phnom Rung to the west and Wat Phu to the east. Just before reaching *Gopura IV*, a stepped basin can be seen off the causeway to the left.

Boundary post between Gopuras V and IV.

Gopura IV

A steep short flight of steps leads up to *Gopura IV*, also cross-shaped, like *Gopura V*. Though less immediately spectacular than *Gopura V*, it is in a more complete condition, and has some particularly fine carvings. From their style, and three dated inscriptions found here, this *gopura* is also later than *Gopura V* – from the late Khleang and early Baphuon periods of the beginning of the 11th century.

Causeway leading up to Gopura IV from Gopura V.

Walk through, and on the far side, turn to look at the south-facing outer pediment, which shows the famous theme of the Churning of the Sea of Milk. The scene is essentially that carved on the lintel from Ku Suan Taeng, now at the Phimai museum (➨ pp 93), but this is a much finer treatment and one of the masterpieces of Preah Vihear. As at Ku Suan Taeng, Mount Mandara is shown as a rather slender pole, around which Vishnu has entwined himself. Here, an even more homely touch is the pot at the base, which represents nothing less than the cosmic sea itself! Vishnu is also present as a turtle to prevent the pivot from boring into the ground as the gods and demons on either side (almost indistinguishable from

Pediment showing the Churning of the Sea of Milk, Gopura IV.

each other) pull alternately on the body of the *naga*. Other gods and characters are present: Brahma above the pole with the sun and moon on either side, Indra on his elephant at the far right, Lakshmi appearing behind the pot on its right side, Shiva's emaciated disciple Bringin on the far left, and next to him the *garuda* who constantly tries to steal the elixir produced by the churning.

Beneath the pediment, the lintel shows Vishnu reclining. Continue south, along another causeway, this time 152m in length and originally lined with 35 pairs of boundary stones, leading up to *Gopura III* (each *gopura* marks a major change in level). To the east of the causeway are the remains of another rectangular pond, known as the "lion-head" pool after the stone head of a lion found built into the south side.

Lintel showing Vishnu reclining Gopura IV.

Gopura III

This is the temple's largest *gopura*, with long extensions to each side. The roofing, instead of being terracotta tile as elsewhere, was originally brick supported by wooden beams. On either side of the wide *gopura* are lateral halls, making this the widest part of the temple.

Inner pediment – Shiva and Uma on Nandin, Gopura III.

As you pass through the *gopura*, stop inside the south porch and turn to examine the south-facing pediment. It shows the common scene of Shiva and Uma seated together on the bull Nandi. They ride through a forest, shown economically as a single tree. Unlike later Angkor Wat-style carvings from the 12th century, this early 11th century treatment leaves plenty of empty space around the figures.

Continue through the porch. A shorter distance, and a smaller change in level, separates *Gopura III* from *Gopura II* – only 10 pairs of boundary stones were installed to mark out the causeway, with a ground-hugging *naga* balustrade on either side. From here, turn to look at the south façade of *Gopura III*. The pediments and lintels over the three doorways are all richly detailed – so much, in fact, that from here the main elements are difficult to make out clearly. The face of the *kala* features strongly.

The main south-facing entrance of Gopura III.

Gopura II and Second Courtyard

The north-eastern corner of *Gopura II* offers one of the best views from

Pediment and naga arch main south-facing door, Gopura III.

the temple. From near the top of the steps, look out beyond the solitary statue of a lion to the escarpment of the Dongreks stretching east. From here on, the succession of buildings is continuous. Behind this *gopura* is the second courtyard (numbered outwards from the central sanctuary as before), in a somewhat ruined state. The main entrance is blocked with stones – enter the courtyard through the smaller doorway on the east, close to the statue of the lion.

East 'library' of courtyard II.

To your right, down the centre of the courtyard, rows of pillars mark the site of what was originally a long hall. This leads between the two magnificent 'libraries', each facing inwards, to the central sanctuary. Stop to look at the eastern 'library', just to the left of the path before you reach the end of the courtyard. An elegant building, with tiered pediments over the doorway and half-pediments on each side, it shows the architectural influence of Banteay Srei. It faces inwards; enter and note the plain rectangular interior, lit only by the small horizontal windows above. What appeared from the outside to be half-roofs, suggesting side-naves, are actually false. Walk around to the back of the library, close up against the outer wall of the courtyard. The rear door also is false, while the lintel and the *nagas'* head-dresses confirm the 'library's' early 11th century date of construction

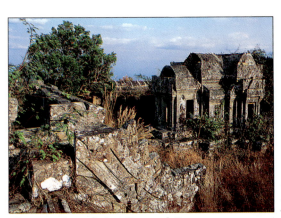

Mandapa, collapsed prang and first court, from gallery roof.

Gopura I and the Central Sanctuary

Continue through the door in the *gopura* nearest to the 'library' into the final, principal courtyard. *Gopura I* itself takes up the entire northern side of the enclosure, while to your left and right the gallery connects it with south *gopura*. Ahead is the collapsed tower and its still-standing *mandapa*. The gallery is intact, with inward-facing windows, and looks much like the cloister of an abbey. The only exits from this courtyard, other than the *gopura* through which you just entered, are two small doors in the middle of the west and east galleries.

Southern blind *gopura*

At the southern end of the enclosure is Preah Vihear's final *gopura* – but it is a false one. There is no exit directly out onto the cliff edge; instead, leave by the small door near the middle of the west gallery wall and follow the path around the outside towards the cliff-top, which is marked by a flagpole. The southern side has a blank face, but two decorated blind doors at each corner, topped with miniature pediments. From here it is only a few steps to the cliff edge and its sheer drop (and in fact, some care is needed if you walk around to the south-east corner, which is within a few metres of the edge). To the south, from the flag-pole, the view over the plains of northern Cambodia is restricted only by the haze.

Corner of the final, cliff-edge blind gopura.

The hills due south are those of Phnom Tbeng. Over to your right a little, to the south-west, another range of hills 50 km distant is Phnom Sandak. It is said that on the clearest days the Phnom Kulen, close to Angkor, can be made out a little over 100 km away, beyond Phnom Sandak.

For all the grandeur of its site, perched on the edge of a giant cliff and with a commanding view over northern Cambodia, Preah Vihear is difficult to visualise as a whole. There is no view that takes in both the temple and the great panorama below. Most temples offer at least one clear, overall view; in this respect, Preah Vihear frustrates. The experience of the visit is certainly great – the series of ascents over the best part of a kilometre, the ornate *gopuras* and wealth of decorative detail – but by the end of it, at the cliff edge, only the imagination can reconstruct an overall sense of the monument. Even if the tower were still standing, there would be no comprehensive view of it from ground-level. Perhaps partly for this reason, it is the five *gopuras* and this last blind one that particularly impress and could be considered the visual hallmark of Preah Vihear.

Other buildings

North of the first courtyard, which contains the *mandapa* and the remains of the tower, stand two rows of massive square-sectioned pillars. These mark the location of a long hall that connected the first and second courtyards. The pillars originally divided this hall into three naves, the central one of which had a ridged roof with finials.

Unidentified shrines north of the temple complex.

Outside the precincts of the temple are two points of interest. South and east of the car park on the Thai side is a viewing pavilion built in the 1980s when access to Preah Vihear was forbidden. This is on the other side of the road, up steps that lead past the bunkers of a Ranger outpost. From here there is a rather unsatisfactory view of the causeways and *gopuras*, mostly obscured by trees, but also a view of two strange shrines, with no parallel at any other Khmer site (they were blocked off without an entrance, but thieves long ago broke in and stole the statues, of which only the base remains). Of more interest is a quite recently discovered rock carving – figures in bas-relief of uncertain period, but possibly representing Kubera, flanked by two female deities, on the vertical cliff face facing north. To reach these, take the steep stairway with railings just off the path to the pavilion.

Best times to visit Early morning and late afternoon, but this depends on the rules of access mentioned below. **Admission** Over the years, this has varied from easy to impossible, due to the political circumstances already mentioned, and advice given here may not be accurate at the time you try to visit Preah Vihear. At the time of writing, the only restriction on visiting the temple is that the time is limited – from early morning to mid-afternoon – but the border is under military control. It is advisable to contact the TAT office in either Bangkok or Ubon Ratchathani (➡ p. 285-87) for the latest information. **Nearby sites** Preah Vihear is relatively far from other Khmer sites. **Location** On and leading up to a triangular promontory of the escarpment formed by the Dongrek Mountains, in Sisaket province. **By car** *From Ubon:* Take Route 24 via Det Udom for 95 km as far as the junction with Route 2085 and turn left in the direction of Kantharalak (11 km from the turn-off). More directly, turn right onto Route 2178 from Route 24 at Warin Chamrap just after crossing the bridge over the Mun River as you leave Ubon. This eventually joins Route 2085; continue south-west, crossing Route 24, to Kantharalak. In either case, from the town of Kantharalak, continue south for another 36 kilometres to Maw I-Daeng, which is as far as you can drive. There is a car park and barrier across the road. Park here and fill in the necessary papers on the Thai side; you will need your passport, and at the time of writing these formalities can be completed only between 0800 and 1430, for visits that are restricted to 0800-1600 (moderate charge). These times and conditions may change. Walk the ½ km to the end of the road, beyond is a natural sandstone pavement that slopes gently down to a stream. Just before the stream is the Thai border post where you will need to check your papers once more. Steps lead down and over a small bridge. From there, climb the path which leads to the temple's first staircase, at the foot of which is a Cambodian post (another moderate charge for admission). 1½ - 2 hrs. *From Surin:* From Route 24, turn right (south) onto Route 221 and continue to Kantharalak, 8 km further on. From here, follow the directions above. 3 hrs. *From Sisaket:* Follow Route 221 all the way, for 64 km, to Kantharalak. Continue as above. 99 km, 1½ hrs.**By bus** *From Ubon*, Surin and Sisaket: Regular bus services go only as far as Kantharalak. From there you can hire a *songthaeo* for the remaining 36 km, but it will be expensive. A cheaper alternative is to share a regular *songthaeo* as far as Ban Phum Sron, 23 km from Kantharalak, and there hire a motorcycle taxi *(motusai rab chang)* and ride pillion for the remaining 13 km (these are available at the junction between Route 221 and Route 2248. **Nearest accommodation and food** There is limited accommodation in nearby Kantharalak (36 km):- Kantharalak Hotel 131/24-25 Sinpradit Rd. tel: (045) 661085. 20 rooms, incl. 3 a/c. On the main street, south of the town centre. Khwan Yeum Hotel 571 Sinpradit Rd. tel: (045) 661126. 21 rooms, incl. 2 a/c. Very basic motel-style, further south than the Kantharalak Hotel and almost on the edge of town.Otherwise, Ubon (➻ p. 285-87) or Sisaket (➻ pp. 278-80).

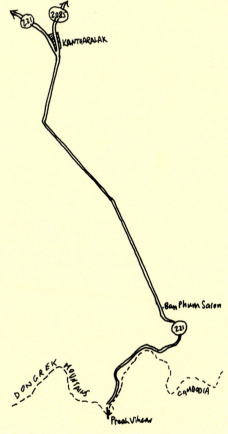

NORTHEAST – LOWER MUN VALLEY

As the Mun River flows eastwards to join the Mekong, the land changes slowly. The level of the plains becomes lower, but the Dongrek Mountains on the southern edge rise to become a very impressive escarpment. A significant part of this area, particularly around Surin, is Khmer-speaking, in contrast to the Lao dialect that is used over most of Isaan. The form of Khmer used is rather different from that in Cambodia, and a local distinction is made between 'high' and 'low' Khmer (that is, upland versus lowland). Within thirty minutes to an hour's drive of the small provincial capital of Surin are a number of interesting sanctuaries, most of them small but all worth visiting. Further east, Ubon Ratchathani is a more convenient base for visiting Preah Vihear, Kamphaeng Yai and Kamphaeng Noi, and is the departure point for overland travel to Wat Phu in Laos (should this be permitted).

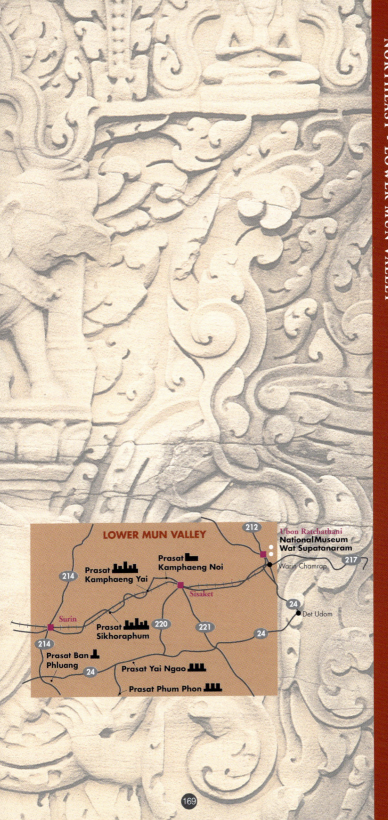

LOWER MUN VALLEY

Prasat
Kamphaeng Yai

Prasat
Kamphaeng Noi

214

212

Ubon Ratchathani
National Museum
Wat Supatanaram

217

Warin Chamrap

Sisaket

Surin

214

Prasat
Sikhoraphum

220

221

24

Det Udom

24

Prasat Ban
Phluang

24

Prasat Yai Ngao

Prasat Phum Phon

The single tower on its high laterite base.

Prasat Ban Phluang 🌢🌢 ❧   ปราสาทบ้านพลวง

Date: **Second half of the 11th century**
Style: **Baphuon**
Reign: **Udayadityavarman II**
Visit: **20 mins**

This finely executed sanctuary is in the form of a single unfinished tower, square and redented, in a pale sandstone. The restoration, by American archaeologist Vance Childress, has been carefully and sensitively carried out, and the simplicity of the site, in a small grassy area set with a few acacia trees, is welcome.

Plan

The tower, on a high laterite platform, stands alone, surrounded by a moat that is broken on the east side by a grassy causeway. To the east is a large *baray*, still in use.

Platform

The base is a high T-shaped platform built of laterite blocks, its three wings projecting north, south and east. The sanctuary faces east, as is usual, and is approached by mounting the steps built into the front, eastern projection of the platform. Once on top, it becomes clear that the base is actually over-sized for the sanctuary as it now exists. Its northern and southern wings make up a rectangular platform 23.3 x 8.4m, while the slightly narrower front platform, 6m wide, projects 7.5m to the east.

There may have been, or intended to have been, an entrance hall on this front projection, while there is sufficient room on either side of the sanctuary, north and south, for other structures. As all the stone recovered during the restoration is accounted for, these open spaces on the platform suggest the possibility that construction was unfinished. Conceivably, an entrance hall might have been built of wood, but there is no evidence.

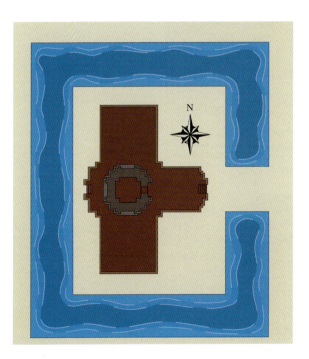

Sanctuary

The upper part of the sanctuary, which would have been the tower, is certainly missing, and there is some doubt as to why this should be. During restoration, the area was searched carefully for all the original blocks, but only those now re-assembled were found. One possible explanation is that the tower was never completed, which could have been due to lack of funds, or to political or dynastic changes. Another is that the upper part might have been in light materials, namely wood, which would have long since rotted.

The eastern door is the sanctuary's only entrance, the other three doorways being false. The lintel above the east door is representative of the very high order of carving that decorates the sanctuary. The proportions are unusually deep, and the motif includes garlands issuing from the mouth of a *kala* placed low on the lintel. Above this fanged, jaw-less head, Indra rides an elephant – a single-headed version of this god's

Kala lintel over east door.

usual mount, Airavata. Indra being, in addition to the god of the sky and rain, the guardian of the East, his position over this doorway is particularly appropriate. The top of the lintel is bordered with a frieze of six meditating *rishis* (ascetics) displaying different *mudras* (gestures).

In the pediment above, standing on another *kala*, the god Krishna lifts a stylised Mount Govardhana in the scene mentioned on page 26. At his feet

Krishna pediment over east door.

Guardian figures at the corners of the tower.

are cattle and their keepers. The surround of this pediment is a highly decorated arch-like frame made up of two undulating *nagas*, each with five heads. Similar *naga* arches grace the pediments on the other three sides of the sanctuary. The bas-relief standing figures at the redented corners are door guardians – *dvarapalas*. The one on the right as you face the doorway is unfinished, with only the basic form roughed out.

Make a clockwise circuit of the sanctuary. On the south side, the lintel shows Indra again, this time on the more common three-headed rendering of the elephant. The pediment above is incomplete, but shows part of a particularly strong carving of a *kala* face. The rear, western face has an uncarved lintel and pediment, while on the north side the lintel has Krishna killing the serpent Kaliya; the pediment shows Indra yet again, on a one-headed elephant. To have three treatments of Indra on the same sanctuary is unusual – even more so in that one of the aspects of the story of Krishna lifting Mount Govardhana on the east face is that he does so to protect the cattle and herdsman from the force of Indra's rain. The reasons for this unusual emphasis on Indra are not known. The lintel below on the north side shows Krishna battling the *naga* Kaliya.

Indra on lintel over south door.

Artefacts

During the excavations, more than 4,000 pottery fragments were recovered, which would have made up at least 270 vases. As these were found directly in front of the entrance and inside the sanctuary, they must have been used as part of the temple's rituals, probably for offerings.

Indra on single headed Airavata on northern pediment.

Krishna lintel over north door.

Best times to visit Early morning gives the best view, particularly with the sun rising over the fields to the east. **Admission** Officially 0730-1800 but in practice unrestricted. Small charge. **Nearby sites** Ta Muen Thom, Ta Muen Toch and Ta Muen (58 km), Phum Phon (33 km), Yai Ngao (29 km). **Location** Ban Phluang lies a short distance south of Route 24, almost due south from Surin, at the village of Ban Phluang in Prasat district, Surin province. **By car** *From Surin:* Take Route 214 south to the cross-roads at Amphoe Prasat. Cross over Route 24 in the direction of Chong Chom, taking care to avoid the speeding trucks and buses at this dangerous junction (from either Khorat or Ubon turn south off Route 24 here). Continue for 3 km; at the 32 km marker turn left onto a small road. After 700m this road turns sharply right; the temple is on your right after another 50m. 33 km, ½ hr. *From Khorat, Phnom Rung and the west:* Take Route 24 east and turn right at Prasat onto Route 214. Follow the directions above. 2½ hrs from Khorat, 45 min. from Phnom Rung. *From Ubon and the east:* Take Route 24 west and turn left at Prasat onto Route 214. Follow the directions above. 3 hrs from Ubon. **By bus** *From any direction,* take a bus as far as Prasat, and there hire a *songthaeo* for the remaining short distance.
Nearest accommodation and food
Surin (•• pp. 283-84).

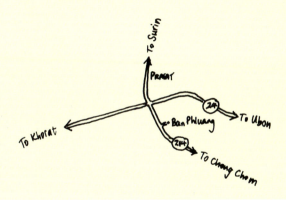

The tower in its palm tree village setting.

brick building remains

brick building remains

tower

laterite

Prasat Phum Phon 🌺 ◝ ปราสาทพูมโพน

Date: 7th century
Style: Prei Kmeng
Reign: Bhavavarman II
Visit: 15 mins

This small temple, featuring a single standing brick prasat and accompanying remains, stands in the middle of quiet, traditional village with a backdrop of palms, and is the earliest Khmer sanctuary still in good condition in the country. Built in the Prei Kmeng style, in the second half of the 7th century, it post-dates Khao Noi slightly (↔ p. 127), but here the structure is original and unreconstructed.

When built, the sanctuary would probably have attracted at least a small settlement, and although there is no historical evidence of continuous occupation, it is quite possible that the village that now surrounds Prasat Phum Phon has been here in some form or another since the seventh century.

Plan

Although only the redented brick tower stands, on its southern side is a rectangular laterite base, which may have supported a laterite or wooden building, and on its northern side the remains of a small brick structure. The three buildings, facing east, were aligned in a north-south row on a low laterite base, and now stand in an open space surrounded by palms. Further north again – some 30m – was another small brick building.

The tower is square in plan and 5.7 metres on each side, with the usual single entrance facing east; the false entrances on the other sides have over them the remains of miniature replicas of the building. Stone was used just for the doorway, but only a small part of the lintel remains: the foliate scrolls are typical of the period.

Detail of door-frame on small building.

The only remains of the small brick building on its northern side are the door-frame, but its construction is unusual for such an early temple. The structural lintel that hangs over the door jambs has a 45-degree mitred joint, not normally found until about three centuries later. 30 metres to the north, another brick structure, measuring 1.6 by 4 metres, faces east. Its decorative lintel and columns have been removed for safety (see below).

Artefacts

A Prei Kmeng-style lintel and columns were recovered from the small brick building north of the tower, and are now in the National Museum, Bangkok.

Brickwork and carved stone over doorway of prang.

Best times to visit Early morning. **Admission** Unrestricted, no charge. **Nearby sites** Yai Ngao (12 km), Ban Phluang (33 km), Sikhoraphum (49 km). **Location** In the village of Ban Dom, in Sangkha district, Surin Province. **By car** *From Surin:* Take Jitbamrung Rd south for two blocks from the Petchkasem Hotel complex, and turn left onto Route 226 (signposted but not very clearly). After 3 km, Route 226 turns left towards Sisaket, but keep to the road going straight ahead, marked Route 2077. This heads south-east to Amphoe Sangkha, 47 km further on. Continue through Sangkha village (the road bends to the right) to the junction with Route 24, 2 km ahead. Cross over Route 24 and head south on Route 2124 for 8 km until the village of Ban Dom. Near the centre of the village, just off the road to the left, the surviving brick prasat stands in a grassy area. 60 km, 1 hr. *From Khorat, Phnom Rung and the west:* On Route 24 heading east, 190 km from Khorat, turn right onto Route 2124 and continue as above. 3 hrs from Khorat, 1 hr from Phnom Rung. *From Ubon and the east:* Drive west on Route 24 as far as the junction with Route 2124, 181 km from Ubon and 136 km from Det Udom. Turn right and continue as above. 2½ hrs from Ubon. **Nearest accommodation and food** Surin (↦ pp. 283-84)

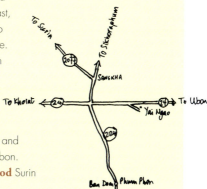

The southern tower.

Prasat Yai Ngao ปราสาทยายเหงา

Date: **First half of 12th century**
Style: **Angkor Wat**
Reign: **Suryavarman II**
Visit: **10 mins**

Two brick towers appear to have been all that was built of this small temple in the Angkor Wat period, though there was almost certainly intended to be a third. Yai Ngao (the name means 'Lonely Grandmother' and probably refers to some local legend) is of marginal interest, chiefly that of the brick bas-relief *nagas* on one of the towers. There is a modern wat on the site.

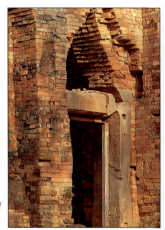

Doorframe of the partially collapsed northern tower.

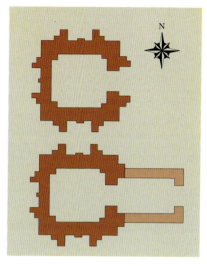

Plan

There are two redented brick towers, each just over 5m square in plan, and facing east. The southern tower carries lightly incised but fine *naga* heads terminating the arch that frames the pediment on the south-facing side, and these are unusually in brick. The northern tower is close to collapse, and shored up by beams.

Artefacts

Miscellaneous parts of antefixes are laid out in front of the towers.

Naga head carved directly into brick.

Best times to visit No special time.
Admission Unrestricted, no charge. **Nearby sites** Ban Phluang (29 km), Phum Phon (12 km), Sikhoraphum (44 km). **Location** Near Ban Sangkha village in the Sangkha district of Surin province. **By car** *From Surin:* Follow the directions for Phum Phon above (↦ pp. 175), as far as the junction with Route 24. There, instead of crossing over onto Route 2124, turn left onto Route 24. After 3 km, a small track leads off to the right. 56 km, 1 hr. *From Khorat, Phnom Rung and the west:* Drive east on Route 24. Look for the signs to Amphoe Sangkha and continue as above. 187 km from Khorat, 2-2½ hrs; 44 km from Phnom Rung, 45 mins. *From Ubon and the east:* On Route 24, 177 km from Ubon, turn left (if you miss the turning, turn back 3 km when you reach Route 2124. 2-2½ hrs from Ubon. **Nearest accommodation and food** Surin (↦ pp. 283-84).

The five towers, with distinctive later (Lao) superstructures.

Prasat Sikhoraphum 🌰🌰🍃

ปราสาทศรีขรภูมิ

Date: 12th century
Style: Angkor Wat (with later, non-Khmer additions)
Reign: Suryavarman II
Visit: 20 mins

Apsara in the Angkor Wat style, central tower.

Little visited, but of great charm and interest, the five towers of Sikhoraphum lie on the edge of a village on the road between Surin and Sisaket. The rural setting adds to the attractiveness of this small monument, but despite its size the layout of the towers and the quality of the carving show that it was of some importance. The name derives from the Sanskrit '*shikara*', meaning the pointed South Indian sanctuary tower which was a model for many Khmer versions (↠ p. 28).

The peculiar shape of the superstructures is due to later rebuilding by the Laos, probably in the 15th or 16th centuries. Although the intricate redenting of the brickwork has some interest, the total effect is ungainly – and, of course, completely out of keeping with the original Khmer architecture that survives in the bases of the towers.

Plan

The arrangement of Sikhoraphum's towers – in a quincunx – is unique in Thailand, although it features in some of Cambodia's most famous temples, such as Pre Rup, East Mebon and Angkor Wat. This comparison itself is rather strange, because the grouping of four towers around a larger central one – as in the number five marked on dice – very clearly represents Mount Meru, and was usually reserved for state temples (↠see p. 22). Against the normal architectural order, we find here, in a relatively unimportant location, a kind of miniature East Mebon, though with an even lower base. The platform, in laterite and sandstone, is only one metre high, and 25m square. The whole is surrounded by a moat, divided into two parts by causeways on the east and west. East of the temple is a *baray*.

Central tower

The most remarkable part of the main tower is the lintel, door frame and surrounding decorations. All in a warm-toned sandstone, they are not only very finely carved, but contain some elements unique in Thailand. The lintel has great vertical depth, and is densely carved throughout. Given that many lintels on the less well-visited sites have had to be removed to museums to prevent theft, it is a particular pleasure to come across this outstanding example of carving in the Angkor Wat style *in situ* here. The focal point of the base of the lintel is a *kala* head placed very low, above which a 10-armed Shiva dances on a pedestal supported by *hamsas*. These mythical birds indicate the celestial location of the dance. The *kala* grasps the hind-legs of two lions; these in turn each hold a lotus from which issues a garland that forms a series of loops around the lintel.

The wealth of surrounding detail repays a closer look. Within the upperloops of the garland on either side are four divinities (the elephant-headed Ganesh is on your right) with *rishis* in attendance on either side. Below these, in the lower loops of the garland, are the smaller figures of lesser divinities, six in all, each riding a crested dragon. As at Phnom Rung, the dragons are not normal members of the Khmer mythological bestiary, and suggest some ultimately Chinese influence.

Lintel over the central tower's main door.

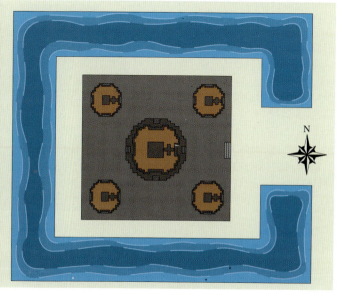

Capital with garuda, surmounted by naga antefix, central tower.

Below the decorative lintel, octagonal colonettes flank the doorway, while the columns carry bas-relief guardians *(dvarapalas)* and *apsaras*. The *apsaras*, which in this period made such a striking appearance at Angkor Wat itself (where 1,700 were carved), are almost completely unknown beyond Cambodia. The only other known instance of such *apsaras* in Thailand is at Prang Pako, Chokchai district in Nakhon Ratchasima province, but these have been removed to Phimai museum. These celestial maidens were for the entertainment of the gods, and the best representations have, as here, some idiosyncrasies. Note the parrot perched near the *apsaras'* shoulder as well as the more usual lotus held in one hand.

Distinctive of this period is the treatment of the feet, which appear awkwardly in profile. This is exactly the same as at Angkor Wat, and shows the stone-carvers unwillingness or inability to deal with foreshortening. The Khmers were by no means alone in facing this difficulty of representing the human figure. The Egyptians adopted a similar solution – torso facing, head and legs in profile – but the Khmer approach looks more uncomfortable to us because of the otherwise naturalistic treatment. The *dvarapalas* carry, as usual, a club.

Above the lintel, the remains of the gable end in two rearing displays of *makaras* disgorging five-headed *nagas*, all magnificently crowned. These *nagas* are, in fact, Baphuon in style – more evidence that artistic style in the region did not correspond to the periods known at Angkor. The capital of the pilaster directly below each *naga* is highly decorated, with a small *garuda* launching out from the corner.

Surrounding towers

The other four towers are of interest principally for the brickwork, which is of a high standard and well-laid, even though by this time in Cambodia, brick had ceased to be used as a building material of any significance. As is typical in Khmer brick buildings, the courses were cemented with a vegetable compound that allowed them to be laid flat against each other. Like the main tower, they each have a single east-facing entrance and three blind doors on the remaining sides. Note the stucco *makara-naga* arch on the south-west tower, much cruder than the stone gable end of the main tower.

Artefacts

Various antefixes and lotus-bud tower finials lie on the low platform.

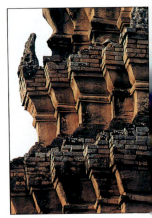

Redented brickwork, south-west tower.

Best times to visit Early morning. **Admission** Officially 0830-1630, but in practice unrestricted. Small charge. **Nearby sites** Yai Ngao (44 km), Phum Phon (49 km), Kamphaeng Yai (40 km). **Location** On the eastern edge of Sikhoraphum village, on the Surin-Sisaket road; Sikhoraphum district, Sisaket province. **By car** *From Surin*: Take Jitbamrung Rd south for two blocks from the Petchkasem Hotel complex, and turn left onto Route 226 (signposted but not very clearly). After 3 km, Route 226 turns left towards Sisaket – continue on this road until 36 km from Surin, just past the junction with Route 2371. A sign marks the small road left to the temple. Turn here and continue for ½ km; the temple is on the left. 36 km, 30-40 mins. *From Kamphaeng Yai*: Head west on Route 226 for 40 km, until just after the Lam Phok reservoir on the left. At the sign, turn right and continue for ½ km. 40 km, 30 mins. *From Sisaket*: As from Kamphaeng Yai. 67 km, 50 min.-1 hr *From Ubon*: To Sisaket, and then as above.
By bus *From Surin*: Regular services. *From Sisaket:* Regular services.
By train The village is conveniently on the line from Bangkok and Khorat to Ubon, and there is a railway station. The temple is just over 1 km from the station - take the road east for about 400m to the market, continue over the cross-roads for another 300m, where the road turns right. After another 200m turn left; the temple lies 300m directly ahead, through the gates of a modern wat. *From Bangkok* (Hualamphong Station): 3 rapid trains daily (8½ - 9 hrs), 3 ordinary trains daily (10 ½ hrs). To Bangkok: same services.*From Khorat:* 1 diesel Sprinter daily in the morning (3½ hrs), 3 rapid trains daily (3½ - 4 hrs), 4 ordinary trains daily (4½ hrs). *From Buriram:* Same trains as from Khorat (1½ hrs).*From Sisaket:* 3 rapid trains daily (1½ - 2 hrs), 4 ordinary trains daily (1½ - 2 hrs). *From Ubon*: 1 express train daily (2½ hrs), 3 rapid trains daily (3 hrs), 4 ordinary trains daily (3½ hrs). **Nearest accommodation and food** Food stalls in the village market (see above). For accommodation, Surin (⟶ pp. 283-84) or Sisaket (⟶ pp. 278-80).

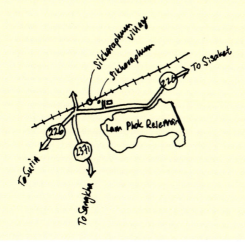

The restored central tower.

Prasat ปราสาทกำแพงใหญ่
Kamphaeng Yai 🏵️ 🏵️

Date: **11th century**
Style: **Mainly Baphuon with some Khleang elements**
Reign: **Udayadityavarman II**
Visit: **30 mins**

Not visible from the road, this important sanctuary is set in the heart of a small village, next to a relatively modern wat. Like Phnom Wan and several other Khmer monuments, it attracted Theravada Buddhist monks and so, in a fashion, its religious function has continued. The sanctuary has been recently restored by the Fine Arts Department – quite well, if a little too thoroughly for some tastes. In the course of the excavations, a magnificent life-size bronze figure representing a guardian was discovered in a very good condition. Now in the National Museum in Bangkok, it further emphasises Kamphaeng Yai's importance.

Plan

The site comprises six similarly-sized structures in a gallery-lined enclosure. The gallery, of laterite blocks with sandstone windows and entrances, has a massive appearance, which has given the temple its modern name, meaning "Large Walls". Aligned to the cardinal points, each of the four gallery walls has in its centre a *gopura*. The principal entrance is the eastern *gopura*, which is slightly larger and more elaborate than the other three.

The rectangular enclosure, just slightly longer east-west than north-south, contains six buildings.

Eastern *gopura*

Enter the temple from right in front of the tall, garish modern *viharn*. This is directly opposite the main eastern *gopura,* which is a very substantial, cross-shaped building – note the side chambers each with their own entrance. There is a Khmer inscription on the left wall, just before you enter the enclosure from here.

Pediment on north side of central tower.

The enclosure

Pause at the inner doorway of the east *gopura* – a good vantage point to survey the buildings and gallery. The latter has sandstone window frames, horizontal like those of the 'libraries' at Preah Vihear. Ahead is the line of three *prasats*, all on the same high base, while in front of these, to your left and right, are the two 'libraries', their entrances facing in the other direction as usual. Walk over to the central, and principal shrine.

Main sanctuary

Pediment on south side of central tower.

The high platform on which the central shrine was built extends to either side, but on closer inspection you can see that this middle section is sandstone, while the wings underpinning the two other towers are of laterite. This central tower is built partly in sandstone and partly in brick (most of which you can see is new reconstruction), but the arrangement is not as simple as at, say, Non Ku. The lintel of the porch is uncarved, while the pediment is badly damaged, but sufficient remains to recognise Shiva dancing – note Shiva's female disciple Kareikalammeyar on the left, easily identified by her drooping breasts. The inner lintel shows Indra riding Airavata, above a *kala* face. Two *simhas* flank the *kala,* and spew garlands which loop upwards.

Make a circuit of the *prasat*. On the south face there is a fine pediment showing Shiva and Uma on Nandin – the bull wears decorations, while the costumes of the figures are in the Baphuon style of the 11th century. The lintel below has a scene from the Ramayana over a *kala* face. Around on the other side, the pediment is carved with Krishna holding up Mount Govardhana (the same scene that appears over the entrance to Ban Phluang), while the lintel, with figures over a *kala* face, is very worn.

The other towers

The towers on either side of the central shrine, extensively rebuilt in new brick, both have very

Central sanctuary from the northeast.

worn lintels, featuring barely discernible figures over *kalas*. Behind the southern tower is another, also newly reconstructed, with an uncarved lintel. It is highly unlikely that this asymmetrical layout was intentional; almost certainly there was intended to be a fifth tower on the other side, which would then have given Kamphaeng Yai a similar arrangement to that of Muang Tam's inner enclosure. The large bronze statue described below was found near the south-west corner.

Southern 'library'

Cross over to the building that faces towards the southern tower, in the position of a 'library'. Its outer lintel is carved with a divinity flanked by two elephants, all above a *kala* face. The inner lintel shows Nandi the bull carrying Shiva and Uma, but in quite a different treatment from the pediment on the main tower. As in the main shrine's inner lintel of Indra, and the south library's inner lintel of Vishnu reclining, the work is clearly by provincial craftsmen: the naïve elements include forest animals, but the bull has been given an almost haughty stance.

Lintel - Vishnu reclining in the northern 'library'.

Northern 'library'

On the other side of the enclosure, the northern 'library' also has two lintels. That over the west-facing porch shows Krishna fighting two horses. Just inside, the inner lintel is of considerable regional interest – the theme is the popular one of Vishnu reclining, but it has been treated here in a more down-to-earth way than normal. As usual, both consorts – Lakshmi and Bhumidevi – cradle Vishnu's legs, but note how his left foot is pressed firmly into Bhumidevi's breast. A point of interest for the dating of styles in Thailand are in the *nagas* at top right. They have just-discernible crowns, which is unusual for this 11th century Baphuon period – until these were analysed recently, it was thought that the earliest appearance of crowned *nagas* was at Phnom Rung.

Lintel in the southern 'library'.

Artefacts

The most famous discovery from Kamphaeng Yai, and quite recent, is one of the finest Khmer bronzes ever found. It is now in the National Museum, Bangkok (➙ pp 234). Excluding the wedge-shaped base,

West facing lintel of the southern 'library'.

intended to fit in a corresponding cavity in stone, it measures 126 cm in height – close to life-size – and depicts a young man with a patrician appearance. Only the hairpiece, right hand and left elbow are missing, and the casting is a very superior piece of work. The dress is definitely 11th century Baphuon in style – pleated sampot and a decorated belt fringed at the back with small hanging pendants. Exactly who he is meant to represent is not entirely certain, but the posture, with hand on hip, suggests that he might have been a guardian figure. If so, of the two possibilities, his human form would make him Nandikesvara (paired with the fanged Mahakala). As a guardian, he would have held a stave in the missing hand.

The face, with its sombre but decisive expression, is particularly fine. The deep insets of the mouth, beard, moustache and eyebrows would have been inlaid, very probably in gold (there are still traces of gilding). The hair was pulled back into a chignon *(jatamukuta)*, and although the lower hairline is carved, the chignon itself has broken off.

Best times to visit Early morning and late afternoon.

Admission By being in the grounds of a wat, entry is unrestricted and there is no charge. **Nearby sites** Kamphaeng Noi (19 km), Sikhoraphum (40 km). **Location** In the centre of the village of Ban Sa Kamphaeng Yai, in the Uthumporn Phisai district of Sisaket province. **By car** *From Surin:* As for Sikhoraphum (•• pp. 178) but continue for another 40 km, until 200m past the railway crossing at the village of Ban Sa Kamphaeng Yai. Turn right into the village; 100m down the lane, turn right into the large and bizarre cement gates of a modern wat. The Khmer temple is within the grounds. *77 km, 1 hr. From Sisaket:* Take Route 226 west from Sisaket. After 20 km the road makes a sharp turn left, due to re-numbering. In the village, turn left at the sign for Wat Sa Kamphaeng Yai – if you cross the railway line, you have gone too far. *27 km, 20-30 mins From Ubon:* To Sisaket, and then as above. **Nearest accommodation and food** Sisaket (•• pp. 278-80), Surin (•• pp. 283-84).

185

Kamphaeng Noi

ปราสาทกำแพงน้อย

Date: *Late 12th to early 13th centuries*
Style: *Bayon*
Reign: *Jayavarman VII*
Visit: *15 mins*

Another hospital chapel, typical of the style, in laterite. Alone it would not be worth a detour, but it is right on the road between Sisaket and Kamphaeng Yai, only 10 minutes drive from the latter. For comparison, and more details about Khmer hospital chapels, look at the other entries – Ta Muen Toch, Prang Ku and the two Kuti Reussis.

Plan

The arrangement is typical of an *arogayasala* – central tower in a small rectangular enclosure entered by an eastern *gopura*, with a 'library' in the south-east corner. A *baray* was built to the east.

All the main structures are in laterite, with sandstone used for the door – and window-frames, and for the lintels. The enclosure wall, also in laterite, measures 20m by 35m, and the tower 5m square, preceded by a porch on the east that juts out 3m. One lintel remains *in situ* over the inner doorway of the *gopura*, but it has been incorrectly replaced. Also, the lintels found here were Baphuon in style; the time difference between these and the temple is so great – almost two centuries – that the explanation is almost certainly that they were re-used from another sanctuary.

Laterite tower from north-west corner of the enclosure wall.

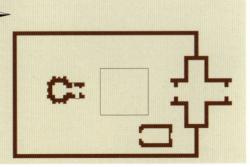

Best times to visit No special time. **Admission** Unrestricted and no charge, because in the grounds of a wat. **Nearby sites** Kamphaeng Yai (19 km), Sikhoraphum (49 km). **By car** *From Sisaket:* Leave Sisaket west on Route 226, as for Kamphaeng Yai. 9 km after the bridge over the river Huai Samran (a tributary of the Mun), look for a sign to the temple and turn right into the grounds of a modern wat – Wat Thep Prasat Sa Kamphaeng Noi. The laterite enclosure and tower lie within the grounds. 5-10 mins. *From Surin:* Follow the directions for Kamphaeng Yai (•• p. 182), and continue on Route 226 for another 19 km. Turn into the gates of the modern wat. 85 km, 1¼ hrs. *From Kamphaeng Yai:* As from Surin, above. 19 km, 20 mins. **Nearest accommodation and food** Sisaket (•• pp. 278-80)

Ubon National Museum

พิพิธภัณฑ์อุบลราชธานี

Visit: 45 mins

Ubon National Museum is housed in an elegant building dating from 1918, which originally housed the provincial government offices. After these became too small, it was handed over to the Fine Arts Department and, after renovation, was opened in 1989 by HRH Princess Maha Chakri Sirindhorn, becoming the first provincial museum in the Northeast. With an emphasis on regional history and culture, the museum has rooms devoted to geography, geology, pre-history, and local handicrafts. One room features the art of the Dvaravati and Chenla periods (6th-9th centuries AD), while two rooms house a collection of Khmer Art from the mid-9th to mid-12th centuries and Thai-Lao art from the 16th to 17th centuries.

Khmer ceramic jar 11th - 13th ccentury.

Admission Wed-Sun 0900-1600, small charge. Telephone (045) 255071. **By car** It is in Ubon Ratchathani town itself on Kuenthani Road. (↦ p. 285 for town map).

Wat Supatanaram, Ubon 🔥

Visit: 15 mins วัดสุปัฏนาราม

Whilst in Ubon, make a short trip to this 19th century wat built under the instructions of King Rama IV in 1853 to house various ancient artefacts. Of interest for this book is Thailand's oldest lintel, in pre-Khmer early 7th century Thala Borivat style. The wat houses a Sukhothai period Buddha image in the Giving Blessing attitude. There is also a Sambor Prei Kuk lintel which is one of the earliest examples of Khmer caving found in Thailand. Various stone inscriptions are also housed there such as that from Manai Cave and the Wat Supatanaram Sanskrit inscription, dating to the 7th century. There is also a sandstone door pilaster with a carved guardian and foliate decoration in Khmer style.

A lintel in the Thala Borivat style (a variety of Sambor Prei Kuk), Note the inward facing short-bodied makaras each bearing small figures.

Stone pilaster with guardians.

Location On the Mun River. **By car** It is in Ubon Ratchathani town itself on Supat road. (➡ p. 285) for town map.

Although the limits of the Khmer Empire were pushed north almost as far as where Vientiane now stands, the influence was clearly less marked, as evidenced by the very few sites north of a line running from Phimai to Ubon Ratchathani. The only temple of real significance is Prasat Narai Jaeng Waeng, near Sakon Nakhon.

Right: Prasat Narai Jaeng Waeng

Prasat ปราสาทนารายณ์เจงเวง
Narai Jaeng Waeng ♥

Date: 11th century
Style: Baphuon
Reign: Udayadityavarman II
Visit: 30 mins

A small sandstone temple on a high laterite platform. The lintels and pediments are all interesting, and there is a fine *somasutra* still *in situ* – one of very few throughout the remains of the Khmer empire. This is, in fact, the most northerly Khmer sanctuary still in good condition. The name is both unusual and reflects the history of the region – Narai is the Thai name for Vishnu, but *jaeng waeng* is old Khmer, meaning 'long legs'. The entire name presumably refers to the reclining Vishnu on the northern pediment. What makes this unusual is that Sakhon Nakhon has for a few centuries been a Lao area, and so the name pre-dates this. (the modern Khmer pronunciation would be *cheung weng*).

Plan

While there may originally have been an enclosure and even a moat, all that remains today is the sanctuary tower, with a single entrance on the east side, covered by a porch.

The sanctuary

Enter through the gate on the south side, and walk around to the right to begin at the eastern entrance. Over the entrance to the porch, only the lintel remains, featuring Indra, guardian of the east, riding the elephant Airavata. Inside, the door to the sanctuary carries a pediment showing Shiva dancing – as at Phimai and Phnom Rung. Here, however, the figure unusually has 12 arms rather than 10. If you have already visited Phimai and Phnom Rung, you should be able to recognise the surrounding figures – the female disciple Kareikalammeyar seated on the left as you face the carving, and Ganesh on the right playing an instrument.

Shiva dancing: pediment over east door.

The pediment has at some point been roofed over – the corbels intrude on both sides. On the lintel below, Krishna fights two *simhas*.

Walk clockwise around the sanctuary tower. On the south side is a lintel divided into an upper and lower band, clearly telling a story. The meaning, however, has not been deciphered, although the presence of a monkey in the central

Lintel on the south side.

Vishnu reclining: the north face of the sanctuary.

porch on the upper band suggests that this might be from the Ramayana.

Continue round to the north side, which has a false door, like the west and south. The pediment, very provincial in style but powerful, is of Vishnu reclining, and has given the temple its local name. The style, and the checked pattern of the *sampot* worn by the god, show the influence of local folk art, and invites comparison with the reclining Vishnu at Kamphaeng Yai (↠ p. 182-184). Below, the lintel carries another scene of Krishna fighting, but here he battles with a single *simha*.

On the platform under the door, a *somasutra* emerges from the *garbhagrha*, as at Phimai and Phnom Rung. Here, however, it retains a finely carved spout in the form of an elephant-headed beast – either a *makara* or a *gajasimha*.

Somasutra outside the north, blind door.

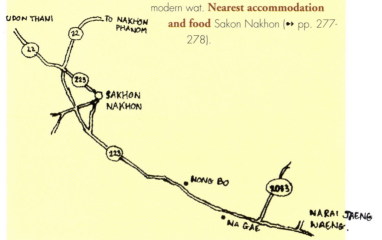

Khon Kaen National Museum 🍃 พิพิธภัณฑ์ขอนแก่น

Opened in 1972, the museum has a good general collection, including artefacts from Ban Chiang and a number of Dvaravati stone *semas* carved with Buddhist scenes. Khmer pieces include a lintel from Ku Suan Taeng in Baphuon style showing Indra on Airavata (↔ p. 96) and several pieces excavated from the hospital chapel site at Ku Noi in Maha Sarakham province. These last include a stone statue of a guardian, possibly Nandikesvara, a stone torso of a four-armed figure, possibly Vishnu, and a stone stele which identifies Ku Noi as one of Jayavarman VII's hospitals. There are also brown stoneware ceramics, and bronzes that include a conch shell decorated with Mahayana Buddhist motifs and small votive Mahayana deities.

Lintel with Vishnu reclining from Ku Suan Taeng.

Lintel showing Indra on Airavata, from Ku Suan Taeng.

Indra on Airavata

Indra, guardian of the East, was frequently shown over the main eastern doorways, and at Ku Suan Taeng was featured on the southern tower, now collapsed. As usual, he rides the three-headed elephant Airavata. Unusually, the style of this lintel is Baphuon (↔ p.39), many decades earlier than the late Angkor Wat period when the temple was built. It may be that the lintel was reused from elsewhere.

Buddha subduing Mara – Khmer bronze 12th century.

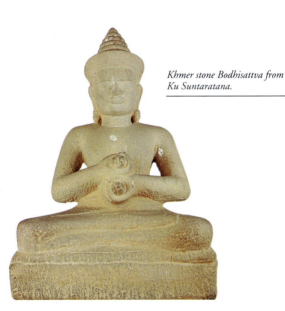

Khmer stone Bodhisattva from Ku Suntaratana.

Admission Wed-Sun 0900-1200 and 1300-1600, small charge.
By car The museum is located in the Provincial Civil Service Centre, north of the town centre. Tel: (034) 236741.**Nearest accommodation and food** Khon Kaen town (•• pp. 258-261).

217

Sirindhorn
Reservoir

Pakxé

Mekong River

Champasak

Wat Phu

Huei Thamo

THAILAND

LAOS

LAOS

LAOS

Present-day Laos lies entirely on the left bank of the Mekong River, but a large part of North-eastern Thailand is Lao-speaking (and even in the early part of this century was often referred to as Siamese Laos). The Mekong close to Vientiane seems to have been the furthest point reached by the Khmers, and at this distance from the capital, the degree of control that they were able to exert is uncertain. Access to the middle reaches of the Mekong, however, was easier – and in particular to one of the most important sites in Khmer history. Wat Phu, near Champasak, can justifiably claim to be one of the most sacred sites in Southeast Asia. Much of this stems from its special location, on the lower slopes of a mountain that is topped with a huge monolith in the form of a natural linga. This virtually guaranteed its importance for Shiva worshippers, and it was no doubt the principal temple for the earlier kingdom of Chenla.

Wat Phu's northern 'palace' and Middle baray.

The south-west gopura is the best preserved at the site.

Huei Thamo ห้วยตาโม

Date: **Late 9th-early 10th century**
Style: **Bakheng**
Reign: **Yasovarman I**
Visit: **45 mins**

Mukhalinga in the south-west gopura.

Little seems to have changed at this unrestored site since de Lajonquière was here at the turn of the century. This overgrown temple of small-to-medium size lies half-buried and half-collapsed in secondary forest on the left bank of the Mekong downriver from Champasak. It makes an interesting addition to a trip to Wat Phu, adding 2-2½ hrs to the journey, and the experience is very much that of exploring an unknown site. The name, Huei Thamo, is taken from the small tributary of the Mekong by the banks of which the temple was built. Locally, it is referred to as 'Oumoung', meaning a subterranean cavern – for no obvious reason. Apart from the style of the lintels and pediments, the temple's date is known from an inscription dated 889, declaring the sanctuary dedicated to Rudani – that is, Durga, consort of Shiva in her terrible aspect.

Plan

The temple is oriented towards the south-east, probably to take advantage of the strip of land partly enclosed by the Huei Thamo stream on one side, and an even smaller dry stream bed on the other.

The enclosure is difficult to make out in its present state. There are traces of a laterite wall which appears to have been originally about 3m high, but it is uncertain (without excavation) where the east wall was. The course of the Huei Thamo and its now-dry small tributary stream seem to have formed part of an effective moat. The best preserved *gopura* is that on the south-west side, and this is the first building that you notice as you approach along the forest trail described below. It is in laterite, with sandstone door- and window-frames, all on a raised laterite base. The north-west *gopura* is in considerably worse condition

At the centre of the enclosure are the remains of three east-facing towers, in brick. Now collapsed because of looters digging in the past, they were arranged two in front and one behind, rather than the more usual single row.

Artefacts

Detail of pediment showing Indra on Airvata.

One of the most interesting pieces from Huei Thamo – and surprisingly still *in situ* – is an unusual *mukhalinga* (literally 'linga with face'). This stone linga has four large faces at its tip, and is in the south-west *gopura*. *Mukhalingas* normally have much smaller faces. Other stone pieces lie scattered among the

trees, including a boundary stone, a lintel featuring Indra on a three-headed Airavata, and *naga* antefixes.

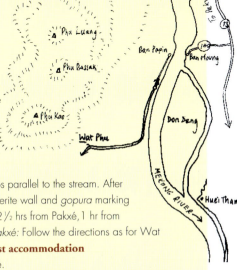

Naga antefix.

Best times to visit Because of its wooded location, any time of the day. **Admission** Unrestricted, no charge. **Nearby sites** Wat Phu (⟶ p 200). **Location** Close to the left (east) bank of the Mekong River, near the village of Ban Tomo, near Champasak. **By boat** *From Pakxé:* Follow the directions for visiting Wat Phu on p. 206, but continue past Champasak, keeping the island of Don Daeng with its broad sandy beach on your left. (During the rainy season, July-January, shallow-draught boats can take the shorter east channel around the island). Round the tip of the island (where the current is quite strong) and land on the beach of the east bank where there are a few small houses – at the point where the small tributary, the Huei Thamo, enters the main river. Cross the beach, climb the steep bank and continue across the narrow strip of land to a crude log footbridge. On the other side of the stream, climb the bank and follow a forest trail to the left that keeps parallel to the stream. After 300m you come to a low laterite wall and *gopura* marking the enclosure of the temple. 2½ hrs from Pakxé, 1 hr from Champasak. **By car** *From Pakxé:* Follow the directions as for Wat Phu (⟶ pp. 268-69.) **Nearest accommodation and food** Champasak, Pakxé.

The northern 'place' blind door.

The main sanctuary.

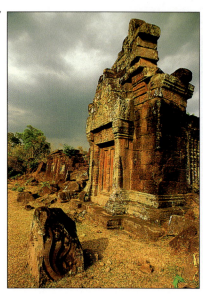

Wat Phu วัดภู

Date: *Existing buildings 11th and 12th centuries, on a much-rebuilt ancient site*
Styles: *Mainly Angkor Wat remaining*
Reigns: *Jayavarman I (pre-Angkorean), Jayavarman VI, Suryavarman II*
Visit: *2 hrs*

With Phimai, Phnom Rung and Preah Vihear, Wat Phu occupies the first rank of Khmer temples outside Cambodia. It also enjoys the distinction of being the oldest religious site used by the Khmers (pre-dating the empire itself), because of its special location at the foot of a distinctive mountain overlooking the middle reaches of the Mekong River. The 1408-metre mountain, now called Phu Kao, which translates as 'Chignon Mountain' (from *'[pom] kao'*, meaning 'hair gathered up'), is topped with a huge monolith. This so obviously represented a natural linga to Shivaites that it was given the Sanskrit name 'Lingaparvata' ('mountain of the *linga'*) and was an evident choice for a sacred site.

There is documentary evidence that the site was the principal sanctuary of the Chenla capital Shreshthapura, founded on the site of the present-day small town of Champasak. One of the first known kings of Chenla, probably ruling in the 5th century, was called Shreshthavarman, which suggests strongly that he founded the capital here. A Chinese 6th century text mentions that 'near the capital there is a mountain called Ling-chia-po-p'o [Lingaparvata], on top of which there is a temple which is always guarded by a thousand soldiers. It is consecrated to a spirit named P'o-to-li, to which human sacrifice is made. Each year, the king goes into this temple and himself offers a human sacrifice during the night'.

Chinese transliterations of foreign names were notoriously off the mark, but the spirit P'o-to-li almost certainly referred to Bhadreshvara, a clue that leads back to the

Cham holy city of My-Son, some 270 km to the north-east, near Danang in Vietnam. In the second half of the 4th century, the Cham king Bhadravarman founded the first shrine at My-Son dedicated to Shiva Bhadreshvara, giving his own name to the cult. Moreover, an inscription recovered from Champasak was made by order of a king Devanika, considered by Coedès to be the same person as another Cham king who ruled between about 455 and 472 and referred to by the Chinese as Fan Shen-ch'eng. The area around Champasak, therefore, may originally have been a part of Champa.

All of this attests to a long history of worship at this site before the Khmers began work on Wat Phu.

Plan

Like Preah Vihear and Phnom Rung, but unusually for a Khmer temple, Wat Phu is laid out on an axis, stretching a kilometre and a half if the basin at its foot is included. All three temples, in fact, take advantage of their special locations, and in the case of Wat Phu this is probably the most picturesque of

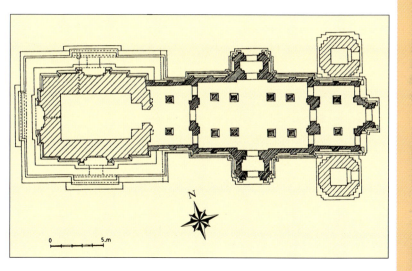

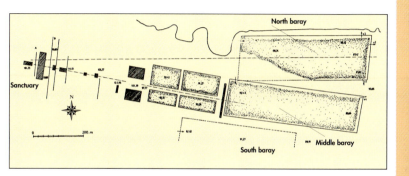

any Khmer site, in or out of Cambodia. The surrounding mountain slopes are forested and the view from the highest part of the temple takes in, on a clear day, the middle Mekong, its valley and the Bolovens Plateau far to the east. Louis Finot commented, "I do not know that the Cambodian architects have ever shown more taste in the choice of a site, more art in the arrangement, more cleverness in combining the accidents of the terrain and the disposition of its edifices, in the manner of producing a seizing impression of nobleness and majesty."

Devata flanking the sanctuary's main entrance.

The sanctuary, with no enclosure, stands at the western end of the complex, on a natural terrace, facing almost due east (98 degrees) along the axis and overlooking the Mekong River in the distance. A series of causeways and staircases follow this line to the Middle *baray*, an artificial basin at the eastern end, and this axis is flanked by the two largest buildings, known as 'palaces'. Smaller basins, now dry, lined the lower causeway, while another, square, basin lies a few hundred metres to the north. The total distance from the sanctuary to the Middle *baray* is 800 metres.

Causeway and basin

Southern 'place' from the upper terrace.

An artificial rectangular basin, 600 metres by 200 metres and still full of water, lies at the foot of the temple, marking the eastern end of the axis. Now referred to as the Middle *baray*, (↔ map on p. 201) it was dug later than most of the surviving temple, probably during the reign of Suryavarman II. An inscription referring to a large basin called the Divakaratataka (named after the king's chief adviser) probably describes this one. The dirt access road now runs along the south side of this to the admissions office. At the western end of the basin there was originally a pavilion; the derelict building now standing in its place was built in 1959 by the last prince of Champasak.

Head of kala on interior lintel of the sanctuary.

Although vehicles can drive on up to the 'palaces', a better sense of the temple is achieved by walking from the office to the start of the lower causeway, which begins at the basin. Almost level, this stretches 250 metres towards the 'palaces' – one of the longest approaches of any Khmer temple. It was originally lined with *nagas* and boundary stones, a few of which are still standing.

The 'palaces'

East blind door, north 'palace'.

The western end of the causeway is flanked on either side by two long, imposing buildings. The ends of these buildings, facing east and west, have impressive gables, pediments and lintels, but the doors are blind; the entrances are in the middle of the long side. Behind each building, though difficult to make out from here, laterite galleries enclose a rectangular courtyard. This kind of complex, in which a group of long buildings or galleries enclose a rectangular space, is not particularly common, but first appeared in Cambodia in the 10th century at Koh Ker. For no really good reason, such buildings are traditionally called 'palaces'.

There are some differences in construction between the two buildings; the south 'palace' is built of sandstone, while in the north 'palace' stone was reserved for the gables, base, cornice, windows and entrances, with laterite used for the main body of the walls. This may, as in other temples at Angkor, have been due to shortage of sandstone or to speed up the construction. The northern 'palace' is the

Krishna killing Kamsa on the inner lintel of the sancuary's south facing entrance.

more imposing when approaching from the east along the causeway, as the gable and pediments on the southern building have collapsed.

The façade of the eastern end of the north 'palace', with its steeply pitched gable and two-tiered triangular pediments, bears some resemblance to the Baphuon-style *Gopura* III at Preah Vihear (though without the upswept gable ends), but the decorative elements place these buildings a little later, at the beginning of the Angkor Wat style. In fact, here at Wat Phu is the last appearance of triangular pediments. The great age of this site means that there has inevitably been a great deal of rebuilding, which complicates the dating.

The lintel features a divinity seated on the head of a *kala,* who grasps the ends of the undulating branch of foliage, a scene repeated on the other lintels of both 'palaces', and on the other pediments also. The lower pediment here, however, features Umamahesvara – a very simple rendering of Shiva and Uma riding Nandi.

Pediment on the northern 'place' with Shiva and Uma on Nandin.

The causeway continues west between the two buildings, to a short flight of steps flanked by the first of the frangipani trees which make such a spectacle of Wat Phu at the height of the dry season. The length of the 'palaces' gives a special prominence to the succession of balustered stone windows. The western ends of both buildings are in good condition, with blind doors, two-tiered pediments and high gables.

Succession of staircases

Above the 'palaces', a shorter causeway on an incline leads up to a staircase and the remains of a pavilion on a terrace. About a third of the way along this causeway, lined with boundary stones and the remains of long gallery walls on either side, a single elongated sandstone 'library' stands on the left, its entrance facing in towards the causeway.

The next staircase, with frangipani trees, leads up to another causeway, even shorter and more inclined. Another staircase leads up to the second terrace, which carries the remains of six square brick buildings, three on each side of the steps. Above this, and past a large stone *dvarapala*, now worshipped locally as a legendary founder of Champasak, a series of laterite-walled terraces lead to the upper level and its sanctuary.

The staircases, flanked by frangipanis.

Upper terrace

This broad terrace, shaded by trees and some 30 metres above the lower levels, is the location for the sanctuary, a modest but stylistically important building. A relatively large antechamber, with two side doors flanking the main entrance, opens to the east. The corner pillars and the side walls of the central porch carry beautifully carved *devatas* and *dvarapalas*. The two outer doors of the antechamber lead into side-naves, and these were possibly the inspiration for the half-galleries that became a feature of the Angkor Wat style. These side-naves and interior doorways gave the builders the opportunity to install some very fine interior lintels. The centre of the sanctuary is now occupied by a group of modern Buddha images, as this upper terrace is now the site of a Buddhist wat. Traces of the original brick roof remain.

On the south side of the sanctuary are the ruins of a small building. Behind this, just below the rock face that towers above, is the sacred spring, and the remains of an associated chapel, small basins, an elevated walkway and stone

Brahma, Shiva and Vishnu carved on the rock face behind the sanctuary.

conduits. Stylistically from the 11th century, evidence of old reconstruction and the discovery of a pre-Angkorean stele and antefix suggest that the original structures were much older.

Behind and to the north of the sanctuary are a number of carvings made directly into some of the large boulders that have fallen from the cliff above. Nearest the sanctuary is a vertical face carved with a bas-relief of Shiva flanked by Brahma and Vishnu. Farther north is a stone deeply carved with the outline of a crocodile; what makes this interesting is that its dimensions are those of a human figure, and it is very deeply incised, suggesting that this might have been the sacrificial stone for the ceremony described by the Chinese in the 6th century. Opposite is another stone carved with a short flight of steps that are surrounded by two serpents (not *nagas*). A little further north, the large head of an elephant is carved on a boulder.

Stone carved with outline of crocodile near sanctuary.

Artefacts

Most have been removed, in particular by the last local ruler, Chao Boun Oum, who renounced his title in 1964. The standing stone figure of a *dvarapala,* on the north side of the steps of the second terrace, is the only statue remaining *in situ.* Two of the most important finds are an elegant inscribed mirror handle (13th century, now in the Musée Guimet, Paris) and a 14-kilo silver pre-Angkorean head of Vishnu (discovered in 1964).

Best times to visit Early morning in particular, as the temple and its axis face east. Late afternoon is also attractive, the lower 'palaces' remaining sunlit until about 2 $\frac{1}{2}$ hours before sunset. The best time of the year is undoubtedly from February to June, when the frangipanis are in bloom. The weather is more comfortable at the beginning of this period; April and May can be extremely hot. The presence of the mountains causes some unpredictability in the weather, and late afternoon convectional clouds are not uncommon. There is a three-day festival leading up to the February full moon (coinciding with the Buddhist Makha Puja), attracting large numbers of people. Whether this is an added attraction to a visit or not depends on personal taste; expectedly, however, the site remains littered for a few weeks afterwards. At a second annual festival, in June, a water buffalo is sacrificed. **Admission** 0800-1100, but in practice there is unrestricted entry. Small charge, and an additional small charge for a still camera. In theory, video and movie cameras attract a substantial charge, officially by negotiation with the Directorate of Monuments.

Nearby sites Huei Thamo (↔ p 198), about 30 mins by boat down river from Champasak or 20 mins from the nearest landing to Wat Phu at Ban Panorn; alternatively a 12- km road detour from the junction of the Ban Moung ferry road with route 13. To combine with a visit to Wat Phu, add 2 – 2½ hours if travelling by boat, 1½ – 2 hours if by car. **Location** Wat Phu is on the lower eastern slope of Phu Kao, 12 km by dirt road from Champasak and 37 km from Pakxé (including a ferry crossing of the Mekong). **Directions** The usual starting point is Pakxé – ↔ p 268-69 for details. From Pakxé, Wat Phu can be reached by road, with a ferry crossing, or by boat to Champasak with a vehicle for the remaining 12 km. **By boat** The more interesting approach by far is down the river. The journey to Champasak takes approximately 1½ hours depending on high or low water, as the latter restricts the channels (high water is July-January, following the July start of the rainy season). A river boat for the return journey to Champasak is normally arranged through a tour agency, but one can also be hired on the Muang Kao side of the river. A less expensive but slower alternative is one of the regular passenger boats sailing between Pakxé and Champasak (ask at the Pakxé ferry landing: there are a few each day). After about 1 hr on the river, the first of a small group of islands is reached: Don Hua Pa Kor (Catfish Head Island). About 20 mins later the peak of Phu Kao, topped with the monolithic linga, comes into view on the far right, appearing behind the larger mountain Phu Bassak. About 15 mins later the boat arrives at the ferry landing of Ban Papin on the right bank, 2 km north of Champasak. Alternatively, continue for another 10 mins to the landing at Champasak's morning market (↔ p 199 to extend the trip to include Huei Thamo, ↔ p 198). With a couple of days' notice, the Pakxé tour agent or guide will arrange for a vehicle to be waiting at Champasak. Otherwise, make arrangements on the spot, but expect some delay due to the shortage of local transport. The final part of the journey is the dirt or mud (depending on the season) road leading south to Wat Phu, 12 km from the centre of Champasak. The road runs by the *baray* at the foot of the temple to the wooden admissions office. 2 hrs. **By car** *From Pakxé:* The land route from Pakxé is quicker than the boat, at about 1½ hrs including the ferry crossing, through mainly forest. Take route 13 south, being careful after 9 km not to continue straight on route 20, which takes off for Saravane; route 13 here bends to the right. From here, the road is paved only in parts. 33 km from Pakxé, turn right onto a signposted road to the ferry at Ban Moung village, 4 km further on. The three small ferries that cross to Ban Papin directly opposite sail on demand and can each take only 2 vehicles. The crossing takes 10 mins. Continue to Wat Phu as described above. To include Huei Thamo in the trip, (↔ p. 198). 1½ hrs. *From Ubon:* If overland travel is permitted from Thailand, cross the border at Chongmek and drive towards Pakxé. the road continues east for 40 km (1 hr) to the small town of Muang Kao, on the west bank of the Mekong River directly opposite Pakxé. 24 km from Chongmek is the village of Ban Phonthong, 2 km beyond which is a bridge, and 1 km after this on the right an unmarked dirt road. It is possible, although not recommended, to reach Wat Phu by this route; the road is in bad condition and the journey of about 60 km would need a 4WD vehicle. See the entry for Pakxé ➥ p. 268-69 for the difficulties of travel into Laos. If expense is not the first consideration, a Bangkok-based travel agency can probably offer the most convenient arrangements. The TAT office on Ubon (➥ p. 285-287) can also give up-to-date information on overland travel. In the context of a tour of the Khmer temples stretching eastward from Khorat Province in Thailand, this would be ideal; Wat Phu would provide an appropriate climax to the journey. This depends, however, on Lao Immigration permitting entry at the border post at Chongmek, 76 km east of Ubon on Thailand's route 217. Alternatively, you could leave Laos by this route: the circular trip would then be Bangkok-Vientiane-Pakxé/Wat Phu-Ubon-Bangkok. In fact, an itinerary based on this could have Wat Phu as the first Khmer temple visited, followed by Preah Vihear, Kamphaeng Yai and so on, all the way to Muang Khaek and Non Ku near Khorat. **Nearest accommodation and food** There is some choice, but proximity needs to be weighed against comfort. Because of the monastery at Wat Phu, there is a *sala* (rest hall) on the upper terrace where it would be possible to spend the night, although in the company of mosquitoes. A donation of a few dollars would be appropriate. In Champasak there is a small government-run guest-house/hotel with rudimentary facilities. The town has a single restaurant opposite, the 'Kin Champa Service'. The best facilities are in Pakxé, and this is where most visitors stay (➥ p. 268).

CENTRAL PLAIN

Although difficult for the Khmers to control because of its distance, the valley of the Chao Phraya was strategically and economically important. This has always been the main rice-growing area of Thailand, while the river provided communications at least as far as Nakhon Sawan. The capitals of Thailand, throughout its history, have been located in this broad valley. When the Khmers first established a base here, it was at the former Mon city of Lvo, or Louvo, now called Lopburi. Another important centre was at the site of Sukhothai, further north. The Tai people had not yet settled the valley – their main wave of immigration took place around the 12th century – but when they did, eventually expelling the Khmers, they too chose the existing cities for their own centres. As a result, there was considerable rebuilding. The Khmer temples that survive are nearly all from the 13th century, following the Bayon style, mainly in laterite, with stucco decoration. At this distance from Angkor (between 400 and 600 km as the crow flies), there was considerable independence, not only in government, but also in the architecture. The term 'Lopburi Style' has some justification for these monuments of the Chao Phraya valley, although for a long time Thai historians used it for all Khmer temples and carvings in Thailand.

Right: Wat Mahathat, Lopburi.

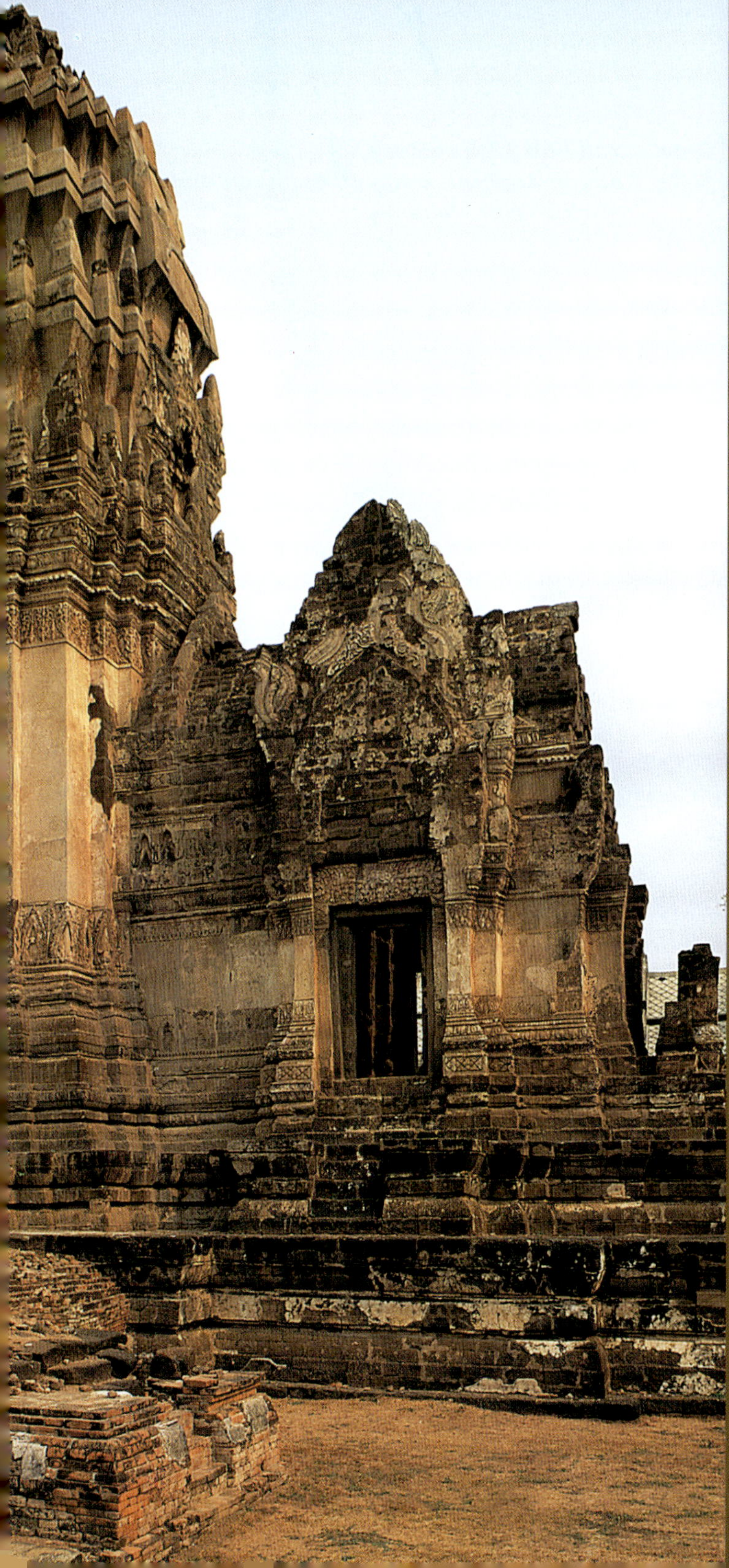

Wat Mahathat, Lopburi

Date: **2nd half 13th century** วัดมหาธาตุ ลพบุรี
Style: **Bayon/Lopburi, but with Baphuon and Angkor Wat elements**
Visit: **1 hr**

Although many times restored and added to, Wat Phra Si Ratana Mahathat (to use its full name) is still an impressive example of late Khmer provincial architecture. This was the principal temple of Louvo, as Lopburi was known, and although the layout and majority of buildings are from the Ayutthaya period (including a fine *viharn*), the tower and its *mandapa* form the Khmer heart of the complex.

Louvo, a former Mon centre, was taken by the Khmers during the reign of Suryavarman I (1002-1050), and became the regional capital for the middle Chao Phraya valley; the earliest Khmer inscriptions from here are dated 1022 to 1025. Louvo remained a Khmer centre for most of the period from the early 11th until the late 13th century, but there are a number of clues that the local rulers or governors attempted to assert their independence. In 1115 Louvo sent an independent mission to China (where it was known as Lo-hu). This was only two years after Suryavarman II succeeded to the throne after a struggle, and the timing of the mission was probably opportune. 40 years later, just after Suryavarman II's death, another independent Louvo embassy was sent to China. The outcome of this is unknown, as is the exact status of Louvo throughout these two centuries, but there were certainly periods during which it functioned as part of the Khmer Empire, both administratively and militarily. In the famous bas-relief at Angkor Wat depicting the parade of the king and princes, the Louvo contingent under its commander Rajendravarman is clearly treated as a well-disciplined Khmer force and an integral part of the army, in contrast to the Siamese mercenaries, depicted as exotic barbarians.

In all events, Louvo had definitely broken away from Angkor by 1289, when it began once more to send embassies to China. This clouded history of Louvo's relationships with Angkor has a direct bearing on the art and architecture that survives. The sanctuary at Wat Mahathat recalls elements of Phimai and Angkor Wat, particularly in the profile of the tower, but the proportions and the building materials are quite different. There is still no general agreement over whether this was simply a provincial version of the Khmer models at Angkor, or whether it was an expression of a locally developed culture. Thai historians have tended to identify a distinct Lopburi school, and it may well be that at this distance from the Cambodian capital, with evidence of attempts at political independence, Wat Mahathat and its neighbouring temples should be considered slightly apart from the mainstream of Khmer architecture. A source of confusion is that the 'Lopburi School' is sometimes applied to all Khmer architecture, in the Northeast as well, and even to all artefacts as far back as the 7th century, which unnecessarily includes some Dvaravati sculpture.

Plan

Although the entire precinct of Wat Mahathat is of considerable interest, most is post-Khmer, and the relevant structure is the central laterite tower and *mandapa*. Wat Mahathat is located close to the centre of the old city of Lopburi, immediately to the west of the railway station. The entrance gate is in the middle of the eastern side; directly ahead is the ruin of a large brick *viharn,* and the Khmer sanctuary lies behind this.

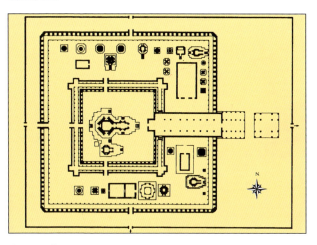

Central sanctuary

Isolated from the surrounding buildings, the sanctuary tower, *mandapa* and the short connecting *antarala* form a single imposing structure in laterite, built on a low, stepped brick platform. The two most immediate impressions are the height and the familiar corncob profile of the tower, like an upwardly-stretched version of the tower at Phimai. Some of the techniques used at Phimai to create an imposing effect have been employed here to an even greater degree. In particular, the base is very high, and its narrow stepped terraces form a concave profile that sweeps up to the main body of the sanctuary. This, combined with the outward bulge at the main cornice level,

The central sanctuary.

gives a waisted effect that enhances the impression of height. The two-tiered arches and pediments over the doorways are also taller and more pointed than those at Phimai.

Stucco-decorated cornice on the tower.

The redenting, the diminishing tiers and the inward-leaning antefixes all contribute to the characteristic curve of the tower. Instead of sandstone, however, the structure is in laterite, originally completely covered in stucco. Traces of stucco decoration remain, some of it, such as on the cornice of the tower, of very high quality. Nevertheless, seeing Wat Mahathat after the major temples of the Northeast leaves an impression of imitation. The use of sandstone throughout the towers of Phimai and Phnom Rung helps to give them coherence; the carving of the *makara-naga* arches, the pediments and so on appear integral to the structure. Using stucco for a similar effect appears more superficial, however substantial the underlying laterite framework. B. P. Groslier considered this use of stucco to reproduce the original Khmer stone architecture to be little more than *trompe l'oeil,* and that such laterite or brick imitation "exaggerates the parts to the detriment of the composition as a whole".

The one remaining in situ lintel, over the south door of the mandapa.

This aesthetic judgement notwithstanding, Wat Mahathat's tower marks an important point in the transition from Khmer sanctuary tower to Thai *prang*. The striving for the effect of height and the elevation of the multi-terraced base evolved into the typical slim, cylindrical *prang* mounted on a massive and elaborate base, such as at Wat Phra Ram in Ayutthaya, and at the later Wat Arun in Bangkok. The concrete restorations to the upper levels of the tower and the concrete beams supporting the northern doorway date to 1983.

Only one of the external lintels, over the south door of the *mandapa*, remains *in situ*. Although the details are not particularly clear, it has an interesting history. The tower was built late in the 13th century, and this lintel is made, not in stone, but in plaster on top of laterite – normal at this late date. However, the design is definitely not from the late 13th century. The figure in the centre holding two animals is probably Krishna, and the garland loops strongly on either side. These and other details are definitely Baphuon in style, from two centuries previously. The mystery is why the carver would have made such an out-of-date design. An ingenious explanation is that this lintel is a copy of an original in stone from the sandstone ruins behind the tower, since lost. By this date, stone carving skills had probably disappeared; builders preferred the less demanding stucco applied to laterite.

Artefacts

A lintel and statuary from Wat Mahathat are on display at the Somdet Phra Narai National Museum nearby. The lintel, depicting Indra riding on Airavata, is in the Angkor Wat style and dates to between 1100 and 1175.

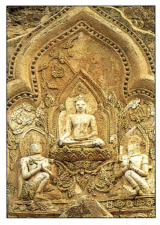

Stucco pediment on the south side of the tower.

Best times to visit Late afternoon, early morning. **Admission** 0830-1700. Small charge. **Nearby sites** All of Lopburi's extant Khmer and Khmer-influenced temples are within easy walking distance of each other. Prang Sam Yod (➥ p. 214) is the most famous, 400m. due north. Also of some interest is Prang Khaek (➥ p. 217) opposite the Provincial Judiciary, the ruined brick tower of Wat Nakhon Kosa on the other side of the railway tracks, and the laterite base of San Phra Kan, this last in the middle of a traffic circle and now overrun by macaques. The museum (➥ p. 218) has a number of rooms devoted to Khmer pieces. **Location** Wat Mahathat is located next to Lopburi railway station, in the centre of town. **Directions and nearest accommodation and food** (➥ Lopburi, pp 261-64).

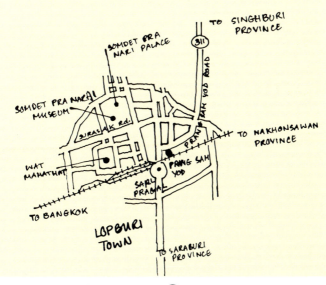

The three towers.

Prang Sam Yod, Lopburi 🪷 ปรางค์สามยอด

Date: **Early 13th century**
Style: **Bayon/Lopburi**
Reign: **Jayavarman VII**
Visit: **20 mins**

The outline of this three-towered laterite sanctuary (the Thai name means 'Three Prangs') is Lopburi's most well-known symbol. Built during the reign of Jayavarman VII, Prang Sam Yod was, like all temples of the Bayon period, consecrated to the Mahayana Buddhist faith of the king. The central sanctuary contained an image of the Buddha under *Naga*; statues of the Bodhisattva Avalokitesvara and Prajñaparamita occupied the other two. Following Jayavarman VII's death, the temple may have been converted to Shivaite use, as a *linga* was enshrined here, as happened at the Bayon and elsewhere.

Plan

The three inter-connected towers are on a north-south axis, each with doorways opening east and west. The building material is laterite, originally covered with stucco, some of which remains. The stucco decorations of the main cornice level at the corners of the towers are of high quality, with remaining 5-headed *nagas*, *kala* face, elephants and a frieze of *hamsas*. The later addition of a *viharn* during the reign of King Narai, when the sanctuary was converted to Theravada Buddhist use, is inappropriately in brick, and spoils the view from the east. There is only limited room to appreciate the temple, as it occupies a relatively small, raised island, surrounded by buildings and traffic. Nevertheless, the juxtaposition of 13th century Khmer architecture and provincial concrete shop-houses has an undeniable appeal.

Rishi carved into the base of a colonette, the south door of the southern tower.

Stucco naga on the cornice of the southern tower.

Stone antefix, western face of central tower: Varuna riding hamsas.

Stucco elephant on cornice, southern tower.

Tower from viharn.

Best times to visit Late afternoon, for the best light on the western side that is uncluttered by later building. **Admission** Unrestricted, no charge. **Nearby sites** San Phra Kan and Wat Nakhon Kosa can both be seen from Prang Sam Yod. Wat Mahathat is a 10-minute walk south, Prang Khaek a 5-minute walk west. **Location** In the centre of Lopburi, just across the railway line from the San Phra Kan traffic circle. **Directions and nearest accommodation and food** (⟿ Lopburi pp 261-64).

Prang Khaek, on a traffic island.

Prang Khaek, Lopburi
ปรางค์แขก

Date: 10th century
Style: some indications of late Bakheng and early Koh Ker
Reign: Unknown
Visit: 10 mins

Even more incorporated into the modern town than Prang Sam Yod, the brick sanctuary of Prang Khaek occupies a small traffic island opposite Lopburi's Provincial Judiciary (San Changwat Lopburi). The sanctuary comprises three towers on a north-south axis, the ruin of a brick *viharn* immediately in front of the middle tower's east door, and another brick building to the south, on the axis of the towers. There is no sign of a base. The central tower is the largest of the three; all are in brick, redented, with traces of the original stucco covering. The profile, particularly of the two flanking towers, has a slightly squat, tapered curve reminiscent of Phnom Rung.

Best times to visit No particular time; the temple is too close to surrounding buildings to catch the early morning or late afternoon sun. **Admission** Unrestricted, no charge. **Nearby sites** Wat Mahathat, Prang Sam Yod, San Phra Kan, Wat Nakhon Kosa (↦ map on p. 261). **Location** Opposite the Provincial Judiciary (San Chiangwat Lopburi). **Directions and Nearest accommodation and food** (↦ Lopburi pp 261-64).

Somdet Phra Narai National Museum, Lopburi ♣

พิพิธภัณฑ์สมเด็จพระนารายณ์

Visit: 30 mins

This small museum in the grounds of the palace houses a collection from various periods of Thai history, as well as a few good Khmer pieces. These include an Angkor Wat-style lintel from the first half of the 12th century recovered from Wat Mahathat and featuring Indra on Airavata, and an 11th-century Baphuon-style lintel from Si Thep, showing Shiva and Uma on Nandi. In addition, there are several stone Buddha images, some votive bronzes, a few Khmer ceramics and 10th- century stucco decorations.

Stone Buddha image.

Admission Wed-Sun 0900-1600, small charge. **Directions** In the grounds of the Narai Ratchanivet Palace, between Ratchadamnoen Rd. and Pratu Chai Rd.

Chantarakasem National Museum, Ayutthaya พิพิธภัณฑ์จันทร์เกษม

Visit: **15 mins**

Ayutthaya is not usually associated with Khmer art and this museum is not worth a visit for the Khmer collection alone, but is interesting nonetheless if you are stopping at the museum already. The modest collection of Khmer pieces include small votive bronzes and several stone Buddhas under *Naga*. Unfortunately, none are attributed to any site.

Stone Ganesh.

Admission Wed-Sun 0900-1630, small charge. **Directions** In the grounds of Chantarakasem Palace, U-Thong Rd, opposite the boat landing stage on the Chao Phraya River. tel: (035) 241586

Sukhothai Historical Park อุทยานประวัติศาสตร์สุโขทัย

Sukhothai is a city that has great importance in Thai history, having once been the capital city for those Tai people who settled this intermontane valley, fed by the Ping, Yom and Nan rivers, from the mid-thirteenth century to the mid-fifteenth century. Over this 200 year period Sukhothai saw the birth of a true Siamese identity and style in architecture, the applied arts and many other areas including the formalisations of the Khmer-derived Siamese script. Today a wealth of ruins

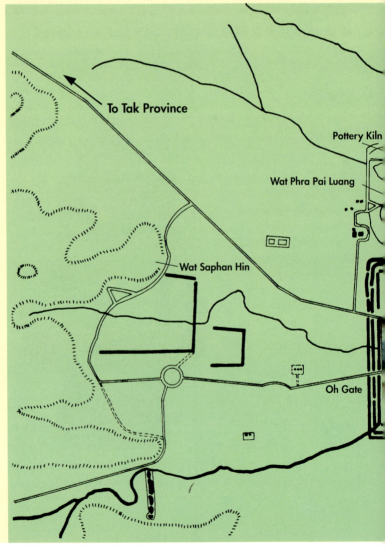

To Tak Province

Pottery Kiln

Wat Phra Pai Luang

Wat Saphan Hin

Oh Gate

may be observed in the Historic Park which has been declared a World Heritage Site by UNESCO.

The rectangular plan of the city with the most important religious building in the middle suggests the influence in the city planning of the Khmer, who always placed the principal shrine in the centre surrounded by ponds and canals.

Although most of the buildings are post-Khmer, evidence of Khmer influences remain. A Khmer style sandstone deity from the mid-12th century has been found close to San Ta Pha Daeng, while the architecture of Wat Phra Pai Luang is similar to Khmer architecture of the Bayon period and was probably constructed at the very beginning of the 13th century.

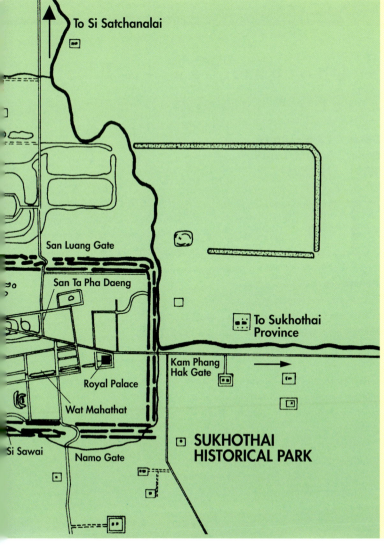

To Si Satchanalai

San Luang Gate

San Ta Pha Daeng

To Sukhothai Province

Kam Phang Hak Gate

Royal Palace

Wat Mahathat

Si Sawai

Namo Gate

SUKHOTHAI HISTORICAL PARK

The laterite sanctuary.

Sukhothai: San Ta Pha Daeng　ศาลตาผาแดง

Date: 13th century
Style: Bayon/Lopburi
Visit: 10 mins

The oldest surviving Khmer building at Sukhothai, this single sanctuary tower stands on an exceptionally high base, which gives it imposing proportions, despite not being particularly large. It was built entirely in laterite, although the superstructure has long since collapsed. There are no traces of the original stucco moulding on the building.

Artefacts

The torsos of five life-size statues were uncovered here, and originally led Boisselier to date San Ta Pha Daeng to the Angkor Wat period, but they, and the site, are now generally regarded as being from the Bayon period.

Best times to visit Early morning and late afternoon. Combine with visits to other Sukhothai sites. **Admission** Included in overall charge to Historical Park from the entrance gate. **Nearby sites** Wat Si Sawai and Wat Phra Pai Luang (both in Sukhothai Historical Park), Wat Mahathat and Wat Chao Chan at Si Satchanalai (55 kms north of Sukhothai town). **Location** In the north section of the Sukhothai Historical Park, 500 m. **Directions** (↦ p.280 an Airport is planned for 1996) **Nearest accommodation and food** Sukhothai (↦ pp.280-82), Phitsanulok (↦ pp. 273-77).

The three towers and southern approach.

Sukhothai: Wat Si Sawai

Date: **The Khmer elements: 13th century**   วัดศรีสวาย
Style: **Bayon/Lopburi**
Visit: **20 mins**

Wat Si Sawai is situated within the city walls some 350 metres to the south of Wat Mahathat (see plan). The temple is surrounded by a laterite wall with the entrance to the south. From the evidence of artefacts it is believed that the site was a Brahmin shrine, featuring three towers in a row on one base, before the founding of the city. In 1907 Crown Prince Vajiravudh visited the site and discovered a statue of Shiva within the *viharn* in front of the tower. Later,

following restoration by the Fine Arts Department, a lintel with Vishnu reclining was discovered. In the Sukhothai period the temple was converted to Theravada Buddhism and three new tower were constructed, as seen today. Some of the stucco decoration shows influence of the Khmer Bayon period but was executed in the mid 14th century. There has been some unfortunate crude restoration of the stucco in recent years.

Artefacts

A worn lintel showing Vishnu reclining is at the nearby Ramkamhaeng National Museum (→ p.226)

Stucco decoration of garuda on prang.

Best times to visit Early morning and late afternoon. Combine with visits to other Sukhothai sites. **Admission** Included in overall charge to Historical Park from the entrance gate. **Nearby sites** San Ta Pha Daeng and Wat Phra Pai Luang (both in Sukhothai Historical Park), Wat Mahathat and Wat Chao Chan at Sri Satchanalai (55 kms). **Location** In Sukhothai Historical Park, 600 m from the entrance gate. **Directions** As for San Ta Pha Daeng above. **Nearest accommodation and food** Sukhothai (→ pp. 280-82), Phitsanulok (→ pp. 273-77).

The northern tower.

Sukhothai: Wat Phra Pai Luang 🌺🌺 วัดพระพายหลวง

Date: **13th century**
Style: **Bayon/Lopburi, with later additions**
Visit: **20 mins**

The largest Khmer temple at Sukhothai, Wat Phra Pai Luang is located north of the triple earthern ramparts that define the later Siamese city. Later additions, both structural and decorative, give the temple a slightly Siamese appearance, but the surviving northernmost sanctuary tower is a fine example of its period – laterite with extensive stucco mouldings in the Bayon style. Noteworthy are the door surrounds ending in *makara* spewing forth *nagas*. The temple was probabably Mahayana Buddhist dating to the reign of Jayavaman VII (1180-1219). A statue of Buddha sheltered by *naga* was found here. Later during the Sukhothai period the temple was converted to Theravada Buddhism, and the architecture reflects the change. In fact, thanks to continued restoration and addition to the stucco, this tower has the most complete appearance of all Khmer sanctuaries built in this manner (more typically, as at the nearby San Ta Pha Daeng, or at Muang Singh in Kanchanaburi, the bare effect of plain laterite is not at all the way that the temples were conceived).

Layout

Originally a line of three towers, facing east as customary, but now only the northernmost survives intact. Of the central and southern towers, only a few courses of the laterite blocks still stand, and these are bare of stucco. All three *garbhagrhas* contain pedestals for *lingas*.

Artefacts

A stone Buddha in meditation may be seem at the Ramkamhaeng National Museum (↦ p.226).

The tower and laterite columns of a viharn on its east side.

Stucco arch from the west face of the tower.

Frieze detail of the above.

Best times to visit Early morning and late afternoon. Combine with visits to other Sukhothai sites. **Admission** Included with general admission to park.**Location** (↦ plan pp. 220-21).

Ramkamhaeng National Museum, Sukhothai ❧

Visit: **_1 hr (incl. non-Khmer exhibits)_**   พิพิธภัณฑ์รามคำแห...

The location of this, one of the most important provincial museums, in the Sukhothai Historical Park, makes it an essential part of any visit to the surrounding temples. It houses most of the artefacts found at Sukhothai, and all the significant Khmer pieces. These, of course, form only a small part of the entire collection, which is principally from the Sukhothai period of Siamese art and architecture (and is fully described in the _Guide to Thailand's Ancient Capitals_).

Specific pieces include:

Lintel, showing reclining Vishnu, from Wat Si Sawai.

Stone 14C Buddha in meditation, Wat Phra Pai Luang.

Plaque: Vishnu from Wat Si Sawai.

Male divinity, 12C- 13C from Wat San Ta Pha Daeng.

Female divinity, 12C- 13C from Wat San Ta Pha Daeng.

Stucco angels in adoration 14C, Wat Mahathat.

Admission Wed-Fri. 0900-1600, small charge. **Location** At the entrance to Sukhothai Historical Park. **Directions** (↦ pp. 220-21) **Nearest accommodation and food** Sukhothai (↦ pp. 280-82), Phitsanulok (↦ pp. 273-77).

Old Si Satchanalai

เมืองเก่าศรีสัชนาลัย

Kala on spire of the laterite gateway of Wat Mahathat.

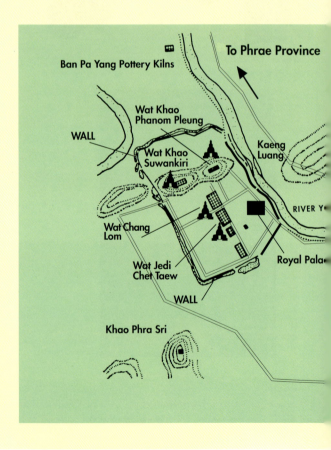

To Phrae Province

Ban Pa Yang Pottery Kilns

Wat Khao
Phanom Pleung

WALL

Kaeng
Luang

Wat Khao
Suwankiri

Wat Chang
Lom

RIVER Y

Wat Jedi
Chet Taew

Royal Pala

WALL

Khao Phra Sri

The historic city of Si Satchanalai is situated in the eponymous district in Sukhothai province, some 530 kilometres from Bangkok and 60 kilometres from Sukhothai. Its main significance lies in the magnificent ruins remaining from the Sukhothai period when Si Satchanalai was virtually a twin capital with Sukhothai (see *Ancient Capitals of Thailand*). Nevertheless there are two *wats* with Khmer remains situated at the site of an earlier town known as Muang Chalieng to the east of the later city in the gooseneck of the River Yom. Both temples should be visited together and visiting details are combined. The atmospheric setting of this site and the main ancient city certainly make Si Satchanalai well worth a visit.

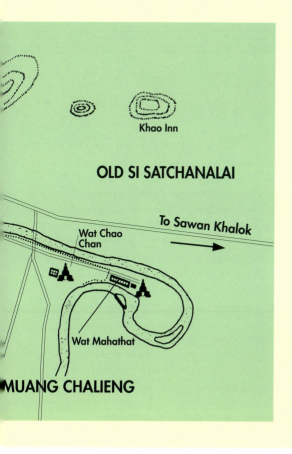

Wat Chao Chan, laterite tower and mandapa at sunrise.

Si Satchanalai: วัดเจ้าจันทร์ ศรีสัชนา
Wat Chao Chan

Date: **13th century**
Visit: **15 mins**

This is one of the oldest temples in the area and was also probably built before the creation of Sukhothai as the royal capital. It is situated close to Wat Sri Rattana Mahathat on the gooseneck of the Yom river. The grounds house the remains of a laterite building in the Khmer style, although of a workmanship of lesser quality than found at other Khmer sites. The building is square in plan with sides of 7 metres and redented corners. Entry is on the east side with the other three sides having niches for Buddha images. The upper part of the building is in three tiers surmounted by a lotus bud. It was previously thought that the temple may have been one of the 'houses with fire' built during the reign of Jayavarman VII, but as the plan is different from other such sites its purpose cannot be definitively established. In fact it was probably built after the reign of Jayavarman VII in the 1230s-50s. On the other hand, it is possible that a very thorough restoration may have obscured some of the evidence.

Best times to visit Early morning and late afternoon. Combine with visit to Sukhothai. **Admission** Unrestricted, no charge. **Nearby sites** Wat San Ta Pha Daeng, Wat Si Sawai and Wat Phra Pai Luang (all in Sukhothai Historical Park, 12 kms from Sukhothai town). **Location Directions Nearest accommodation and food** There is limited accommodation at Si Satchanalai (➛ Sukhothai entry pp. 220-221); otherwise, Sukhothai (➛ pp. 278-280) or Phitsanulok (➛ pp. 273-77).

Wat Mahathat: tower at sunrise.

Si Satchanalai: วัดมหาธาตุ
Wat Mahathat 🌺 ศรีสัชนาลัย

Date: **13th century**
Style: **Bayon and later stucco**
Visit: **20 mins**

Four-face finial on laterite gateway.

The temple is situated to the east of Wat Chao Chan on the banks of the Yom river. Important features of the *wat* include the large laterite tower on a square base with projecting steps and porch at the front. Inside is a small *stupa* believed to have housed a Buddha relic. The tower is thought to have been built in Khmer style during the first half of the 13th century. From its size it was clearly an important temple which was then renovated during the Sukhothai and Ayutthaya periods, giving it a more the appearance of a Siamese *prang*. In front is a large *viharn* constructed from laterite; its upper part has collapsed leaving only the base, columns and some walls. The walls and entrance gate have stucco decoration which, although executed later by Siamese craftsmen, shows the influence of the earlier Khmer style, in particular the entrance portal being topped with a four-face tower reminiscent of the Bayon. Although the temple was built in the Mahayan Buddhist tradition, during the Sukhothai period this changed to the Theravada school.

Best times to visit Early morning, late afternoon **Admission** Unrestricted, no charge, being in the grounds of a wat. **Nearby sites** Wat Chao Chan nearby; San Ta Pha Daeng, Wat Si Sawai and Wat Phra Pai Luang (all in Sukhothai Historical Park, 12 kms from Sukhothai town). **Location and accommodation and food** Phitsanulok (➺ pp. 273-77).

SOUTHWEST

Muang Singh
Kanchanaburi
323
Nakhon Pathom
4
BANGKOK
Bangkok
National Museum
Ratchaburi
35
35
Samut Sakhon
GULF OF
THAILAND
4
Phetchaburi
Wat Kamphaeng Laeng

Muang Singh represents the westernmost outpost of the Khmer empire. It has recently been restored, or over-restored in the views of some commentators.

Bangkok is included by virtue of the National Museum with its excellent collection of important Khmer pieces from sites all over the country.

Finally Wat Kamphaeng Laeng, while not worth a special trip, is interesting to combine with other historic sites in Petchaburi, or as a stopover on the way to the seaside at Cha-um and Hua Hin.

East entrance to central enclosure, Prasat Muang Singh.

National Museum, Bangkok 🍃🍃 พิพิธภัณฑ์พระนคร

Visit: (Khmer section) 45 mins

This is the country's premier museum and houses, among its other important collections, the finest Khmer exhibits. Specific pieces include:

From Phnom Wan:

An early lintel, Preah Kô-style, featuring a *kala* and foliate garlands, from which emerge two triple-headed *nagas*.

Bronze water jar on pedestal in front of nine-petalled lotus.

From Phimai:

The important statue of Jayavarman VII in the posture of the Buddha, almost identical to that from Angkor, carved when Jayavarman was younger, and now at the National Museum in Phnom Penh, Cambodia.

From Ku Suan Taeng:

A lintel showing Vishnu reclining, in a relatively late style, with an almost invisible *naga*.

Krishna killing the naga Kaliya from Phnom Rung.

From Phnom Rung:

A lintel showing Krishna killing the serpent Kaliya.

From Muang Tam:

Two stone guardian figures, probably a pair and if so Nandikesvara and Mahakala.

From Sdok Kok Thom:

The famous inscription from 1052 AD, which describes the foundation of the Khmer Empire by Jayavarman II, and so one of the most important in Khmer epigraphy. At the time of writing, however, it is not on display.

From Phum Phon:

A Prei Kmeng-style lintel and columns from the small brick building at the north end of the group.

The recently discovered bronze statue from Prasat Kamphaeng Yai.

From Kamphaeng Yai:

One of the finest Khmer bronzes ever found – a near-life-size statue, sensitively modelled and in excellent condition. It probably represents the guardian Nandikesvara, in Baphuon style and dress.

From Muang Singh:

Two statues of a 'radiating' Lokesvara, one the product of true Khmer craftsmanship, the other a provincial imitation – but nonetheless interesting for the energy of its vernacular treatment.

In addition, there are many fine unattributed bronzes (notably a fine, intricate *garuda* chariot fitting), ritual artefacts and ceramics.

'Radiating' Lokesvara from Muang Singh.

Gold square with flower design.

Bronze frieze.

Bronze dancers at the base of a pedestal.

Head of Buddha under naga, *c13C, from Wat Na Phra Men.*

Khmer 13C stone statue from Muang Singh.

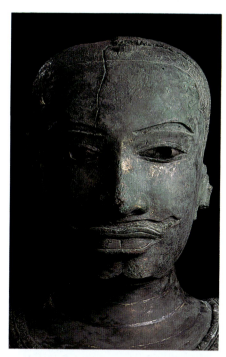

Head of bronze statue, Kamphaeng Yai.

Bronze Panya Paramita.

Admission Wed-Fri 0900-1600, small charge. **Location** On the north-west corner of Sanam Luang, near the Grand Palace.

Central enclosure from SW corner, Kanchanaburi.

Muang Singh 🔴 🌿 ปราสาทเมืองสิงห์

Date: **Late 12th to early 13th centuries**
Style: **Bayon**
Reign: **Jayavarman VII**
Visit: **1 hr**

Although known from the turn of the century, excavation and restoration was undertaken only recently at this westernmost Khmer site so far known. The modern name 'Prasat Muang Singh' means 'Sanctuary of the City of the Lion', and for once the popular name may reflect the original. The inscription on the stele at Preah Khan at Angkor, still *in situ*, mentions Srijayasimhapura ('City of the Victorious Lion') as one of the places to which Jayavarman VII had sent a Jayabuddhamahanatha statue.

Muang Singh's importance lies in its strategic location, on the route west to the Three Pagodas Pass that crosses into Burma. No doubt it was a garrison town to guard and protect this western limit of the empire, but also it was probably an important trading centre.

Plan

The laterite sanctuary is at the heart of a much larger city, and the entire remains form an extensive microcosm of the universe. The city limits are enclosed by an earthern rampart topped with a laterite wall, measuring about 800m by 1400m (compare this with the city of Phimai described on page 70 and the city of Angkor Wat). The shape is not quite rectangular, as the southern border follows the bank of the Kwae Noi river. Within this large enclosure is a series of seven concentric moats and earth ramparts on the north, east and west – representing the surrounding seas and mountains of the celestial universe.

Within these is the temple itself, with an outer enclosure wall of laterite measuring 81m by 104m – a tenth of the size of the city. The central part consists of a rectangular gallery, broken at the cardinal points by four *gopuras*, containing the sanctuary.

The temple

Enter through the east *gopura*, of which little more than the façade and side walls have been reconstructed. The stepped profile is unusual, and compares with the earlier, and sandstone, *gopura* at Sdok Kok Thom (↦ p.132). The gallery to your right as you enter is reasonably complete, with ridge finials on the curved roof. In the north-east section, next to the northern *gopura* is a carving of Avalokitesvara, the Compassionate Bodhisattva.

It needs to be said that the restoration at Muang Singh is, at the least, controversial. The speed at which it was undertaken precluded proper records being made, and some of the reconstruction is suspect. The tallest part of the temple is now the west *gopura*, but the profile of its tower does not correspond exactly to any known form. Some of the trees which invaded the sanctuary since its abandonment have been left *in situ*, which is fine, but the surround with flowers and seating in the north-east corner of the enclosure is, of course, a nonsense. Despite its appearance now, this was not a municipal park!

The central sanctuary has entrances on all four sides. It contains a copy of a statue of Avalokitesvara now in the National Museum, Bangkok (↦ p. 235).

Other buildings

Some 30m west of the temple is an unrestored group of buildings. Because of the lack of work done on them, it is impossible at the moment to say what their function was, and what relationship they had with the main sanctuary.

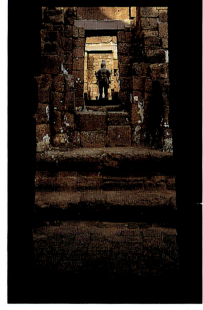

Vishnu statue through door of sanctuary, Kanchanaburi.

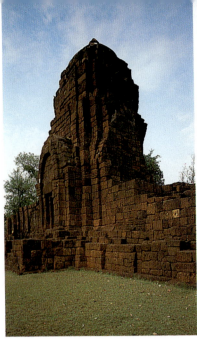

Artefacts

There is a small collection of statues and stucco decorations near the main entrance to the site, but the two most important pieces – two versions of a statue of Lokesvara – are now at the National Museum, Bangkok.

West entrance to central enclosure.

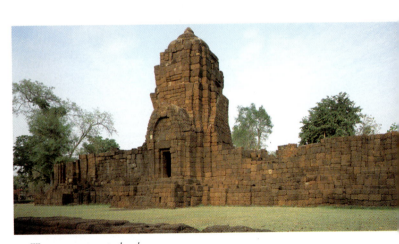

West entrance to central enclosure.

Best times to visit No special time. **Admission** 0830-1600, small charge. **Nearby sites** A few km east is the site of another sanctuary, as yet unexcavated, known locally as Muang Krut, the 'City of Garuda'. This suggests that the area was more populous than was at first thought. **Location** On the left bank of the Kwae Noi River, in Kanchanaburi province. **By car** *From Kanchanaburi:* Leave town north-west on Route 323, and 45 kms, from town, is located on a steep bank of the Kwai Noi river the waterway narrows and becomes fast flowing. *From Bangkok:* Take Route 4 heading west, and after Nakhon Pathom, where Route 4 veers south follow the sign to Kanchanaburi on Route 323 **Nearest accommodation and food** Kanchanaburi (➟ pp.256-59).

Surviving Towers Kamphaeng Laeng.

Phetchaburi : Wat วัดกำแพงแลง
Kamphaeng Laeng

Date: **13th century**
Style: **Bayon/Lopburi**
Visit: **15 mins**

Although not *en route* to any of the other monuments, and not really worth the journey for its own sake, this late period Khmer site has considerable charm. Located in a quiet backwater of the rather old-fashioned town of Petchburi, the laterite temple is now in the grounds of a modern Buddhist *wat.*

Plan

Surrounded by a laterite wall, the compelx comprises five structures – four towers each on a stepped base, and a shrine built to a cross-shaped plan. The orientation is, as usual, to the east, with the four-porched shrine at the front looking out over a small artificial pond. The towers are in a slightly unusual configuration: a row of three at the front, with the remains of a single tower directly behind and centred. All the buildings are of laterite, which is typical of the period, and would originally have been covered with stucco, of which there are a few remaining fragments.

Artefacts

In 1956, a statue of Shiva's consort Uma was found in one of the towers.

Best times to visit Early or late in the day. **Admission** Being in the grounds of a wat, entry is free. **Nearby sites** None. The nearest is Muang Singh (↦ p. 238) **Location** In the town of Petchaburi, east of the river (Menam Petchaburi). **By car** *From Bangkok* take Route 4 (the main road to Southern Thailand), and turn off at the sign for Petchaburi – watch out for the prominent royal palace of Khao Wang on an isolated hill to the left of the road. Immediately past the hill, take Ratwithi Road across the Petchaburi River. The road bends to the right; at the bend turn left and continue. The road curves right and becomes Pho Karong Road: Wat Kamphaeng Laeng is on your right,(↦ the town map on pp. 269-271). **By Train** *From Bangkok* (Hualamphong Station): trains daily. **Nearest accommodation and food** Phetchaburi (↦ pp 269-271).

SUGGESTED ITINERARIES

By far the majority of Khmer sites in Thailand are in the **Northeast** of the country. A single visit, therefore, is invariably centred on **the Khorat Plateau**; some of the monuments in the central plains can be taken in as a side trip, but are probably better included in a journey to some of the country's other attractions. Those to the north of Bangkok, for example, could be incorporated into a **trip to Sukhothai** (see *Guide to Thailand's Ancient Capitals*). In the west, **Muang Singh's isolated location in Kanchanaburi** is one the reasons for its importance – it represents the westernmost limit of Khmer building on a significant scale – but it makes a pleasant excursion with an overnight stop, particularly if combined with a river trip.

Although many visitors will already be on organised tours that include some monuments on a different schedule, these itineraries are designed for independent travel and to make the most of the time available. In any case, apart from a few annual festivals, such as the **elephant round-up in Surin** and the **candle festival in Ubon Ratchathani**, virtually all of the southern Khorat Plateau's interest to visitors lies in its Khmer heritage. The other significant attraction – regional cuisine – can be fully appreciated within these itineraries.

The major sites of the upper Mun Valley – **Phimai, Phnom Rung and Muang Tam** – should on no account be missed. Further east, **Preah Vihear (known in Thai as Khao Phra Viharn)** is one of the most important and spectacular temples in the whole of the Khmer empire, and is worth a complete journey – provided that political conditions on the border between Thailand and Cambodia permit entry. For reasons that have been explained, it has been largely inaccessible for long periods, and although the itineraries assume that it can be visited, this should be checked in advance. **Banteay Chhmar** is another Cambodian temple that is so close to Thailand (northeast of Aranyaprathet) and so spectacular that it begs to be included in an itinerary, but the possibility again depends on border conditions. Political considerations and accompanying travel restrictions may also make it difficult to include **Wat Phu in Laos** conveniently. Again, this is a major site and well worth the visit if at all possible.

These are monuments of the first rank. Following them are a large number of small-to-medium sites, and rating them in order of visitability involves personal judgement. Some are more immediately satisfying than others, by reason of the setting, the standard of restoration, or the quality of the surviving architecture and *in situ* decoration. Certain sites are of more archaeological than visual interest, but it is expected that those with prior knowledge of Khmer archaeology will construct their own itinerary from the main section of this guide.

A second consideration is location – a site of only moderate interest might be so close to an already-planned route that it would not represent much of a detour. The recommended itineraries below give a balanced selection of attractive sites, including all the most important, that can be visited within the time periods, the shortest one of which is two days with one overnight stop.

A car or minibus is the ideal way of visiting the temples, although obviously more expensive than train and bus. Public transport is perfectly practical for the majority of them, although it slows down any itinerary and prevents some visits at the best times of day. Using the network of buses in the Northeast takes time and, on some of the country roads, may involve some discomfort. The shortest time allowed for each itinerary is based on private transport; allow longer if you are using public transport. Private transport could be arranged from Bangkok, but as the major provincial towns can be reached by plane, train or air-conditioned bus, an alternative would be to travel directly to Khorat, for example, and hire a vehicle there.

The light is a consideration that we have tried to take into account in these itineraries, as it can have a great impact on the experience of a visit. Thailand is within the tropics, so that for the larger part of the day the sun – in fine weather – is high and the lighting harsh. Almost without exception, the temples look their best early in the morning and late in the afternoon in clear weather; the temperature is more pleasant at these times, also. Nearly all of the photographs in this guide, and in the companion book *Palaces of the Gods*, were taken at these times.

Most Khmer temples were built to face east, so that in most cases the approach and best overall view are from this direction. Ideally, then, the best time to visit would be at sunrise. Given the distance from the nearest towns, however, this demands a certain dedication in rising early, which may not fit in with the other needs of a holiday. We recommend that at least one dawn visit be attempted; the first rays of the sun striking a tower and eastern *gopura*, and the peace and silence in some sites, more than compensate for the discomfort of a pre-dawn start.

In this monsoonal region, the most pleasant and visually attractive time to visit is the winter dry season. From November to February the air is generally clear, giving reliable sunrises and sunsets, and although midday temperatures are still quite high, the evenings can be cool, and sometimes even chilly, because of the height of the Khorat Plateau. After February the temperature increases, and from this time until about the end of May the conditions can be extremely hot and dusty, although the light early and late in the day is still good. When (or rather if) the rains break around May, cloudy skies and high humidity prevail until about the end of October.

1. Quick tour of the near Northeast *1 overnight*

Day 1 Bangkok – lunch by Lam Takhong Reservoir – check-in Khorat hotel – Phimai Museum – Phimai – sunset at Phnom Wan – overnight Khorat.

Day 2 Phnom Rung – Muang Tam – Non Ku, Muang Khaek & Muang Gao – Si Khiu quarries – return Bangkok, National Museum.

2. Northeast highlights *2 overnights*

Day 1 Bangkok – lunch by Lam Takhong Reservoir – check-in Khorat hotel – Phimai Museum – Phimai – sunset at Phnom Wan – overnight Khorat.

Day 2 Phnom Rung – Muang Tam – check-in Surin hotel – Ta Muen Thom, Ta Muen Toch Ta Muen – overnight Surin.

Day 3 Ban Phluang – Phum Phon – Yai Ngao – Sikhoraphum – Non Ku, Muang Khaek & Muang Gao – Si Khiu quarries – return Bangkok, National Museum.

.3. Northeast highligh with Preah Vihear *3 overnights minimum*

Day 1 Bangkok – lunch by Lam Takhong Reservoir – check-in Khorat hotel – Phimai Museum – Phimai – sunset at Phnom Wan – overnight Khorat.

Day 2 Phnom Rung – Muang Tam – check-in Surin hotel – Ta Muen Thom, Ta Muen Toch & Ta Muen – overnight Surin.

Day 3 Ban Phluang – Phum Phon – Yai Ngao – Surin – *then either* Preah Vihear if visitable or Sikhoraphum – Kamphaeng Yai – Kamphaeng Noi – overnight Ubon Ratchathani.

Day 4 Early morning return to *either* Preah Vihear if visitable *or* Kamphaeng Yai – Non Ku, Muang Khaek & Muang Gao – Si Khiu quarries – return Bangkok, National Museum.

4. The Royal Road to Phimai *A 1-day special tour - see entry under the same heading, page 154*

Ta Muen Thom – Ta Muen Toch – Ta Muen – Ban Kruat – Muang Tam – Kuti Reussi #1 – Kuti Reussi #2 – Ban Bu – Phnom Rung – Phimai.

5. Comprehensive Northeast tour *5 overnights minimum*

Day 1 Bangkok – lunch by Lam Takhong Reservoir – Si Khiu quarries – Non Ku, Muang Khaek & Muang Gao – check-in Khorat hotel – Mahawirawong Museum – Phnom Wan – Phimai – overnight Khorat.

Day 2 Early morning return to Phimai – Phimai Museum – Ku Suan Taeng – check-in Surin hotel – Ta Muen Thom, Ta Muen Toch & Ta Muen – Ban Phluang – overnight Surin.

Day 3 Sunrise at Phnom Rung – Muang Tam – Ban Bu – Sikhoraphum – Kamphaeng Yai – Kamphaeng Noi – Ubon Museum – overnight Ubon Ratchathani.

Day 4 Narai Jaeng Waeng – late afternoon at Preah Vihear – overnight Ubon Ratchathani.

Day 5 Early morning return to Preah Vihear – Yai Ngao – Phum Phon – Bai Baek – Ban Kruat quarries & kilns – Sdok Kok Thom – overnight Aranyaprathet.

Day 6 Sunrise at Khao Noi – Prachinburi Museum – return Bangkok, National Museum. *Alternatively:* After sunrise at Khao Noi, drive to Banteay Chhmar. Then, either spend two hours there during the late morning and return to Aranyaprathet, continuing on to Prachinburi Museum and Bangkok, or attempt to stay overnight near Banteay Chhmar, returning to Aranyaprathet the next morning.

6. Southern Laos 1 *overnight from arrival at Pakxé*

Day 1 Pakxé - boat to Huei Thamo - boat to Champasak - (by vehicle) late afternoon at Wat Phu (by vehicle) – overnight Pakxé.

Day 2 Early morning return to Wat Phu (by vehicle) or continue on to Mekong River falls.

7. Laos and the Northeast combined *4 overnights from arrival at Pakxé*

Day 1 Pakxé – boat to Huei Thamo – boat to Champasak – (by vehicle) late afternoon at Wat Phu – (by vehicle) overnight Pakxé.

Day 2 (overland to Ubon Ratchathani) – check-in Ubon hotel – Ubon Museum – late afternoon at Preah Vihear – overnight Ubon Ratchathani.

Day 3 Early morning return to Preah Vihear – Kamphaeng Noi – Kamphaeng Yai – Sikhoraphum – check-in Surin hotel – Phum Phon – Ban Phluang – Ta Muen Thom,

Ta Muen Toch & Ta Muen – overnight Surin.

Day 4 Sunrise at Phnom Rung – Muang Tam – Ban Kruat quarries – check-in Khorat hotel – Phimai – sunset at Phnom Wan – overnight Khorat.

Day 5 Early morning return to Phimai – Phimai Museum – Mahawirawong Museum – Non Ku, Muang Khaek & Muang Gao – Si Khiu quarries – return Bangkok, National Museum.

8. Lopburi side-trip from Northeast tour *1 additional overnight*

(detour at Saraburi from Khorat) – check-in Lopburi hotel – Wat Mahathat – Prang Sam Yod – Prang Khaek – Lopburi Museum – overnight Lopburi – return Bangkok, National Museum.

9 Central Thailand *2 overnight*

Day 1 Bangkok – check-in Lopburi hotel – Wat Mahathat – Prang Sam Yod – Prang Khaek – Lopburi Museum – overnight Lopburi.

Day 2 Check-in Phitsanulok hotel – Sukhothai: San Ta Pha Daeng, Wat Si Sawai, Wat Phra Pai Luang, Museum – Si Satchanalai: Wat Mahathat and Wat Chao Chan – overnight Phitsanulok.

Day 3 Return Bangkok, National Museum.

10. Western Thailand *1 overnight*

Day 1 Bangkok – check-in Kanchanaburi hotel – Muang Singh – overnight Kanchanaburi.

Day 2 Optional river trip – return Bangkok, National Museum.

11. Western and Central Thailand *3 overnights*

Day 1 Check-in Kanchanaburi hotel – Muang Singh – overnight Kanchanaburi.

Day 2 Check-in Lopburi hotel – Wat Mahathat – Prang Sam Yod – Prang Khaek – Lopburi Museum – overnight Lopburi.

Day 3 Check-in Phitsanulok hotel – Sukhothai: San Ta Pha Daeng, Wat Si Sawai, Wat Phra Pai Luang, Museum – Si Satchanalai: Wat Mahathat and Wat Chao Chan – overnight Phitsanulok.

Day 4 Return Bangkok, National Museum.

TEMPLES RANKED BY INTEREST

🔥🔥🔥 *Major sites of first rank architecturally.*
Worth a complete journey.

Phimai
Phnom Rung
Banteay Chhmar
Ta Muen Thom
Preah Vihear (Khao Phra Viharn)
Wat Phu

🔥🔥 *Temples of considerable interest.*
Worth half a day's travelling time.

Phnom Wan
Muang Tam
The Royal Road to Phimai
Ban Phluang
Sikhoraphum
Kamphaeng Yai
Wat Mahathat, Lopburi
Wat Phra Pai Luang, Sukhothai
National Museum, Bangkok

🔥 *Temples of general interest. Worth an hour or two's travelling time.*

Si Khiu quarries
Muang Khaek
Mahawirawong Museum, Khorat
National Museum, Phimai
Kuti Reussi #2
National Museum, Prachinburi
Khao Noi
Sdok Kok Thom
Ta Muen Toch
Phum Phon
National Museum, Ubon
Wat Supatanaram Museum, Ubon
Narai Jaeng Waeng
National Museum, Khon Kaen
Huei Thamo
Prang Sam Yod, Lopburi
Somdet Phra Narai National Museum, Lopburi
Wat Si Sawai, Sukhothai

Wat Mahathat, Si Satchanalai (although higher ranking for its non-Khmer buildings)
Ramkamhaeng National Museum, Sukhothai
Muang Singh

Other temples. Worth a stop en route.

Non Ku
Muang Gao
Prang Ku
Ku Suan Taeng
Kuti Reussi #1
Ban Bu
Ta Muen
Yai Ngao
Kamphaeng Noi
Prang Khaek, Lopburi
Chantarakasem National Museum, Ayutthaya
San Ta Pha Daeng, Sukhothai
Wat Chao Chan, Si Satchanalai

✎ *Temples in an attractive location.*

Phnom Wan
Phnom Rung
Kuti Reussi #2
Muang Tam
Khao Noi
Banteay Chhmar
Ta Muen Thom
Ta Muen Toch
Preah Vihear (Khao Phra Viharn)
Ban Phluang
Phum Phon
Sikhoraphum
Huei Thamo
Wat Phu
Muang Singh
Sukhothai temples
Si Satchanalai temples

FESTIVALS

JANUARY

Agricultural Fair, Maha Sarakham. Early in the month, featuring agricultural exhibitions, local handicrafts and cultural performances.

Elephant Round-up, Chaiyaphum.

FEBRUARY

Phra Nakhon Khiri Fair, Phetchaburi. A fair centred on the City on the Mount (Phra Nakhon Khiri), the hill dominated by a 19th century palace.

Phra Phut Chinnaraj Fair, Phitsanulok. Festival honouring one of Thailand's most revered Buddha images, in Wat Phra Si Ratana Mahathat. In addition to the religious ceremonies, there is folk theatre, *ramwong* dancing and bazaars.

Wat Phu Festival. For the three days before the February full moon (coinciding with the Buddhist Makha Puja) there is a popular festival that attracts large numbers of people.

King Narai Reign Fair, Lopburi. The fair celebrates the reign of King Narai the Great, the Ayutthayan monarch best known for his promotion of diplomatic relations with European powers during the mid-1600s. It features homage-paying ceremonies, processions, various entertainments and bazaars.

MARCH

Lam Duan Flower Festival, Sisaket. A three-day festival at the beginning of the month with a non-specific mix of cultural performances, handicrafts and bazaars.

Tao Suranari Fair, Khorat. A 10-day event at the end of March and beginning of April, celebrating the city's heroine, Khunying Mo. The wife of the Deputy Governor, she defeated an invading Laotian army in the 19th century by getting its troops drunk and then, with a small force of women, killing them. The fair features parades, bazaars and cultural performances.

APRIL

Dok Khun – Siang Khaen Festival, Khon Kaen. Coinciding with Songkran, the traditional Thai New year, this festival combines merit-making religious ceremonies with the usual folk entertainment.

Ordination Festival with elephant procession, Haad Sieo (Si Satchanalai).

A two-day mass ordination of monks in which the young men ride in procession on elephants through the village.

Phnom Rung Festival. What began as an annual Buddhist pilgrimage has been developed into something of a tourist occasion. The festival is timed to coincide with the alignment of the temple's principal axis with the rising sun, and lasts for a few days. Check dates for the year with TAT.

MAY

Rocket Festival, Yasothon. Known in Thai as the 'Bun Bang Fai', this quite ancient festival features the launching of black powder rockets, some of considerable size, in what is essentially an attempt at rain-making. It is held during the second weekend of the month, and timed for the expected (but by no means reliable) start of the annual monsoon.

The town of Yasothon is the centre of the celebrations, but rockets are made and launched throughout the area (formerly the festival took place along much of the middle reaches of the Mekong River). The rockets, some of which are the world's largest using black powder, are made locally over the two to three weeks prior to the festival. On the first day there is a parade in town and the rockets are blessed; on the afternoon of the second the rockets are launched. The majority of celebrants are very noisy, enthusiastic and drunk.

JULY

Candle Festival, Ubon Ratchathani. Intricately carved giant candles (usually 2 metres tall by 25 cm in width) are paraded through the town and presented to temples, in celebration of the Buddhist festival of 'Khao Pansa'. This marks the beginning of the three-month retreat of the monks to study, during the rains, and takes place on the full moon of the eigth lunar month, which is usually July. There are drama and dance performances also, and merit making.

SEPTEMBER

Boat Races, Phitsanulok. Annual regatta on the Nan river.

OCTOBER

Wax Castle Festival, Sakon Nakhon. A celebration of the end of the annual Buddhist Rains Retreat (Ok Phansa) with beeswax representations of temples and shrines paraded through the town and presented to the temples; festivities continue the following day. See the Ubon Candle Festival above.

Boat Races, Phimai. More races on the Mun River, together with various entertainments and bazaars.

Boat Races, Buriram. This annual regatta is staged on the Mun River in Buriram's Satuek district. Celebrations include processions and cultural perfomances with elephants.

Loi Krathong and Candle Festival, Sukhothai. One of the major celebrations of this nationwide festival is at the Sukhothai Historical Park. Taking place at the full moon of the 12th lunar month, Loi Krathong is traditionally celebrated by releasing small floats containing a candle into the water. This has been developed at Sukhothai into an event of some size, normally booked up well in advance.

Elephant Round-up, Surin. What was once a genuine round-up performed by the local Suai people, traditional elephant trainers, has become a well-publicised tourist event. There are usually at least a hundred elephants, which race and perform various other field events.

Chinese banquet for Monkeys, Lopburi. More than 500 simian recipients of local Chinese culinary largesse, dining at Prang Sam Yod, put more than the usual strain on city centre traffic and tourists. Table manners not to be expected.

Silk Fair, Khon Kaen. As the centre of Thailand's tradi-tional silk production, the city hosts a fair lasting several days that includes process-ions and cultural shows.

Kite Festival, Buriram. Kite flying is normally a March activity in Thailand, but here in the Northeast, Buriram has a competition in December, featuring battles of the sexes between male (Chula) and female (Pakpao) kites.

TOWN INFORMATION

Facilities in the provincial capitals and other major towns are listed here. Local accommodation near the sites, which is usually modest, is listed at the end of each temple entry.

Hotels		
✪✪✪✪	Expensive
✪✪✪	Medium price
✪✪	Inexpensive
✪	Low budget

Note: these prices are approximate at the time of writing, and are liable to change.

Banking hours are Mon-Fri 08.30-15.30. Post Office hours are Mon-Fri 08.30-16.30, Sat 09.00-12.00. Most buses for towns listed here leave from Mor Chit 1 Bus Terminal except for Sukhothai, Phitsanulok, Kanchanaburi and Phetchaburi (see entries).

ARANYAPRATHET

Bangkok 298 km – Prachinburi 150 km – Khorat 250 km – Lahan Sai 118 km. Aranyaprathet is a bustling border town which has grown as a result of the international community working in the nearby refugee camps over the past 20 years. It has no sites of interest in town but is convenient for visiting.

By car *From Bangkok:* Leave on the airport expressway north to Rangsit (9 km from Don Muang airport), and turn right onto Route 305 in the direction of Nakhon Nayok (75 km from Rangsit). There, join Route 33 heading east, all the way to Aranyaprathet, 162 km further on. 3½-4 hrs.

From Khorat: Take Route 304 south through Pak Thong Chai and crossing the mountains east of Khao Yai, as far as Route 33 at Kabin Buri (150 km). Turn left (east) onto Route 33 and continue all the way to Aranyaprathet, 95 km further on. *From Phnom Rung:* 179 km. At the T-junction with Route 2075, turn right, and at Lahan Sai 1 km further on, turn right onto Route 2075. After 16 km, this joins Route 348, which continues south over the mountains directly to Aranyaprathet, 118 km from Lahan Sai (note that at Ta Phraya, Route 348 makes a right turn at a nominal cross-roads). *From Muang Tam:* Take the road that leads due west from the village of Ban Khok Muang, leaving Muang Tam on your right. At the T-junction after 6 km, turn right, and continue as from Phnom Rung above.

By bus *From Bangkok:* a/c buses daily every hour from 05.30-17.00, non-a/c buses daily every hour from 05.30-16.30 (5 hours), from the Mor Chit 2 Bus Terminal, Kamphaengphet Rd. Tel: (02) 9361880, 9360657 non a/c, a/c. *From Khorat:* daily to Chonburi. At Kabinburi change to the bus which runs from Prachinburi to Aranyaprathet. 14 buses daily from Khorat to Chonburi from 03.30-16.45.

By train *From Bangkok:* (Hualamphong Station) 2 ordinary daily (5½ hrs.) 06.00, 13.10. Tel: (02) 223 7010, (02) 223 7020.

Tourist information *(Gan thongthio)*

None in town. The nearest is the TAT office in Pattaya at 382/1 Chaihat Rd, South Pattaya, Amphoe Bang Lamung, Pattaya City, Chonburi.
Tel: (038) 427667.

Police station *(Sathaanee tamruad)*

Mahadthai Rd, opposite the Tessabaan and Amphoe.
Tel: (037) 231203 or 191 in an emergency.

Local administrative offices *(Tessabaan and Amphoe)*

Both on Mahadthai Rd, a short distance south-west of the clock tower *(hor naligar)*, and opposite the police station. Tessabaan tel: (037) 231062, 231111. Amphoe tel: (037) 231016, 231800.

Hospitals *(Rong phayabaan)*

Aranyaprathet Hospital, Suwanasorn Rd, almost next to the clock tower.
Tel: (037) 231180, 231190.

Post and telegraph office *(Praisanee)*

Suwanasorn Rd, just north-east of the clock tower.
Tel: (037) 231006/7, 231728.

Railway station *(Sathaanee rodfai)*

At the end of Mahadthai Rd, 100m north-east of the clock tower.
Tel: (037) 231698.

Bus stations *(Baw Kaw Saw)*

Ratuthit Rd, 100m south-east of junction with Mahadthai Rd.
Tel: (037) 231262.

Banks with currency exchange *(Thanaakaan laek ngoen)*

Thai Farmers Bank, 73/5 Bumrungrad Rd. Tel: (037) 231072.
Krung Thai Bank, 135 Chao Phaya Bodin Rd. Tel: (037) 231031.
Thai Military Bank, 73/16 Bumrungrad Rd. Tel: (037) 231280, 231290.

Accommodation *(Rong raem)*

Inn Pound ✪✪ 152 Tanawit Rd, Ban Mai Nong Sai. Tel: (037) 232116, fax: (037) 232115. 154 a/c rooms. Aranyaprathet's first large hotel, a short distance out of town, 2 km north on Route 348. Facilities include an attractive swimming pool, and restaurant with music. The rooms are just adequate, though not up to the standard that the exterior and public areas would lead you to expect – low building standards in a hotel obviously not built to last. Price: 400-600 baht.

Inter Hotel ✪✪ 108/7 Soi Ban Aran, Ban Aran Rd. Tel: (037) 231291, 231848, 232352, fax: (037) 232352. 40 a/c rooms. Recently rebuilt, neat hotel, centrally located. Despite the address, the directions to follow are: turn right at the clock tower and then left onto Ratuthit Rd. After 200m turn right down Soi Chatasingh (Soi 1) – the hotel is signposted. Price: 450 baht.

Aran Garden Hotel 1 ✪ 59/1-7 Ratuthit Rd. Tel: (037) 231105, 231836. 29 non a/c rooms (with fan). The older of the pair – basic, and typical of the kind of small Chinese hotel that has long been a common feature of provincial towns. Price: 120-170 baht.

Aran Garden Hotel 2 ✪ 110 Ratuthit Rd. Tel: (037) 231070, 231905/7, 231837. 43 rooms, incl 13 a/c. New hotel from the same owners, just along the road, rooms. Price: a/c 380 baht, fan 160-220 baht.

Restaurants *(Raan ahaan)*

Ploen Restaurant, Jitsuwan Rd. Tel: (037) 231627. The best of several restaurants in this street in the centre of town.

Somjit Pochana, Ratuthit Rd (opposite *Aran Garden Hotel 1*). Tel: (037) 231246. Simple and straightforward corner restaurant, popular for breakfast.

Outside town

There are three garden restaurants on Route 348, just north of the junction with Route 33 and before the *Inn Pound*. They are:– *Suan Ahaan Daeng Thong,* • *Suwan Ahaan Sabai Jai* • *Seafood Talae Pao Phai* opposite Aranyaprathet market. The most delicious dish is *Yam Pla Krob (crispy fish salad).*

Food stalls

At the market on Jitsuwan Rd. Also in the night market.

BURIRAM

Bangkok 410 km – Khorat 151 km – Surin 111 km – Phnom Rung 74 km.

By car *From Khorat:* Drive south on Route 304 to Route 24; follow this east, turning left on Route 218. *From Phimai:* leave to the south on Route 2163, turning east onto Route 2162 at Hin Dad; continue via Lamplaimai to Buriram. *From Surin:* Take Route 2078 west. *From Ubon Ratchathani and the east:* Take Route 24 and turn right on Route 219.

By bus *From Bangkok:* Four a/c buses daily and seven non-a/c from the Mor Chit 2 Bus Terminal Kamphaengphet Rd, (5 hrs). Tel: (02) 9361880, 9360657 non-a/c, a/c. *From Khorat:* Seven buses daily, (2-2½ hrs). *From Surin:* Frequent buses from the Surin Bus Station on Jitbumrung Rd, (1½ hrs), tel: (044) 511756.

By train *From Bangkok* (Hualamphong Station): Two diesel sprinters daily (5½ hrs), one express train daily in the evening (6½ hrs), three rapid trains daily (6½ hrs), three ordinary trains daily (9 hrs). *To Bangkok:* Same services, tel: (02) 223 7010, 223 7020. *From Khorat:* Same trains as from Bangkok (sprinter and express 1 ½-2 hrs, rapid and ordinary 2-2½ hrs). *From Surin:* Four diesel sprinters daily (45 mins), one express train daily in the evening (45 mins), three rapid trains daily (45 mins), five ordinary trains daily (55 mins).

Tourist information *(Gan thongthio)*

None in Buriram. The nearest is the TAT office in Khorat.

Police station *(Sathaanee tamruad)*

Jira Rd. Tel: (044) 611234 or 191 in an emergency.

Local administrative offices *(Tessabaan)*

Pipat Rd. Tel: (044) 611442.

Hospitals *(Rong phayabaan)*
Buriram Provincial Hospital, Nasathaanee Rd. Tel: (044) 611262. Located
on the road that runs parallel to Niwat Rd on the other side of the railway line.

Post and telegraph office *(Praisanee)*
Romburi Rd, near the clock tower. Tel: (044) 611142.

Railway station *(Sathaanee rodfai)*
Niwat Rd, next to the clock tower, at end of Romburi Rd. Tel: (044) 611202.

Bus stations *(Baw Kaw Saw)*
Thani Rd. Tel: (044) 611595, 612534

Banks with currency exchange *(Thanaakaan laek ngoen)*
Bangkok Bank, 100 Soonthonthep Rd. Tel: (044) 612718.
Thai Farmers Bank, 132 Soonthonthep Rd. Tel: (044) 611036.
Siam Commercial Bank, 28/30 Thani Rd. Tel: (044) 612911, 612909.

Accommodation *(Rong raem)*
Vongthong Hotel ✪✪✪ 512/1 Jira Rd. Tel: (044) 612540, 620858,
620860-2 Fax: (044) 620859. 71 rooms all a/c. Prices 600-1,400 baht.
Thepnakorn Hotel ✪✪ 139 Jira Rd. Tel: (044) 613400/2, fax: (044)
613400. 30 a/c rooms, incl four suites. Motel, 1 km east of town. Pric440-
540 baht.

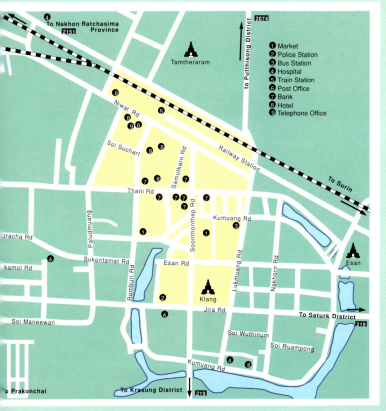

Thai Hotel ✪✪ 38/1 Romburi Rd. Tel: (044) 611112, 611132, fax: (044) 612461. 96 rooms, 20 a/c. Near clock tower and railway station. Price: fan 150 baht, a/c 360-440 baht.

Buriram Hotel ✪✪ 148 Niwat Rd. Tel: (044) 611740, 612504, fax: (044) 612147. 84 rooms, 42 a/c. rooms. Price: 400-600 baht.

Grand Hotel ✪ 137 Niwat Rd. Tel: (044) 611089, 611179. 96 rooms, 5 a/c. rooms. Price: 400 baht, fan 160-200 baht.

Chai Charoen Hotel ✪ 114-6 Niwat Rd. Tel: (044) 611559. 39 rooms. Price: 80-120 baht.

Niwat Hotel ✪ 89/10-2 Niwat Rd. Tel: (044) 611640. 20 rooms. Price: 50-70 baht.

Restaurants *(Raan ahaan)*

Porn Phen, Romburi Rd, near the Thai Hotel. Tel: (044) 611553

Viangchan, 31/17 Thani Rd. North-eastern food. There appear to be three restaurants with the same name – this was the only one tried. Very typical: no ambience, but authentic Isaan food – bile sauce, etc.

Maitrichit Restaurant, 169/ 2-4 Soonthonthep Rd. Tel. (044) 611538.

Food stalls

There is a small night market in front of the railway station.

Car rental *(Chao rod)*

Phnom Rung Tours, 131 Buriram-Prakonchai Rd. Tel: (044) 612046, fax: (044) 61269.

Buriram Transport, Jira Rd. Tel: (044) 611905, 611491.

Torket, 265- 71 Soonthonthep Rd. Tel: (044) 611366.

CHAIYAPHUM

Bangkok 342 km – Khorat 117 km – Khon Kaen 170 km – Phitsanulok 326 km – Phimai 108 km. Chaiyaphum is a small town and the accommodation refects this, being functional and characterless.

By car *From Bangkok:* On the way to Khorat, leave Route 2 at the Si Khiu interchange, taking Route 201, (another 128 km). 1³/₄ hrs. *From Khorat:* Take Route 2 north, and after 8 km, at Choho, turn left onto Route 205. Continue for 54 km until the intersection at Nong Bua Khok. Turn right here onto Route 201, which reaches Chaiyaphum after 55 km. Alternatively, 84 km north on Route 2 on the way to Khon Kaen, take Route 202 left for 61 km. 1 ¹/₂ hrs. *From Phimai:* Take Route 206 12 km west to join Route 2. Turn right and continue as above. 1¹/₄ hrs. *From Khon Kaen:* Take Route 2 south in the direction of Khorat, and turn right onto Route 202. At Chaiyaphum, take the road that goes east from the roundabout at the town's southern entrance, passing the hospital, for 2 km. 2¹/₂-2³/₄ hrs.

By bus *From Bangkok:* 10 a/c buses and 20 non a/c buses from Mor Chit 2 Bus Terminal Kamphaengphet Rd. Tel: (02) 9363659 non a/c, a/c (6 hrs). *From Khorat:* Frequent buses (2 hrs).

Tourist information *(Gan thongthio)*

See TAT Khorat, page 265.

Police station *(Sathaanee tamruad)*

Harouthai Rd, near Phra Ya Lae Momument. Tel: (044) 811318.

Local administrative office

Harouthai Rd, opposite Police Station. Tel: (044) 811378.

Hospitals *(Rong phayabaan)*

Chaiyaphum Provicial Hospital, Bannakarn Rd.
Tel: (044) 811644, 811640, 822365.

Post and telegraph office *(Praisanee)*

Bannakarn Rd, opposite Chaiyaphum Rd Vocational School.
Tel: (044) 811080, 821600.

Bus stations *(Baw Kaw Saw)*

Niwesrat Rd, near Chaiyaphum Electricity Office. Tel: (044) 811344.

Banks with currency exchange *(Thanaakaan laek ngoen)*

Bangkok Bank 273/96 Ratchathan Rd. Tel: (044) 811662/3
Thai Farmers Bank 69/1 Harouthai Rd. Tel: (044) 811267/9
Siam Commercial Bank 376/213 Harouthai Rd. Tel: (044) 812303.

Accommodation *(Rong raem)*

Loet Nimit Hotel ✪✪ 1/447 Niwesrat Rd. Tel: (044) 811522/3.
79 rooms a/c and fan. Price: 200-600 baht, suites 800 baht.

Sirichai Hotel ✪ 565 Nonmuang Rd. Tel: (044) 811543, fax: 812299.
92 rooms a/c and fan. Price: 190-550 baht, suites 800 baht.

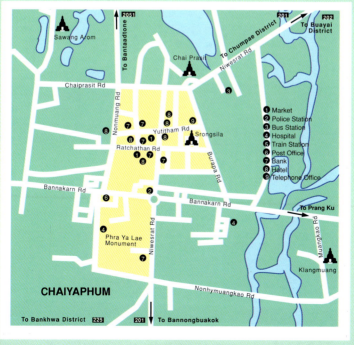

Restaurants *(Raan ahaan)*

Looktarn Harouthai Rd, Amphoe Muang. Tel: (044) 812728.
Chanphan Burapa Rd, Amphoe Muang. Tel: (044) 811094.

Food stalls

Behind Provincial Administration Office.

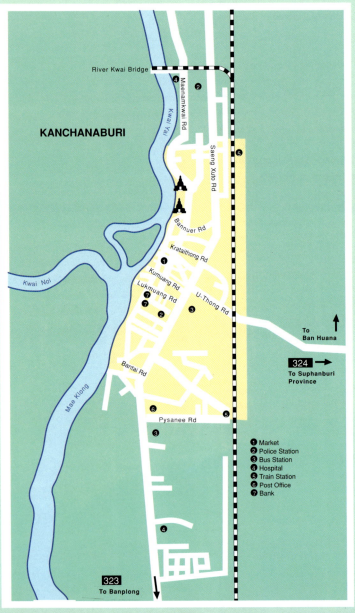

Bangkok 128 km – Nakhon Pathom 65 km – Lopburi 212 km. Kanchanaburi is situated in beautiful countryside on the River Kwai and is closely associated with the bridge of that name and the history of the Second World War. There is a British cemetary there. Apart from the Khmer temple, it is worth a visit for the above features.

By car *From Bangkok:* Take Route 4 and turn right onto Route 323, (2 hrs). An alternative is to take Route 338 (the Pin Klao-Nakhon Chaisri Rd) and then join Route 4 as above, (2 hrs). *From Lopburi:* One can take a somewhat cross-country route. Take Route 3196 to junchtion with Route 3267. Turn right to Ang Thong. Take 3195 to junction with Route 340. Turn left to Suphanburi and there take Route 321 to U-Thong and then 324 to Kanchanaburi.

By bus *From Bangkok:* Frequent a/c and non-a/c buses leave the Southern Bus Terminal, Boromraja Chonanee Rd, every 20 mins (06.00-22.00 a/c, 04.30-19.30 non a/c), $2^1/_2$-3 hrs. Tel: (02) 434 5557/8 non a/c, (02) 435 1199 a/c. *From Lopburi:* Possible but involving changes at Singhburi and Suphanburi.

By train *From Bangkok:* Two trains daily from Bangkok Noi Station, Thonburi, tel: (02) 411 3102, 08.00, 13.45 ($2^1/_2$ hrs). The special tourist train on weekends and holidays from Hualamphong Station is a day trip, and does not take in Muang Singh. Tel: (02) 223 7010, 223 7020.

Tourist information *(Gan thongthio)*
The TAT office is on Saeng Xuto Rd. Tel: (034) 511200, fax: (034) 511200. Open daily 08.30-16.30.

Police station *(Sathaanee tamruad)*
Saeng Xuto Rd. Tel: (034) 511560 or 191 in an emergency.
Tourist Police, tel: (034) 512795.

Local administrative offices *(Tessabaan)*
Lukmuang Rd. Tel: (034) 511502, 514788, 514533/4.

Hospitals *(Rong phayabaan)*
Pahon Ponpayuhasena Hospital (Kanchanaburi Provincial Hospital), Saeng Xuto Rd. Tel: (034) 511233, 512448.
Preeshaweth Hospital, (Private), Saeng Xuto Rd. Tel: (034) 611683.

Post and telegraph office *(Praisanee)*
Saeng Xuto Rd. Tel: (034) 511131, 512200.

Railway station *(Sathaanee rodfai)*
290 Saeng Xuto Rd. Tel: (034) 511285.

Bus stations *(Baw Kaw Saw)*
Saeng Xuto Rd. Tel: (034) 511182.

Banks with currency exchange *(Thanaakaan laek ngoen)*
Bangkok Bank 2 U-Thong Rd. Tel: (034) 511212, 512710/1
Thai Farmers Bank 160/80-2 Saeng Xuto Rd. Tel: (034) 511203, 511774
Siam Commercial Bank 274/6 Saeng Xuto Rd. Tel: (034) 513008, 513307.

Accommodation *(Rong raem)*

In town are various functional hotels on Saeng Xuto Rd.

There are several pleasant hotels and restaurants on the river and out of town.

River Kwai Hotel ✪✪✪ 284/15-6 Saeng Xuto Rd. Tel: (034) 513348-9, 513348-9, 511565, 511184. Fax: 511269. Bangkok office: (02) 251 6970, 251 9008 ex.410, 251 6970. 190 rooms. Price: 1,450-1700 baht.

Si Muang Kan Hotel ✪ 131/113 Saeng Xuto Rd. Tel: (034) 511609. 60 rooms. Price: a/c 270-480, fan 200 baht.

Out-of-town accommodation

Kasem Island resort ✪✪✪✪ 27 Bann Tai Village. Tel: (034) 513359. Bangkok office tel: (02) 255 3603, fax: (02) 255 3604. 30 bungalows and rafts. Price 750 baht.

Felix River Kwai Resort ✪✪✪✪ 9/1 Mu 3 Tamakarm, Amphoe Muang. Tel: (034) 515061-83, fax: (034) 515095. Bangkok office, tel: (02) 255 3410-9, 255 5767. 255 rooms. Price: 3,776-17,655 baht.

River Kwai Village ✪✪ Bangkok office, tel: (02) 251 7552, 255 2350, 251 7828. 60 rooms. Price:220-1,200 baht.

Kwai Yai River Hut ✪✪ Bangkok office 37 Soi Lung Suan Purnjit Rd. Tel: (02) 252 9337. 20 rafts. Price 850.

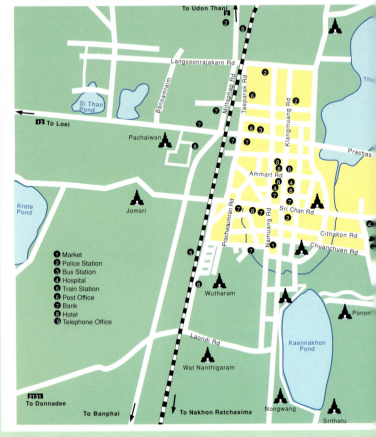

Restaurants *(Raan ahaan)*

Ban Naur, Rimnamnamuang Rd. Tel: (034) 512326.

Thong Nathii, Rimnamnamuang Rd. Tel: (034) 512944.

Phae Kan, Rimnamnamuang Rd. Tel: (034) 513251.

Sabai-jit, 284/54-5 Saeng Xuto Rd. Tel: (034) 511931.

Namkrung Restautant, 328/1 Song Kwae Rd.

River Kwai Restautant, near Bridge over the River Kwai.
Tel: (034) 512540,512541.

Food stalls

Saeng Xuto Rd opposite the Police Station.

Car rental (Chao rod)

BT Travel, Saeng Xuto Rd. Tel: (034) 511967.

KHON KAEN

Bangkok 449 km – Khorat 190 km – Udon Thani 115 km – Phitsanulok
307 km. Khon Kaen is a fast-developing city with the largest university in the
Northeast. This expansion has led to an improvement in hotel
accommodation, although not in atmosphere.

By car *From Bangkok:* Take Route 1. At Saraburi turn onto Route 2 to
Khon Kaen (6-7 hrs). *From Khorat:* Take Route 2 to Khon Kaen (2- 2$^1/_2$
hrs). *From Phitsanulok:* Take Route 12 (5-6 hrs).

By bus *From Bangkok:* 17a/c buses daily and non-a/c every hour
from the Mor Chit 2 Bus Terminal, Kamphaengphet Rd. Tel: (02)
9361880, 9360657 non-a/c, a/c. (6 hrs).

By train *From Bangkok:* Hualamphong Station: Five trains daily
(express 7 hrs, rapid 8 hrs). Tel: (053) 223 7010, 223 7020

By plane *To and from Bangkok:* Two Thai Airways International flights
daily, three Fri-Sun, 50 mins. Tel: (02) 535 2081/2, 523 6121.
To and from Chiangmai: Two flights weekly, 1$^1/_2$ hrs. Chiang Mai
Airport, Sanaambin Rd. Tel: (053) 211644, 211515.

Tourist information *(Gan thongthio)*

15/5 Prachasamosorn Rd, nr. Sosesukorn Hotel, Amphoe Muang.
Tel: (043) 244498/9, fax: (043) 244497.

Police station *(Sathaanee tamruad)*

Klangmuang Rd. Tel: (043) 211162, or 191 in an emergency.

Local administrative offices *(Tessabaan)*

Soonrajakarn Rd. Tel: (043) 236882.

Hospitals *(Rong phayabaan)*

Provincial Hospital, Sri Chan Rd. Tel: (043) 236005, 237137.
Sri Nakarin Hospital, (Khon Kaen University) Mittaphap Rd.
Tel: (043) 237902.
St. Paul Hospital, (Private) 45/36-9 Phimphasut Rd.
Tel: (043) 237683, 237688.
Mokul Hospital, 157-161 Sri Chan Rd. Tel: (043) 238934,237822.

Post and telegraph office *(Praisanee)*

194/1 Soonrajakarn Rd. Tel: (043) 241223, 221486.

Airline offices *(Gan binthai)*

Thai Airways International, 183/6 Maliwan Rd.
Tel: (043) 236523, 239011.

Airport *(Sanaambin)*

Khon Kaen-Loei Rd. Tel: (043) 238803, 243037.

Railway station *(Sathaanee rodfai)*

Ruanrom Rd. Tel: (043) 221112.

Bus stations *(Baw Saw Kaw)*

Prachasamosorn Rd. Tel: (043) 237472 (non a/c)
Klangmuang Rd. Tel: (043) 239910 (a/c).

Banks with currency exchange *(Thanaakaan laek ngoen)*

Bangkok Bank, 254 Sri Chan Rd. Tel: (043) 225144/6.
Also at 147 Prachasamosorn Rd. Tel: (043) 237689, 237677
Thai Farmers Bank, 145/29 Prachasamosorn Rd. Tel: (043) 241597,
237719. Also 318/1 Namuang Rd. Tel: (044) 225131/3.
Siam Commercial Bank, 491 Sri Chan Rd. Tel: (043) 242200/5.

Museums *(Phiphithapan)*

Khon Kaen National Museum, Langsoonrajakarn Rd, Amphoe Muang.
Tel: (043) 236741. Wed-Sun 09.00-16.00. Small admission fee.

Accommodation *(Rong raem)*

Raja Orchid Khon Kaen (Sofitel) ✪✪✪✪ 9/9 Prachasamran Rd, Tel:
(043) 322155, Fax: (043) 322150. The newest and most luxurious hotel in
the Northeast. 213 superior rooms. 79 deluxe rooms and suites. Coffee
shop, Thai, Chinese and Vietnamese restaurants, Karaoke, discotheque,
health club and swimming pool. Price: 2,000 baht, suites 4,200.

Charoen Thani Princess ✪✪✪✪ 260 Sri Chan Rd. Tel: (043) 220400-
10, Fax: (043) 220438. Bangkok office Tel: (02) 721 8240. A new,
international standard hotel. 320 a/c rooms. Facilities: swimming pool, three
restaurants (Chinese, Internat. and Thai). Price: 1,271-3,000 baht.

Kaen Inn ✪✪✪ 56 Klangmuang Rd. Tel: (043) 237744. Bangkok office
tel: (02) 247 1661-2. 162 a/c rooms. Price: 800 baht, suites 1,500 baht.

Khon Kaen Hotel ✪✪✪ 43/3 Phimpasut Rd. Tel: (043) 244881-5, fax:
(043) 242458. 134 a/c rooms incl.suites. Price: 700-1,800 baht.

Kosa Hotel ✪✪✪ 250-2 Sri Chan Rd. Tel: (043) 225014/8. Has newly
opened wing with better rooms. 200 rooms. Price: 900-1,800 baht.

Rose Sukhon Hotel ✪✪ 1/11 Klangmuang Rd. Tel: (043) 236941,
238576-9. A low-rise hotel decorated in Thai-style, situated near the museum.
Price: 550-1,500 baht.

Restaurants *(Raan ahaan)*

Jerat Restaurant, Klangmuang Rd, opposite the municipal market.
Isaan dishes a speciality.

Gai Yang Thiparot, next to the Roma Hotel. Isaan dishes also a
speciality.

Raja Somtham, Klangmuang Rd, in front of the Raja Theater.

Food stalls

At the municipal market, off Klangmuang Rd.

Car rental *(Chao rod)*

Car Rent Center, 98/14 Phousajiga Rd, behind Farry Plaza.
Tel: (043) 243545. Rate per day 1,200 baht with driver.
Air Booking Travel Center, Sri Chan Rd, Amphoe Muang.
Tel: (043) 236562. Rate per day 1,200 baht with driver.

LOPBURI

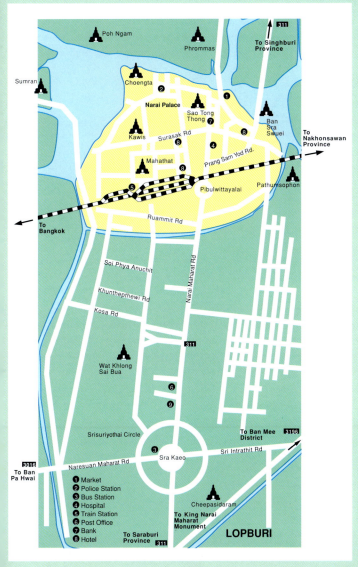

To Singhburi Province

Poh Ngam

Phrommas

Sumran

Choengta

Narai Palace

Sao Tong Thong

Ban Sra Swuei

To Nakhonsawan Province

Kawis

Surasak Rd

Mahathat

Prang Sam Yod Rd.

Pibulwittayalai

Pathumsophon

To Bangkok

Ruammit Rd

Soi Phya Anuchit

Naral Maharat Rd

Khunthepthewi Rd

Kosa Rd

Wat Khlong Sai Bua

To Ban Mee District

Srisuriyothai Circle

To Ban Pa Hwai

Naresuan Maharat Rd

Sra Kaeo

Sri Intrathit Rd

❶ Market
❷ Police Station
❸ Bus Station
❹ Hospital
❺ Train Station
❻ Post Office
❼ Bank
❽ Hotel

Cheepasidaram

To King Narai Maharat Monument

To Saraburi Province

LOPBURI

261

Bangkok 153 km – Ayutthaya 98 km – Phitsanulok 259 km – Khorat 198 km.
Lopburi was an extremely important town during the Ayutthaya period. In
particular in the reign of King Narai it was regarded as the second capital.
Three hundred years later during the Second World War, the Prime Minister,
Pibul Songkram planned to move the administration there. Today, apart from
its historic sites, it retains little old-world charm. It is also famous for its annual
'monkey party'.

By car *From Bangkok:* Take the expressway north past Don Muang airport.
Stay on Route 1 through Saraburi to Lopburi (driving time about $2^1/_4$-$2^1/_2$ hrs).
From Kanchanaburi: Lopburi can also be incorporated in a trip to Muang
Singh near Kanchanaburi (see page 238). Take Route 324 to Suphanburi,
then take Route 3195 to Ang Thong. *From Ang Thong:* Take Route 3267 to
Phra Phutthabat district and take Route 1 to Lopburi. *From Khorat:* An
alternative itinerary is to drive to Lopburi as a side-trip from a tour of the
Northeast. Returning from Khorat on Route 2 (see page 264), turn right at
Saraburi onto Route 1 north; Lopburi is 45 km further on (about 45 mins).

By bus *From Bangkok:* Regular departures from Bangkok's Mor Chit 2
Terminal, about every 20 mins from 05.20-20.30 (3hrs). *From Kanchanaburi:*
Including Lopburi in a trip to Muang Singh is possible by bus, but
considerably more inconvenient than by car. Travel first to Suphanburi (2 hrs);
there change buses for Singhburi ($2^1/_2$ hrs) at the junction of Malimaen Rd
and the road signposted to Sri Prachan. There are frequent buses from
Singhburi bus station to Lopburi (30 mins). *From Phitsanulok:* Non a/c buses
run from Phitsanulok to Khorat which pass Lopburi. Depart Phitsanulok 05.45,
07.30, 08.30, 11.00. *From Khorat:* To include Lopburi as a side-trip from a
Northeastern tour, take the direct bus service from Khorat (4 hrs).

By train *From Bangkok:* Lopburi lies on the Northern Line, and the railway
station is conveniently located for Wat Mahathat. Against this advantage,
most of the departures from Bangkok's Hualamphong station are ordinary
trains, nearly all of which having only unreservable 3rd class seats.
Departures are approximately every hour between 04.30 and 20.00, and
the journey takes $2^1/_2$-3 hrs. There are four rapid trains (early morning, mid-
afternoon, early and late evening), and one express train at 18.00 (the only
train with 1st class seats). By taking a morning train from Bangkok (or
Ayutthaya), Wat Mahathat and the other Lopburi sites can be visited as a
stop-over before continuing to Phitsanulok (for Sukhothai and Si Satchanalai)
or Chiangmai. *From Phitsanulok:* Every Northern Line train passes Phitsanulok
to Lopburi and an ordinary train leave from Phitsanulok to Lopburi at 16.00,
from Lopburi to Phitsanulok 18.00. *From Khorat:* The train from Khorat and the
Northeast stops at Saraburi, from where regular buses can be taken to
Lopburi (see Khorat, page 264).

Tourist information *(Gan thongthio)*

HM The Queen's Celebration Building c/o Lopburi Provincial Hall, Narai
Maharat Rd, Amphoe Muang.
Tel: (036) 422768, fax: (036) 422769.

Police station *(Sathaanee tamruad)*

Lopburi Police Station, Narai Maharat Rd, near King Narai the Great Monument. Tel: (036) 4411013. Ta Hin Police Station, Phra Ram Rd, behind Narai Palace. Tel: (036) 411015.

Local administrative offices *(Tessabaan)*

Narai Maharat Rd, near Lopburi School. Tel: (036) 411037.

Hospitals *(Rong phayabaan)*

Lopburi Provincial Hospital, Pahonyothin Rd, near King Narai the Great Monument. Tel: (036) 411250, 411267/8.

Benjarom Hospital, (Private), 116 Mu 8 Lopburi-Banprak Rd, Amphoe Muang. Tel: (036) 413622, 413602.

Post and telegraph office *(Praisanee)*

1 Narai Maharat Rd, near Lopburi Local Administrative Office. Tel: (036) 411011 • 2 Tahin Post and Telegraph at Prang Sam Yod Rd. Tel: (036) 411804.

Railway station *(Sathaanee rodfai)*

Na Phra Kan Rd, near Wat Phra Sri Rattana Mahathat. Tel: (036) 411022

Bus stations (Baw Kaw Saw)

Narai Maharat Rd, near Sra Kaeo roundabout. Tel: (036) 411888.

Banks with currency exchange *(Thanaakaan laek ngoen)*

Bangkok Bank, Lopburi Branch, 70/74 Surasongkram Rd. Tel: (036) 411023, 411084 • *Bangkok Bank,* Sra Kaeo roundabout Branch, 226/29-31 Narai Maharat Rd. Tel: (036) 412561 • *Thai Farmers Bank,* 100 Surasongkram Rd. Tel: (036) 411615, 411419 • *Thai Farmers Bank,* Sra Kaeo Circle, 424/426 Narai Maharat Rd. Tel: (036) 412207, 413911 • *Siam Commercial Bank,* 223/231 Surasongkram Rd. Tel: (036) 412880, 412706.

Museums (Phiphithapan)

Somdet Phra Narai National Museum in Narai Ratchaniwet Palace on Ratchadamnoen Rd not far from Lopburi Station. Tel: (036) 411458. Mon-Sun 9.00-16.00. Small admission fee.

Accommodation *(Rong raem)*

Lopburi has a reasonable selection of hotels, of which the best and most expensive is the Lopburi Inn. The cheaper accommodation is near the temples.

Lopburi Inn ✪✪✪ 28/9 Narai Maharat Rd, Lopburi 15000. Tel: (036) 412300, 412609, 412802, 412457, fax: 411917. 136 rooms incl. suites, all a/c. 500-1,600 baht. Lopburi's principal hotel. Located on the main road from Bangkok, 4 km before the centre of the old town, and so convenient only with a private vehicle. Most tour groups stay here.

Asia Lopburi Hotel ✪✪ 1/ 7-8 Surasak Rd. Tel: (036) 411892, 411555, fax: (036) 411892. 111 rooms. Fan 140 baht, a/c 400 baht.

Muang Thong Hotel ✪ 1/5-7 Prang Sam Yod Rd. Tel: (036) 411036. 27 rooms. Price: single with fan 120 baht, double with fan 150 baht.

Nett Hotel ✪ 17/1-2 Soi 2, Ratchadamnoen Rd. Tel: (03 6) 411738. 29 rooms. Price: fan 150 baht, a/c 300-450 baht.

Sri Indra Hotel ✪ 3-5 Na Phra Kan Rd. Tel: (036) 411261, 413258.
26 rooms. Price: fan 120-180, a/c 300.

Restaurants *(Raan ahaan)*

Bua Luang, 229/129-32 Narai Maharat Rd. Tel: (036) 413009.
Garden restaurant, considered one of the best in town. 2 km south of Lopburi
Inn.

Maha Sarakham, 226/8-10 Narai Maharat Rd. Tel: (036) 411014.

Anodat, 226/21 Narai Maharat Rd.

Food stalls

Behind Lopburi Station, Sra Kaew Circle.

NAKHON RATCHASIMA (KHORAT)

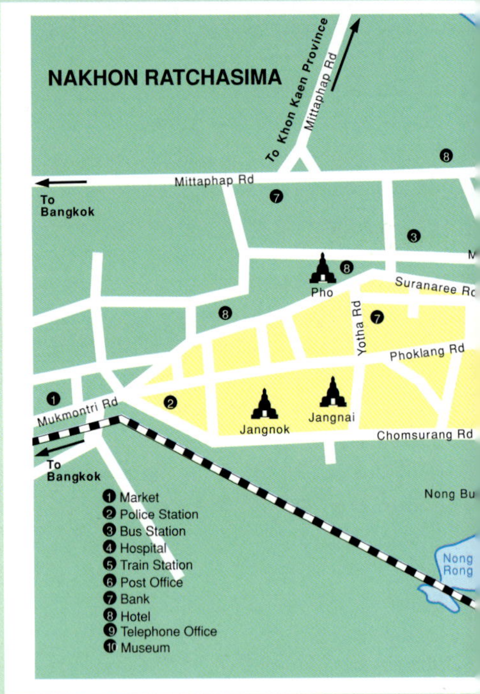

Bangkok 256 km – Buriram
151 km – Surin 198 km –
Khon Kaen 190 km – Phnom
Wan 20 km – Phimai 61 km –
Muang Khaek and Non Ku 38
km – Phnom Rung 126 km –
Phitsanulok 464 km – Lopburi
198 km. Popularly known as
Khorat (by losing the first
syllable and the last three), this
provincial capital is the
gateway to the Northeast – the
first major centre that you
reach on the road or railway
up to the plateau. It is also a
bustling and very fast-growing
commercial centre, which can
make accommodation often
hard to find, and it is by no
means picturesque.
Nevertheless, Isaan's
infrastructure funnels through
the city, and for transport,
communications and

NAKHON RATCHASIMA

To Khon Kaen Province
Mittaphap Rd
Mittaphap Rd
To Bangkok
Pho
Suranaree Rc
Yotha Rd
Phoklang Rd
Mukmontri Rd
Jangnok
Jangnai
Chomsurang Rd
To Bangkok
Nong Bu
Nong Rong

❶ Market
❷ Police Station
❸ Bus Station
❹ Hospital
❺ Train Station
❻ Post Office
❼ Bank
❽ Hotel
❾ Telephone Office
❿ Museum

information (the TAT office is well-staffed and efficient), Khorat is a good base
from which to start.

By car *From Bangkok:* Take Route 1 north to Saraburi, and turn east onto Route
2, which leads directly to Khorat. 3¹/₂-4¹/₂ hrs depending on traffic in

Bangkok. Alternatively, a slower journey is on Route 304 via Minburi, Chachoengsao, Phanom Sarakham, Kabin Buri and Pak Thong Chai. 273 km – about 5 hrs. *From Buriram:* Take Route 218 south-west until Route 24 near Nang Rong. Turn right here and continue to Chok Chai; turn right onto Route 224 into Khorat. 151 km. *From Surin:* Drive south on Route 214 until the junction with Route 24. Turn right and continue as above. 198 km.

By bus *From Bangkok:* A/c buses daily (every 20 mins. from 4.00-22.30) and 50 non-a/c from the Mor Chit 2 Bus Terminal, Kamphaengphet Rd. Tel: (02) 9361880, 9360657 non-a/c, a/c, (4-4^1/$_2$ hrs). *From Buriram and Surin:* Regular bus services. About 2 and 2^1/$_2$ hrs respectively. *From Khon Kaen:* Regular bus services. 3 hrs.

By train *From Bangkok:* (Hualamphong Station) two diesel sprinters daily (4 hrs), one express train daily in the evening (5 hrs), three rapid trains daily (5 hrs), three ordinary trains daily (6 hrs). *To Bangkok:* same services. Tel: (02) 223 7012, 223 7020.

By plane *To and from Bangkok:* One Thai Airways International flight daily, 40 mins. Tel: (02) 535 2081/2, 280 0070-80, 234 3100-19.

Tourist information *(Gan thongthio)*

TAT, 2102-2104 Mittaphap Rd. Tel: (044) 213666, fax: (044) 213667. Open daily 0830-1630. The Khorat TAT office, located next to the Sima Thani Hotel, is responsible for approximately the four provinces of Nakhon

Ratchasima, Buriram, Surin and Chaiyaphum provinces. This includes Phimai, Phnom Wan, Phnom Rung, Muang Tam, Muang Khaek, Non Ku, Muang Gao, Prang Ku.

Police station *(Sathaanee tamruad)*
Supphasit Rd, near intersection with Chainarong Rd. Tel: (044) 242010. Dial 191 for emergency.

Local administrative offices *(Tessabaan)*
Mahadthai Rd. Tel: (044) 243798.

Hospitals *(Rong phayabaan)*
Maharat Provincial Hospital, Chang Phuak Rd. Tel: (044) 254990.
Montri Hospital (private), Mukmontri Rd. Tel: (044) 251707.

Post and telegraph office *(Praisanee)*
Chomsurangyat Rd. Tel: (044) 245380. Mon-Fri 08.30-16.30, Sat 9.00-12.00.

Airline offices *(Gan binthai)*
Thai Airways International, 14 Manat Rd. Tel: (044) 257211, Airport (Sanaambin). Located in the air force base, so permit required to enter. In practice, this means taking the Thai Airways limousine. For information, call Thai Airways office.

Railway stations *(Sathaanee rodfai)*
Nakhon Ratchasima Station, Mukmontri Rd. Tel: (044) 242044.
Jira Junction, Rajapikul Rd. Tel: (044) 242363.

Bus stations (Baw Kaw Saw)
Old bus station (Terminal 1) *(Baw Kaw Saw Gao)* Burin lane, off Mittaphap Rd, one block east of turn-off to Khon Kaen. A/c buses (tel: 245443) and non-a/c buses (tel: 242899) to Bangkok, Phitsanulok, Chiangmai and to other parts of Nakhon Ratchasima province (such as Phimai). Also to Surin for Phnom Rung. New bus station (Terminal 2) *(Baw Kaw Saw Mai)* Mittaphap Rd. 1 km north of turn-off to Khon Kaen. Buses to other Northeastern provinces, and buses passing Khorat for Bangkok (tel: 256007/9).

Banks with currency exchange *(Thanaakaan laek ngoen)*
All the major banks are well represented here with several branches.

Museums *(Phiphithapan)*
Mahawirawong Museum, Ratchadamnoen Rd in Wat Sujinda.
Tel: (044) 242958.

Accommodation *(Rong raem)*
Rajapruk Grand Hotel ✪✪✪✪ 31 Mitraphab Rd. Tel: (044) 261277 Fax:(044) 261278. 159 rooms, all a/c, Price: 1,200-1,500 baht.
Sima Thani Hotel ✪✪✪✪ Mittaphap Rd. Tel: (044) 213100. Fax: (044) 251109. Bangkok office: (02) 234 5599, fax: 236-8320. 267 rooms, all a/c, incl. 14 suites. Khorat's first hotel to international deluxe standards, with atrium and a full range of facilities, including three restaurants (Chinese, Thai) and Pub, coffee shop, swimming pool with bar, health club with sauna and gym. It is located on the main highway from Bangkok, just before town, a few minutes by car or tuk-tuk. Price: 1,600 baht, suites 2,200 baht.
Royal Princess Hotel ✪✪✪✪ 1137 Suranaree Rd. Tel: (044)

256629/35, fax: (044) 256601. 186 rooms. Part of Dusit Group, this modern hotel was opened recently. Facilities include swimming pool, three restaurants (chinese, Thai and coffee shop), a pub and discotheque. It is slightly outside town on the road to Surin. Price: 2,120 bath, suites 5,800-10,593 baht.

Chomsurang Hotel ✪✪ 2701/2 Mahadthai Rd. Tel: (044) 257088/9. 170 rooms, all a/c. Khorat's previous top hotel, now rather faded and in need of renovation. Facilities include restaurant and swimming pool. Price: 950-1070 baht.

Khorat Hotel ✪✪ 191 Asdang Rd. Tel: (044) 242444. 115 rooms.

Sri Pattana Hotel ✪✪ 346 Suranaree Rd. Tel: (044) 246323. 182 rooms. Facilities include coffee shop and swimming pool. Price: 500-1,200 baht.

King's Hotel ✪✪ 1756 Mittaphap Rd. Tel: (044) 253360, 241362. 62 rooms. Inexpensive and good value for its level, although some way out of town (near the Sheraton on the main road from Bangkok). Price: 450-500 a/c, fan: 270-400 baht.

R.C.N. Plaza Hotel 62 Mukmontri Rd., 90 rooms , all a/c., Price: 800-2,500 baht.

Khorat Doctor's Guest House, 78 Suebsiri Rd. Tel: (044) 255846. Six rooms. Extremely good value, and popular. Price: 100-150 baht.

Restaurants *(Raan ahaan)*

Samran Lap, 153-155 Wacharasarid Rd. Tel: (044) 241472. Although probably unfair to single this out among so many good Isaan restaurants, in our experience it is consistently excellent. Unpretentious and busy. Specialities include *suk soda, plaa chonnabot.*

Suan Sin, 163 Wacharasarid Rd. Tel: (044) 243636. Similar to the above.

Suan Phak, 154-156 Chumphon Rd. Tel: (044) 255877/8. Convenient location near the Thao Suranaree monument. Popular at lunch-times.

The Spider, 221-223 Chumphon Rd. Tel: (044) 257210.

Dot Pub, 179 Mahadthai Rd. Tel: (044) 253300.

Thaweephan, Suebsiri Rd. Tel: (044) 257775.

Ban Kaew, 105/17-15 Chomsurangyat Rd. Tel: (044) 246512.

Food stalls

Night market on Manat Rd.

Car rental *(Chao rod)*

United Eastern Tour, Mittaphap Rd, next to TAT office. Tel: 258713/4.

Motorbike rental *(Chao motusai)*

Virjyarnyon, 554-556 Phoklang Rd. Tel: 245421.

Bangkok (by road) 763 km – Ubon Ratchathani 116 km

By plane *From Vientiane:* Daily flight in the morning (1¼ hrs). Travelling this way entails entry into Laos through Vientiane, and so would be better combined with visits to other, non-Khmer sites in the country. Lao tourism has been late developing, due to the political consequences of the Vietnam War and the 1975 Communist take-over, and the regulations controlling entry, exit and internal travel may change. At the time of writing, independent travel is largely discouraged, and the easiest, but most expensive way of visiting Pakxé and Wat Phu is through one of several travel agencies with offices in Vientiane. Bangkok is the most convenient city outside Laos in which to make these travel arrangements; the agency will organise visa, internal travel permit, transportation and accommodation, although at a relatively high mark-up (two or three times the actual cost of arrangements within Laos).

By car *From Ubon:* Potentially, Pakxé can be reached overland from Ubon by road and ferry, so that Wat Phu could be integrated into a trip taking in the temples in Northeastern Thailand. Should the overland route become possible for foreign visitors, take a taxi from Ubon (500-600 baht), or a private vehicle, to Chongmek by way of route 24 south across the Mun River to

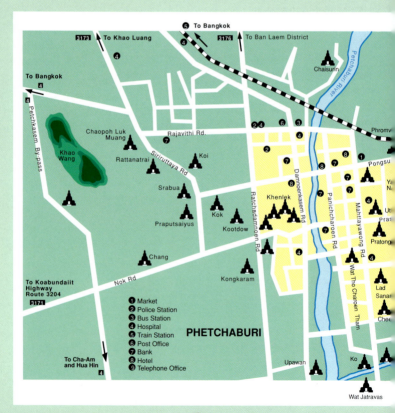

To Bangkok

3173 To Khao Luang

3176 To Ban Laem District

Chaisurin

Petchaburi River

To Bangkok

Petchkasem By-pass

Phromv

Chaopoh Luk Muang

Rajavithi Rd.

Khao Wang

Rattanatrai

Siriruttaya Rd

Koi

Pongsu

Srabua

Khenlek

Damnoenkasem Rd

Panichcharoen Rd

Y

Ut Pras

Kok

Kootdow

Praputsaiyus

Ratchadamnoen Rd

Pratong

Chang

Nok Rd

Kongkaram

Mahtiayawong Rd

Wat Tho Charoen Tham

Lad Sanar

Chee

To Koabundaiit Highway Route 3204

3171

❶ Market
❷ Police Station
❸ Bus Station
❹ Hospital
❺ Train Station
❻ Post Office
❼ Bank
❽ Hotel
❾ Telephone Office

PHETCHABURI

To Cha-Am and Hua Hin

Upawan

Ko

Wat Jatravas

Warin Chamrap, turning left onto route 217 (76 km). At the Chongmek border crossing (about 1 hr from Ubon), the formalities are casual. The Thai immigration does not close, but the Lao immigration hours are 07.00-11.30 and 13.30-16.30 (the hours closed can be interrupted for 50 baht). The road continues east for 40 km (1 hr) to the small town of Muang Kao, on the west bank of the Mekong River directly opposite Pakxé. 24 km from Chongmek is the village of Ban Phonthong, 2 km beyond which is a bridge, and 1 km after this on the right an unmarked dirt road. It is possible, although not recommended, to reach Wat Phu by this route; the road is in bad condition and the journey of about 60 km would need a 4WD vehicle. At Muang Kao, a car ferry crosses the Mekong in 15 mins. to land at Pakxé (car with passengers 2950 *kip* one-way; foot passengers 50 *kip*). Its hours are 08.00-about 11.30 and 14.00-17.00/18.00. Small river boats carry passengers for 100 *kip*.

Accommodation *(Rong raem)*

Pakxé Hotel, ✪✪✪✪   In front of Pakxé morning market. Tel: (007) 856 31 212131, 212045. Price: US$ 10-13.

Auberge du Champa ✪ Pakxé's most comfortable hotel, converted from a large colonial house in the centre of town (all the accommodation and eating places are within a few minutes walk of each other). Spacious rooms, some with balconies. Price: US$20 single, $30 double.

Champasak Palace Hotel ✪✪✪ Ban Phra Bat. Tel: (007) 856 31 212263, 212779-80. Fax: (007) 856 31 212781. Price: US$ 40-140.

Food

The most popular restaurant in Pakxé is on the ground floor of the Souksamlane. Busy, friendly; Lao food and some Western dishes.

To Banlaem District
3178
Pokarong Rd
Kamphengleng
an Rd
Petchplee
hburi Rd
Rd

PHETCHABURI

Bangkok 123 km – Ratchaburi 54 km – Cha-Am 25 km. Phetchaburi is a pleasant town, as Thai towns go, having many old temples, several of which are in the surrounding limestone hills. Most famous is the Khao Wang complex built by King Rama IV. Some old wooden houses in 'gingerbread style' may still be seen in the town centre. The town is also famous for its egg custard (*kanom moh gaeng*) and other sweets.

By car *From Bangkok*: Either take Route 4 to Phetchaburi (166km), or from Bangkok take Route 35 (Thonburi- Paktoh) to Paktoh and change to Route 4 (121km) 2hrs.

By bus *From Bangkok:* Frequent a/c and non-a/c buses from the Southern Bus Terminal, Borómraja Chonnanee Rd. Tel: (02) 435 1199 a/c, 434 5557/8 non a/c (2 hrs).

By train *From Bangkok:* (Hualamphong Station) three express trains daily, four rapid trains daily, four ordinary trains daily. Tel: (02) 223 7010, 223 7020. Bangkok Noi Station, Thonburi, tel: (02) 411 3102.

Tourist information *(Gan thongthio)*

Cha-Am Office 500/51, Phetkasem Rd, Amphoe Cha-Am. Tel: (032) 471005, 471006, fax: (032) 471502. Daily 08.30-16.30.

Police station *(Sathaanee tamruad)*

Rajavithi Rd near the Vocational College. Tel: (032) 425500.

Local administrative offices *(Tessabaan)*

Rajavithi Rd near Police Station. Tel: (032) 427046, 424159.

Hospitals *(Rong phayabaan)*

Phra Chom Klao Hospital (Provincial Hospital), Rod Fai Rd, near the railway station. Tel: 032) 428082.

Noi Kao Chalern Hospital (Private), 60/30-5 Sesaintr Rd. Tel: (032) 425592.

Vetjabandit Hospital (Private), 125 Matayawong Rd. Tel: (032) 426108.

Post and telegraph office *(Praisanee)*

Rajavithi Rd. Near Local administrative office. Tel: (032) 425146, 425571.

Railway station *(Sathaanee rodfai)*

Rod Fai Rd, near Phra Chom Klao Hospital. Tel: (032) 425211.

Bus stations *(Baw Kaw Saw)*

Sesaintr Rd, near Aroonpradit School.

Banks with currency exchange *(Thanaakaan laek ngoen)*

Bangkok Bank, 122 Panitchaoen Rd. Tel: (032) 425024, 427047-8

Thai Farmers Bank, 18/15 Surinroechai Rd. Tel: (032) 426245

Siam Commercial Bank, 2 Damnoenkasem Rd. Tel: (032) 426575, 424188.

Museums *(Phiphithapan)*

Phra Nakhon Kiri National Museum, Khaowang Rd. Tel: (032) 425600. Daily 09.00-16.00.

Accommodation *(Rong raem)*

Phetchaburi is near the popular seaside resorts of Cha-Am and Hua Hin, both with international standard hotels and at the other end of the scale, small bungalows. Cha-Am is about 25 km and Hua Hin 35 km.

In town:

Petchakasem ✪ 86/1 Phetchakasem Rd. Tel and fax: (032) 425581. 50 rooms. Price: fan 220 baht, a/c 450 baht.

Khao Wang ✪ 174/1-3 Rajavithi Rd. Tel: (032) 436167, fax: (032) 410750. 50 rooms. Price: fan 300 baht, a/c 550 baht.

Out of town:

Dusit Resort and Polo Club ✪✪✪✪ Phetkasem Rd. Between Cha-Am and Hua Hin. Tel: (032) 520009, fax: (032) 520296. Bangkok office tel: (02) 236 0450-9. Large, luxurious hotel popular with Bangkok high society. Includes Italian, Thai and French restaurants, night club, swimming pool, tennis, sailing, etc. 316 rooms. Price: 4,000-20,000 baht.

Regent Cha-Am ✪✪✪✪ Phetkasem Rd, Cha-Am. Tel: (032) 471480-86, fax:(032) 471491-2. Bangkok Office tel:(02) 267 2669, fax: (02) 253 5143. Very large slightly older beach front hotel with two different wings and individual bungalows. Range of restaurants (Thai, Chinese, Coffee Shop), discotheque, swimming pools. Extensive gardens. Popular for conferences. 650 rooms. Price: 2,000-14,000 baht.

Cha-Am Phoem Suk, Ruam Chit Rd. Tel: (032) 471347. Bungalows. Price: 800 baht.

Cha-Am Villa, Ruam Chit Rd. Tel: (032) 471010 Bungalows Price: 200-800 baht.

Methavalai ✪✪✪ Ruam Chit Rd, Beach front hotel with swimming pool. Tel: (032) 471028-9, 471145-6. Price: 300, 1,000-1,500 baht.

Hua Hin

Hua Hin is about to be ruined by tasteless high rise hotels such as the Melia just as Cha-Am has been. However the Sofitel retains much of its charm having been very sympathetically extended.

Sofitel Central Hotel ✪✪✪✪ Tel: (032) 512021-38, Bangkok office: (02) 541 1234, fax: 541 1464. An elegant, colonial style, low-rise hotel (formerly the old Railway Hotel) on Hua Hin beach with tasteful rooms and two-room bungalows. Various restaurants, two pools, tennis courts. Easy access to bustling market and golf course. 195 rooms. Price: 4,943-9298.

Royal Garden Village ✪✪✪ Tel: (032) 520250-5, fax: (032) 520260, Bangkok office: (02) 476 0021-2. Attractive hotel some 5 km before Hua Hin Town with rooms in Thai-style buildings set in beautiful gardens running down to the beach. 162 rooms. Two restaurants, swimming pool, tennis courts. Price: 2,900 baht, suites 7,000 baht.

Hua Hin Palace Hotel Pleasant small hotel within 200 yards of beach on the way to Kao Tao 30 mins. Price: 300-500 baht.

Restaurants (Raan ahaan)

Both Cha-Am and Hua Hin have excellent seafood restaurants. In particular the seafood market at Hua Hin has several good restaurants. Thais also love to eat from stalls in the night market at Hua Hin.

Ban Kanom Thai, 130 Phetchaburi Rd. Located on Bangkok road some 10 mins before Phetchaburi Town. Tel: (032) 428526-7.

Phetch Pinkaeo, 80 Phetchaburi Rd. Tel: (032) 425110.

Num Taien, Arnamai Rd opposite Krung Thai Bank. Tel: (032) 425121

Food stalls

On Surinroechai Rd. Near Phetchaburi Theater.

Car rental (Chao rod)

Avis (office in Dusit Resort and Polo Club at Cha-Am). Tel: (032) 520008-9 Price: 1,200- 3,000 baht/day.

Bicycle rental (Chao jakayan)

Cha-Am Beach.

PHIMAI

Bangkok 317 km – Khorat 61 km – Khon Kaen 130 km – Chaiyaphum 85 km – Buriram 150 km – Surin 234 km. Situated at the confluence of the Mun and Khem rivers, Phimai is a small fairly quite town whose main importance is its outstanding Khmer temple. A wider range of accommodation may be had at Khorat, approximately 45 mins drive away.

By car See the entry for Phimai temple, page 70.

By bus See the entry for Phimai temple, page 70.

Tourist information *(Gan thongthio)* See TAT Khorat.

Police station *(Sathaanee tamruad)*

On the west of the town, across the Lam Chakarat River; next to the Amphoe. Tel: (044) 471018, or 191 in an emergency.

Local administrative offices *(Amphoe)*

On the west of the town, across the Lam Chakarat River; next to the police station. Tel: (044) 471617.

Hospital *(Rong phayabaan)*

Phimai Hospital Just north of the river on Route 206. Tel: (044) 471288.

Post office *(Praisanee)*

Immediately to the west of the temple. Tel: (044) 471342.

Bus station *(Baw Kaw Saw)*

For Khorat buses: around the corner from the Phimai Hotel, close to the Pratu Chai (Victory Gate).

Banks with currency exchange *(Thanaakaan laek ngoen)*

All the major banks are represented here with several branches.

Museums *(Phiphithapan)*

Phimai National Museum Tha Songkarn Rd. Nai Muang Sub-district, Phimai District. Tel: (044) 471167. Open Wed-Sun. Small admission fee.

Accommodation *(Rong raem)*

Phimai Hotel ✪ Chomsudasadet Rd. Tel: (044) 471306, fax: (044) 471940. Modest accommodation, around the corner from the bus station, close to the Victory Gate. 40 rooms. Price: with fan 180, a/c 350 baht.

Old Phimai Guest House Chomsudasadet Rd. Tel: (044) 471918. Simpler than the Phimai Hotel, with small rooms and dormitory beds in a large teak house. Close to the temple entrance. 10 rooms. Price: with fan 120, a/c 300 baht.

Restaurants *(Raan ahaan)*

Bai Toey Restaurant Chomsudasadet Rd. Tel: (044) 471725.

Rim Mun Restaurant North-west of town on the 206 by-pass, by the bridge over the Mun River. Tel: (044) 471692, 471232.

Sai Ngam Restaurant Close to the park containing a giant banyan tree known as Sai Ngam and a few minutes' drive north of town on Route 206, past the museum but before the hospital. Tel: (044) 471983.

Pai Reua Restaurant Garden restaurant next to the city's west gate *(Pratu Hin)*. Tel: (044) 471210.

Food stalls

Day-time market: Two blocks east of Chomsudasadet Rd. Night market: one block east of the south-east corner of the temple.

Bicycle rental *(Chao kakayan)*

At Old Phimai Guest House, 214 Mu 1 Chomsudasadet Rd.
Tel: (044) 471918, 25 baht per day.

PHITSANULOK

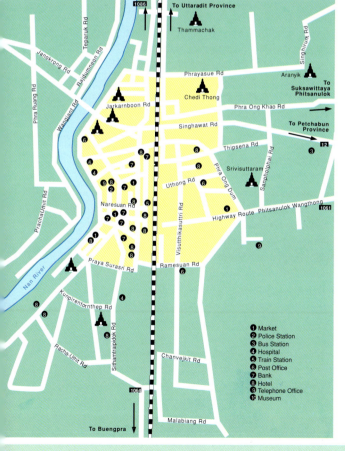

Bangkok 377 km – Sukhothai Historical Park 72 km – Si Satchanalai 115 km – Khon Kaen 307 km – Khorat 464 km. Capital of its province, Phitsanulok (population 75,000) has the widest choice of facilities within reasonable driving distance of Sukhothai and Si Satchanalai, and is a pleasant stop for one or two nights. It also has a Khmer temple of moderate interest, Wat Chulamani. The town's other principal attractions are Wat Phra Si Ratana Mahathat (locally called Wat Yai, the 'Big Temple'), containing the nationally famous Chinnaraj Buddha (Phra Phut Chinnaraj) and having a fine Ayutthaya-style *prang;* the Nan River with its houseboats, the only legally-permitted ones in the country; and a privately owned folk museum with the country's largest collection of traditional rural artefacts and utensils.

Phitsanulok has something of a reputation for good eating, and is known for the bizarrely-prepared dish *phak bung loi faa*, literally 'swamp cabbage thrown in the air'. At a number of inexpensive road-side restaurants and food-stalls, the stir-frying of this green aquatic vegetable has been elevated to a performance, in which the cook throws the cooked *phak bung* (less the plate) across the street where a waiter attempts to catch it. Local competition has inspired increasing acrobatics: waiters may sometimes be seen perched on window ledges of buildings opposite demonstrating their catching ability.

By car *From Bangkok:* Take the expressway past Don Muang airport and continue along Route 1 until the turning for Ayutthaya and Nakhon Sawan on Route 32. Continue north on Route 32 to Nakhon Sawan (240 km from Bangkok), and then Route 117 for the remaining 104 km to Phitsanulok. *From Khon Kaen:* Take Route 12 west directly to Phitsanulok (307 km). *From Khorat:* Either take Route 2 north to Khon Kaen and continue as above, or take Route 2 north for 77 km, turning left onto Route 202 for the next 61 km to Chaiyaphum, followed by Route 201 to Chum Phae (102 km) where it joins Route 12 west to Phitsanulok. *From Lopburi:* 259 km.

By bus *From Bangkok:* Frequent buses from the Mor Chit 2 Bus Terminal, Kamphaeng Phet Rd. Tel: (02) 9363659 non a/c, a/c (5 hrs), 11 a/c buses, 5 non a/c buses. Private companies also operate from the same terminal – Phitsanulok Yanyon Tour, Thawon Farm Tour (tel: (02) 271 3010, 278 3875). *To Bangkok:* same services. Frequent buses also run from the following destinations: *Sukhothai:* (1 hr), *Kamphaeng Phet:* (3 hrs), *Uttaradit:* (2 hrs), *Nakhon Sawan:* (2 hrs), *Chiangmai:* (5^1/$_2$ hrs), *Khon Kaen:* (5 hrs), *Khorat:* (6 hrs), *Lopburi:* (3^1/$_2$ hrs).

By train *From Bangkok* (Hualamphong Station): Three diesel sprinters daily (5^3/$_4$ hrs), one express train daily (the Chiangmai train) at 18.00 (6 hrs), four rapid trains daily (6 hrs), four ordinary trains daily (9 hrs). *To Bangkok:* same services (express train from Chiangmai leaves at 01.00). *To Chiangmai:* one express train daily at midnight (7 hrs), three rapid trains daily (7 hrs), one ordinary train daily (9 hrs). Tel: (02) 223 7010, 223 7020.

By plane *To and from Bangkok:* Two Thai Airways International flights daily, morning and afternoon; additional morning flight Tue-Thur-Sat (45 min.). *To and from Chiangmai:* Daily flights, 2 hrs. *To and from Lampang:* four flights weekly, 35 mins. *To and from Mae Sot:* four flights weekly, 50 mins. *To and from Nan:*

three flights weekly, 55 mins. *To and from Tak:* four flights weekly, 35 mins.

Tourist information *(Gan thongthio)*

TAT, 209/7-8 Surasi Trade Centre, Boromtrailoknat Rd. Tel: (055) 252742-3. Open daily 08.30-16.30. Youth Hostel *(Baan Yaowachon)*, 38 Sanaambin Rd. Tel: (055) 242060.

Police station *(Sathaanee tamruad)*

Boromtrailoknat Rd, near Naresuan Rd. Tel: (055) 240199, 258777.

Hospitals *(Rong phayabaan)*

Provincial Hospital, (Phutha Chinnaraj), Sithamtraipidok Rd.
Tel: (055) 258812-9.

Phitsanuvej Hospital, Khun Phiren Rd. Tel: (055) 252762-3, 258318, Private.

Ruam Phaet Hospital, 212/79 Boromtrailoknat Rd. Tel: (055) 242574.
Private.

Post and telegraph office *(Praisanee)*

Communications Authority of Thailand, Phutta Bucha Rd. Tel: (055) 258013.

Airline offices *(Gan binthai)*

Thai Airways International, 209/26-28 Boromtrailoknat Rd. Tel: (055) 258020,251671, Open Mon-Fri in town. Sat-Sun at the Airport 08.00-17.00.

Airport *(Sanaambin)*

Phitsanulok Domestic Airport, Sanaambin Rd. Tel: (055) 258029.

Railway station *(Sathaanee rodfai)*

Phitsanulok Railway Station, Ekathotsarod Rd. Tel: (055) 258005.

Bus station *(Baw Kaw Saw)*

Phitsanulok Bus Station, Phitsanulok-Lom Sak Rd. Tel: (055) 242430.

Banks with currency exchange *(Thanaakaan laek ngoen)*

Bangkok Bank, 35 Naresuan Rd. Tel:(055) 238370, 259448-9.

Krung Thai Bank, 31/1 Naresuan Rd. Tel: (055) 242112, 258748.

Thai Farmers Bank, 144/1 Boromtrailoknat Rd. Tel: (055) 258599, 258744.

Bangkok Metropolitan Bank, 147-53 Boromtrailoknat Rd.
Tel: (055) 242982-4.

Siam Commercial Bank, 1/14 Sithamtraipidok Rd. tel: (055) 259635, 259311.

Accommodation *(Rong raem)*

Pailyn Hotel ✪✪✪ Boromtrailoknat Rd. Tel: (055) 252411-5, fax:(055) 258185. Bangkok office tel: (02) 215 7110. 240 rooms, all a/c. Comfortable large hotel, central, close to the river. Facilities: restaurant, beauty salon, traditional massage, car rental. Price: 1,413-1,060 baht. Suites: 4,120 baht.

Rajapruk ✪✪✪ 99/9 Phra Ong Dam Rd. Tel: (055) 258788-9, fax: (055) 251395. Bangkok office tel: (02) 215 4612. 123 rooms, all a/c. Large hotel east of the town centre, close to the bus terminal. Facilities include restaurant, swimming pool, coffee shop. Price: 600 baht standard single. Suites 1,500 baht.

Thep Nakorn ✪✪ 43/1 Sithamtraipidok Rd. Tel: (055) 251817, fax: 251897. Bangkok office tel: (02) 233 0196-7. Price: 700-2,500 baht.

Amarin Nakorn ✪✪ 3/1 Chao Phrya Rd. Tel: (055) 258588, 258945, fax: (055) 258945. Bangkok office tel: (02) 2357 399. 132 rooms, all a/c. Facilities include 24- hr coffee shop and beauty parlour. Very central location, near to the railway station. Price: 640-1,800 baht.

Topland Hotel and Convention Centre ✪✪✪ 68/33 Ekathotsarod Rd. Tel:(055) 247800-14. 260 rooms, all a/c. Price 1,500-3,000 baht.

Amarin Lagoon Hotel ✪✪✪ 52/299 Pra Ong Khao Rd. Tel.(055) 214149-56. 305 rooms, all a/c. Price 1,500-3,000 baht.

Nan Chao Hotel ✪✪ 242 Boromtrailoknat Rd. Tel: (055) 259511-3, fax: (055) 259 632. Bangkok office tel: (02) 2781749. 134 rooms. Price: 620-2,500 baht.

Wang Nam Yen ✪ km.46 Phitsanulok-Lomsak Rd. tel: (055) 252 753. Bangkok office tel: (02) 2510054. Price: 600-2200 baht.

Rajapruk Guest House ✪ Phra Ong Dam Rd. tel: (055) 258 477, 258 788. 40 rooms with fan. Price:140-260 baht.

Youth Hostel (Baan Yaowachon) 38 Sanaambin Rd. Tel: (055) 242060. Although a little way from the centre of town, on the way to the airport, this youth hostel converted from an old house in its own grounds is good value. Dormitory rate: 50 baht, double rooms: 130 baht (third person 40 baht). 10 baht discount for IYH card. Located on the No. 4 bus route between the railway station and airport, 100m south of the junction of Sanaambin Rd and Naresuan Rd.

No. 4 Guest House 11/12 Ekathotsarod Rd. No telephone. Four rooms with fan. Unpretentious restored teak house.

Restaurants (Raan ahaan)

Song Kwae, floating restaurant moored off Phutta Bucha Rd.

Rim Nan, floating restaurant moored off Phutta Bucha Rd.

Topland Coffeeshop, Topland Department Store, 5th floor. Tel: 252555. The store, one of the town's biggest, is located between Boromtrailoknat and Naresuan Roads.

Gweitiw Gai, Wat Jan Rd. Named after its speciality, chicken noodle soup, this very popular, inexpensive restaurant is open only for breakfast and lunch.

Gweitiw Hoi Kaa, Phutta Bucha Rd, north of Naresuan Bridge and Wat Mahathat. Noodles, only for breakfast and lunch. The name means the 'hanging legs noodle restaurant', because of the seating in this old wooden house – you sit on the edge of the upstairs floor with your legs hanging out.

Food stalls

Night market along Phutta Bucha Rd south of Naresuan Rd. Includes establishments throwing and serving *phak bung loi faa*.

Car rental (Chao rod)

Golden House Tour, 55/37-38 Sithamtraipidok Rd. Tel: (055) 259973, 251731. Minibus: 1,000 baht/day excl. fuel, incl. mileage.

Phitsanulok Tour Center, 55/45 Sithamtraipidok Rd. Tel: (055)

242206. Cars and Minibus. Available with driver.

Phitsanu Agency Travel, 230/19 Rachamanu Rd.Tel: (055) 251611.
Cars and Minibuses. Only available with driver. Price: 1,200 baht /day.

Pailyn Hotel (see above) Minibus available with driver. Price: 2,500 baht
per day's trip (e.g. to Sukhothai and Si Satchanalai) incl. fuel and mileage.

Motorbike rental (Chao motusai)

Landi Motor, 110/127 Phra Ong Dam Rd. Tel: (055) 242687. Opposite
Bangkok Bank. Price: 150 baht per 24 hrs, 12 hrs: 100 baht.

SAKON NAKHON

Bangkok 674 km – Ubon 286 km – Khon Kaen 205 km – Khorat 311 km.
This medium-sized town is situated near the Thai-Laos border and on the edge
of very beautiful Lake, Nong Han. The area is well-known for its forest
monasteries.

By car *From Bangkok:* Take Route 1 and turn on to Route 2 at Saraburi, turning
on Route 23 at Ban Phai to Maha Sarakarm, and turning on Route 213 to
Sakon Nakhon.

By bus *From Bangkok:* Four a/c buses daily and four non-a/c from the Mor
Chit 2 Bus Terminal, Kamphaengphet Rd. Tel: (02) 9361880, 9360657
non-a/c, a/c, (10 hrs).

By plane *To and from Bangkok:* Daily Thai Airways International flights, 1 hr.
To and from Khorat: three Thai Airways International flights weekly, 50 mins.

Tourist information (Gan thongthio)

None in Sakon Nakhorn. The nearest is the TAT office in Nakhon Phanom
c/o Provincial Administration Office, Abhibanbancha Rd, Ampoe Muang.
Tel: (042) 513490/1, fax: (042) 513492.

Police station (Sathaanee tamruad)

Chaiphasuk Rd near Wat Photri. Tel: (042) 711506.

Local administrative offices (Tessabaan)

Sun Ratchakan Rd. Tel: (042) 711203.

Hospitals (Rong phayabaan)

Provincial Hospital, Charoen Muang Rd. Tel: (042) 711615.
Nasai Tongsiri Hospital (Private), 492 Sakon Nakhon-Nakae Rd, Amphoe
Muang. Tel: (042) 711520, 712031.
Moo Somboon Hospital (Private), 1446/47 Robmuang Rd.
Tel: (042) 712800.

Post and telegraph office (Praisanaee)

Chaiphasuk Rd, near Police Station. Tel: (042) 711049.

Airline offices (Gan binthai)

1446/73 Yu Wattana Rd. Tel: (042) 712259/60. Mon-Fri 8.00-17.00.

Airport (Sanaambin)

Sukkasem Rd. Tel: (042) 713346

Bus stations *(Baw Kaw Saw)*
Ratpattana Rd, near the market. Tel: (042) 712860.
Banks with currency exchange *(Thanaakaan laek ngoen)*
Bangkok Bank 1324/20 Sukkasem Rd. Tel: (042) 711410, 711501.
Thai Farmers Bank 1714/2 Sukkasem Rd. Tel: (042) 711211, 711534.
Siam Commercial Bank 1353/4 Sukkasem Rd. Tel: (042) 711529, 712529.

Accommodation *(Rong raem)*
Imperial Hotel ✪✪ 1892 Sukkasem Rd. Tel: (042) 711119, 711887, 713320 fax: (042) 711889. 230 rooms a/c and fanned. Facilities include coffee shop, Prices: with fan 390 baht, single a/c 490 baht, deluxe 790 baht.
Dusit Hotel ✪✪ 178-4 Yuwa Wattana Rd. Tel: (042) 711198-9, 712200-1, fax: 713116. 102 a/c rooms Facilities include restaurant, swimming pool. Price: 300-650 baht, Suites 750 baht.
Araya Hotel ✪✪ 1432 Premprida Rd. Tel: (042) 711097. 59 rooms. Price: fanned rooms 150 baht, a/c rooms 300 baht.
Restaurants *(Raan ahaan)*
There is a cluster of acceptable restaurants on Premprida Rd.
Kwao Anothai 1709/16-17 Premprida Rd. Tel: (042) 711542.
Best House 1659/1 Premprida Rd. Tel: (042) 713166.
Koa Phai 384/4 Sukkasem Rd. Tel: (042) 712235.
Suan Luk 1865/15 Ratpattana Rd. Tel: (042) 711783.
Tim laab ped Highly authentic northeastern cooking at this small family restaurants that serves only duck and pork dishes.
Food stalls
Sukkasem Rd and Sri Kun Muang Market on Pasukchai Rd.

SISAKET

Bangkok 571 km – Khorat 272 km – Buriram 230 km – Surin 101 km – Ubon 60 km. Srisaket is a small town which is not on the main highway. Its major attraction is Preah Vihear. At time of publication a new hotel was being planned.

By car *From Bangkok:* Follow directions to Khorat, at Khorat turning on Route 226 to Sisaket.

By bus *From Bangkok:* Two a/c buses daily and two non-a/c from the Northern Bus Terminal, Kamphaengphet Rd. Tel: (02) 9361880, 9360657 non-a/c, a/c (8 hrs).

By train *From Bangkok:* (Hualamphong Station): one express train daily in the evening (9 hrs), three rapid trains daily (9-9½ hrs), three ordinary trains daily (11½ hrs). To Bangkok: same services.

From Khorat: One diesel sprinter daily in the morning (5 hrs), one express train daily after midnight (4 hrs), three rapid trains daily (4½ hrs), four ordinary trains daily (4½ hrs). *From Buriram and Surin:* Same trains as from Khorat (most 2½ hrs and 1½ hrs respectively). *From Ubon:* One express train daily (1 hr), three rapid trains daily (1 hr), four ordinary trains daily (1-1½ hrs).

Tourist information *(Gan thongthio)*
None in Sisaket. The nearest is the TAT office in Ubon Ratchathani at 264/1 Khuan Thani Rd, Amphoe Muang. Tel: (045) 243770-1, fax: 243771.

Police station *(Sathaanee tamruad)*
Thepha Rd. Tel: (045) 611199 or 191 in an emergency.

Local administrative offices *(Tessabaan)*
Na Salaklang Rd. Tel: (045) 611046.

Hospitals *(Rong phayabaan)*
Provincial Hospital, Kasikam Rd. Tel: (045) 611503.

Post and telegraph office *(Praisanee)*
Thepha Rd. Tel: (045) 612898, 612421.

Railway station *(Sathaanee rodfai)*
Karn Rodfai 2 Rd. Tel: (045) 611525.

Bus stations *(Baw Kaw Saw)*
Kwang-Heng Rd. Tel: (045) 612500.

Banks with currency exchange (Thanaakaan laek ngoen)
Bangkok Bank 975/6 Kukhan Rd. Tel: (045) 611538 • *Thai Farmers Bank* 1492/4 Kukhan Rd. Tel: (045) 611023 • *Siam Commercial Bank* 980/4

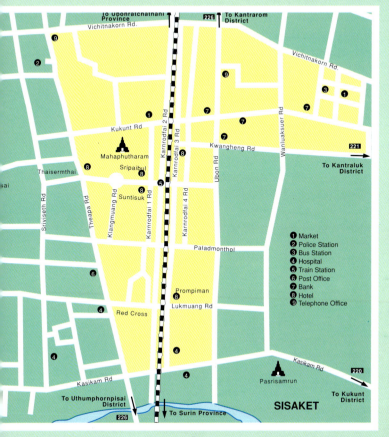

Kukhan Rd. Tel: (045) 611514.

Accommodation *(Rong raem)*

Prompimarn Hotel ✪✪ 849/1 Lak Muang Rd. Tel: (045) 612677, 612757, fax: 612696. 123 rooms, air conditioned and fanned. Price: 280-450 baht.

Santisuk Hotel ✪ Soi Wat Phra Toh (behind railway station). Tel: (045) 611496. 39 rooms (fanned) 60-120 baht.

Sisaket Hotel ✪ 384-5 Sisaket Rd. Tel: (045) 611846. 68 rooms, air-conditioned and fanned. Price: 100-300 baht.

Restaurants *(Raan ahaan)*

Mittraphap Restaurant 431/5 Paladmonthol Rd. Tel: (045) 611369.
Erawan Restaurant 11/7-8 Ubon Rd. Tel: (045) 611948.

Food stalls

Luksue Rd, in front of Srikasem Theatre.

SUKHOTHAI

Bangkok 427 km – Phitsanulok 58 km – Si Satchanalai 58 km – Kamphaeng Phet 188 km. Sukhothai is one of Thailand's ancient capitals dating back to the 13th century. Today the historic sites are contained in the Historic Park which has been declared a World Heritage Site. The moden town is medium-sized and unremarkable.

By car *From Bangkok*: Take Route 1 and turn on to Route 32 to Nakhon Sawan, then turn on to Route 117 to Phitsanulok, and Route 12 to Sukhothai *From Phitsanulok:* take Route 12. *From Si Satchanalai*: Take Route 101. *From Kamphaeng Phet:* Take Route 101.

By bus *From Bangkok*: Three a/c buses daily and six non-a/c from the Mor Chit 2 Bus Terminal, Kamphaeng Phet 2 Rd. Tel: (02) 537 8054-5 non-a/c, 537 8062 a/c, (7 hrs). *From Phitsanulok*: Every 30 mins 06.00-18.00. *From Si Satchanalai*: 06.40, 09.00,11.30, and non a/c buses. *From Kamphaeng Phet*: 06.00-15.00.

By train *From Bangkok:* Regular trains to Phitsanulok and from there a bus to Sukhothai.

Tourist information *(Gan thongthio)*

None in Sukhothai. The nearest is the TAT Office in Phitsanulok.

Police station *(Sathaanee tamruad)*

253 Nikornkasem Rd, near the gaol. Tel: (055) 611199.

Local administrative offices *(Tessabaan)*

360 Jarodvithithong Rd. Tel: (055) 611025.

Hospitals *(Rong phayabaan)*

Sukhothai Provincial Hospital Jarodvithithong Rd. Tel: (055) 611782.

Post and telegraph office (Praisanee)
Nikornkasem Rd. Tel: (055) 611645.

Airline offices (Gan binthai)
Bangkok Airways plan to begin services in 1996. Tel: (055) 681390.

Airport (Sanaambin)
On the road from Sukhothai to Sawankhalok District. Tel: (055) 612803-4
by Bangkok Airway from and to in every Monday, Wednesday, Friday, and
Sunday, departure at 07.30 am.

Bus stations (Baw Kaw Saw)
Prasertphong Rd. Tel: (055) 613296.

Banks with currency exchange (Thanaakaan laek ngoen)
Bangkok Bank 48/2 Singhawat Rd. Tel: (055) 611751.

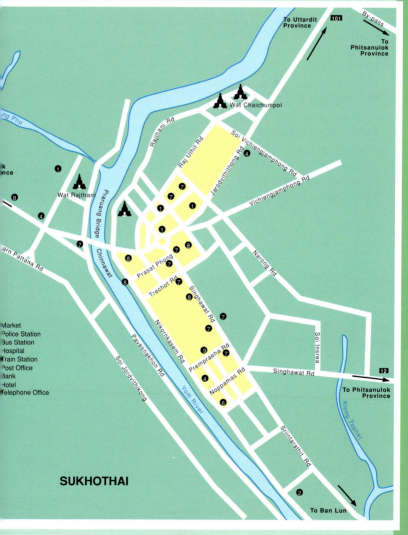

SUKHOTHAI

Thai Farmers Bank 134 Jarodvithithong Rd. Tel: (055) 611932-3.
Siam Commercial Bank 44 Singhawat Rd. Tel: (055) 611641.

Museums *(Phiphithapan)*
Ramkhamhaeng National Museum near the Sukhothai Historial Park.
Tel: (055) 612 167, Wed-Sun 09.00-16.00. Small admission fee.

Accommodation *(Rong raem)*

Pailyn Hotel ✪✪✪✪ 10 Moo 1 Jarodvithithong Rd., Sukhothai 64200.
Tel: (055) 613310-5, fax: (055) 613317. Bangkok office: Markotel Co.
Ltd., 2nd floor Ocean Building, 140/1-2 Phetchaburi Rd., Bangkok 10400,
tel: (02) 215 7110, 215 7112, fax: 215 5640. 323 rooms, all a/c.
Sukhothai's first large luxury hotel, located 4 km from the Historical Park and 8
km from the town centre. Facilities include restaurant, coffee shop, swimming
pool, discotheque, sauna, beauty salon. Specifically designed for tour
groups; rather isolated. Price: 800 baht standard single – 1000 baht deluxe
single/double excl. service charge and tax. Suites 1,500-2,500 baht.

Northern Palace Hotel ✪✪✪✪ 43 Singhawat Rd. Tel: (055) 611193-
4, fax (055) 612038. 67 rooms. Price: 850-1,500 baht, restaurant, coffee
shop, snooker club, swimming pool.

Rajathani Hotel ✪✪✪✪ 229 Jarodvithithong Rd. Tel: (055) 611031,
611308, fax: (055) 612 878. 81 rooms. Restaurant, bar, cocktail lounge,
coffee shop, shopping arcade, tour counter. Price: 680-900 baht.

Restaurants *(Raan ahaan)*

Kho Cheng Heng, 41/2 Nikornkasem Rd. Tel: (055) 611 501
the most delicious dish is flavoured duck with five Chinese spices.

Pranom, 56/1 Singhawat Rd. Tel: (055) 611 618.

Nam Karng, Sukhothai Cultural Center, 214 Jarodvithithong Rd.
Tel: (055) 611 049.

Food stalls
Oppsite Hong Theater.

Si Satchanalai

Wang Yom ✪✪ 78/2 Moo 6, Tambon Si Satchanalai. Tel: (055)
611179, 612277 ext. 279. 15 a/c cottages at 1,500 baht, 10
non-a/c huts at 1,200 baht (prices include American breakfast for 2).
Certainly the most convenient location for Si Satchanalai, being 2 km
south of the visitor centre on the road. On the river the Wang Yom has
extensive if over-manicured gardens, and a restaurant-cum-gift shop.
The same care has not been lavished on the accommodation,
however, which is over-priced for the spartan rather tired rooms.

Banggalow 59 1 km. from the District Hall.
10 rooms. Price: 150 baht.

Restaurants *(Raan ahaan)*

Kang Sak, pleasant situation on the banks of the Yom River by the
Keng Kuang rapids, within the park. A normal stop for tour groups, the
food is nevertheless well-prepared. Tel: (055) 642427, 611179,
612277.

Bangkok 457 km – Ubon Ratchathani 227 km – Buriram 111 km – Khorat 198 km – Phnom Rung 87 km – Ta Muen Thom 90 km – Sikhoraphum 36 km – Kamphaeng Yai 77 km. Surin is a medium-size town famous for its Thai silk. The annual elephant round-up is also held here.

By car *From Bangkok:* As for Khorat; then take Route 224 south as far as Chok Chai, turning left onto Route 24. Follow this east for 143 km to Prasat, and turn left onto Route 214. Surin lies 28 km ahead (450 km, 6-6½ hrs).*From Khorat:* See above (198 km, 2½ hrs-3 hrs). *From Buriram:* Take Route 226, 50 km. *From Ubon:* Take Route 226,190 km. 2½-3 hrs .

By bus *From Bangkok:* Four a/c buses daily and 17 non-a/c from the Northern Bus Terminal, Kampheangphet Rd. Tel: (02) 9363659 non-a/c, a/c, (7hrs).

By train *From Bangkok* (Hualamphong Station): one express train daily in the evening (7½ hrs), three rapid trains daily (8-9 hrs), three ordinary trains daily (10 hrs). To Bangkok: same services.*From Khorat:* One diesel sprinter daily in the morning (3 hrs), one express train daily after midnight (2½ hrs), three rapid trains daily (2½-3 hrs), four ordinary trains daily (5 hrs). *From Buriram:* Same trains as from Khorat (45 mins-1 hr). *From Sisaket:* One express train daily (1½ hr), three rapid trains daily (1½-2 hrs), four ordinary trains daily

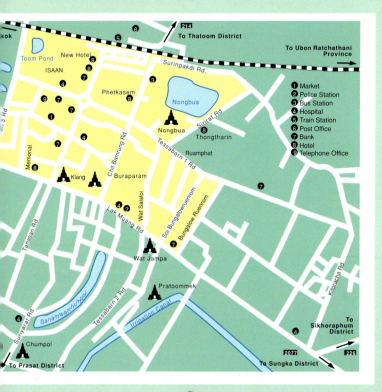

1. Market
2. Police Station
3. Bus Station
4. Hospital
5. Train Station
6. Post Office
7. Bank
8. Hotel
9. Telephone Office

(1½-2 hrs). *From Ubon*: one express train daily (2½ hrs), three rapid trains daily (3 hrs), four ordinary trains daily (3-3½ hrs).

Tourist information *(Gan thongthio)*
See TAT Khorat, page 265.

Police station *(Sathaanee tamruad)*
Lak Muang Rd. Tel: (044) 511007.

Local administrative offices *(Tessabaan)*
Lak Muang Rd. Tel: (044) 512039.

Hospitals *(Rong phayabaan)*
Provincial Hospital Tambon Nai Muang. Tel: (044) 511757.

Post and telegraph office *(Praisanee)*
Nai Muang Rd. Tel (044) 511009.

Railway station *(Sathaanee rodfai)*
Tanasan Rd. Tel: (044) 511295.

Bus stations *(Baw Kaw Saw)*
Chit Bamrung Rd. Tel: (044) 511756.

Banks with currency exchange *(Thanaakaan laek ngoen)*
Bangkok Bank 252 Tanasan Rd. Tel: (044) 512013.
Thai Farmers Bank 353 Tanasan Rd. Tel: (044) 511360.
Siam Commercial Bank 415 Chit Bamrung Rd. Tel: (044) 512062.

Accommodation *(Rong raem)*
Thong Tarin Hotel ✪✪✪ 60 Sirirat Rd. Tel: (044) 514281/8, fax: (044) 511580. 243 a/c rooms. New hotel with grandiose lobby and comfortable, if slightly small rooms. Facilities include restaurant, night-club, cocktail lounge and discotheque. Price: 880-1,500 baht.

Phetkasem Hotel ✪✪✪ 104 Chit Bamrung Rd. Tel: (044) 511274, 511576, fax: (044) 514041. 162 a/c rooms. Facilities include restaurant, discotheque, cocktail lounge and swimming pool. Price: 760-1,300 baht.

Saeng Thong Hotel ✪✪ 155-161 Tanasan Rd. Tel: (045) 512099, 511302, fax: (044) 514329. 125 rooms. Price: with fan 180-500 baht, a/c 320-750 baht.

New Hotel ✪✪ 22 Tanasan Rd. Tel: (044) 511341, 511322. 96 rooms. Price: with fan 150 baht , a/c 430 baht.

Memorial Hotel ✪ 646 Lak Muang Rd. Tel: (044) 511288, 511637. 56 rooms. Price: with fan 200 baht , a/c 400 baht.

Restaurants *(Raan ahaan)*
Sai Yen, 328 Chit Bamrung Rd. Tel: (044) 511878. Highly typical and locally popular; inexpensive. Nothing has been spent on the decor, other than to roof over a large area surrounding a tree (which gives the restaurant its name), but the food is authentic. Specialities include *goy* – chopped and highly seasoned raw meat, with bile if you ask for it, and, in season, *yam kai mot daeng* – a spicy salad of red ants' eggs.

Suan Nga Chang, 520 Kochasan Rd. Tel: (044) 513179. Pleasant garden restaurant with wide menu and elephant show at the weekend.

Food stalls
Near clock tower.

UBON RATCHATHANI

Bangkok 629 km – Khorat 370 km – Surin 227 km – Sakon Nakhon 286 km. Situated on the Mekong River the city has many beautiful Northeastern style temples. Kaeng Sapoe rapids some 5 km outside town are a popular picnic destination. Ubon has a good practical museum with several items of Khmer Art from the mid-9th to mid-12th centuries. *By car From Bangkok and Khorat*: Take Route 226 which a goes due east until it approaches Det Udom, where it turns north-west to Ubon. *From Surin:* The fastest route is also Route 226, which you join at Amphoe Sangkha after take Route 2077; the more interesting journey which takes in Si Khoraphum, Kamphaeng Yai and Kamphaeng Noi, is Route 2080, to Sisaket, continuing on Route 2193 or 24 to Warin Chamrap, where you turn left to cross the river into Ubon.

By bus From Bangkok: Five a/c buses daily and 15 non-a/c from the Northern Bus Terminal, Kamphaengphet Rd. Tel: (02) 9361880, 9360657 non-a/c, a/c, (9½hrs). *From Khorat:* seven buses daily, 5 hrs.

By train From Bangkok (Hualamphong Station): one express train daily in the evening (10 hrs), three rapid trains daily (10-10½ hrs), three ordinary trains daily (13 hrs). To Bangkok: same services. *From Khorat:* One express train daily after midnight (5 hrs), three rapid trains daily (5½ hrs), four ordinary trains daily (5½ hrs). *From Buriram and Surin:* Same trains as from Khorat (most 3½ hrs and 2½ hrs respectively). *From Sisaket:* One express train daily (1 hr),

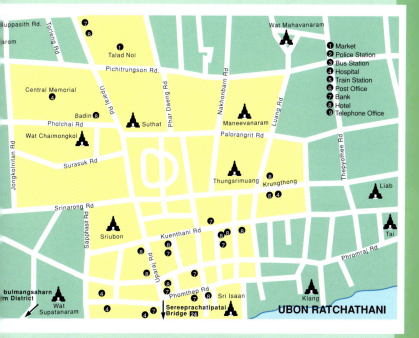

three rapid trains daily (1 hr), four ordinary trains daily (1-1½ hrs).

By plane *To and from Bangkok*: One daily departing BKK in the afternoon and Ubon in the early evening. Thai Airways International 1 hr. flight.

Tourist information *(Gan thongthio)*

TAT, 264/1 Kuenthani Rd. Tel: (045) 243770-1, fax: (045) 243771. Open daily 08.30-16.30.

Police station *(Sathaanee tamruad)*

Sapphasit Rd. Tel:(045) 254216 or 191 in an emregency.

Local administrative offices *(Tessabaan)*

Uparaj Rd. Tel: (045) 254693.

Hospitals *(Rong phayabaan)*

Provincial Hospital, Sapphasit Rd. Tel: (045) 244973,244970-4.
Rom Gao Private Hospital, Uparaj Rd. Tel: (045) 254660, 244658-60.

Post and telegraph office *(Praisanee)*

Luang Rd. Tel: (045) 254001, 242 168. Pathummarai Rd. Tel: (045) 255103.
Rajathani Rd. Tel: (045) 254935.

Airline offices *(Gan binthai)*

Thai Airways International, 364 Chayangkun Rd. Tel: (045) 244450-1, 244265.

Airport *(Sanaambin)*

Thepyothee Rd. Tel: (045) 244452, 254527. About 20 km from town.

Railway station *(Sathaanee rodfai)*

Warinchamrab Rd. Tel: (045) 254004.

Bus stations *(Baw Kaw Saw)*

380 Thepyothee Rd. Tel: (045) 254527.

Banks with currency exchange *(Thanaakaan laek ngoen)*

Bangkok Bank, 49 Ratchabut Rd. Tel: (045) 254074 • *Thai Farmers Bank*, 75/18 Chayangkool Rd. Tel: (045) 255710 • *Siam Commercial Bank*, 367 Uparaj Rd. Tel: (045) 241765.

Museum (Phiphithapan)

Ubon National Museum. See page 188, Khunthani Rd. Tel: (045) 255071. Open Weds-Suns 09.00-16.00. Small admission fee.

Accommodation *(Rong raem)*

Lai Thong Hotel ✪✪ 50 Pichit Rangsan Rd., Tel: (045) 264271 Fax: (045) 264270. 124 rooms, Price: 1,100-1,650 baht including breakfast.

Pathumrat Hotel ✪✪✪ Chayangkul Rd. Tel: (045) 241501-8. Bangkok Office tel: (02) 254 5803, 255 7546. 169 rooms. Price: 550-2500 baht.

Ubon Hotel ✪✪ 2 Ubonket Rd. Tel: (045) 241045/7, 241046. 120 rooms. Price: 200-500 baht, a/c and fan.

Krung Thong Hotel ✪✪ 24 Srinarong Rd. Tel: (045) 241609, fax: (045) 242308. 130 rooms. Price: 200-300 baht.

Ratchathani Hotel ✪✪ Kuenthani Rd. Tel: (045) 254599, 254497. 100 rooms. Price: 350-700 baht.

Sri Isaan Hotel ✪ 60 Ratchabut Rd. Tel: (045) 254204. 26 rooms. Price: 80-140 baht.

Restaurants *(Raan ahaan)*

Sakhon, 12/6-7 Pha Daeng Rd. Tel: (045) 254101 The most delicious dish is minced duck, often half-cooked.

Hong Fa, 302-304 Chayangkul Rd. Tel: (045) 313311-2.

Sariphon Restaurant, 478/1-2 Promrat Rd. Tel: (045) 254397.

Indochin, 12/10 Suppasit Rd. Tel: (045) 254126 (Vietnamese food).

Yim Yim Photchana, 156 Srinarong Rd. Tel: (045) 255251.

Car rental (Chao rod)

Ch.Watana. Tel: (045) 242202

Also via TAT office.

Glossary

Abhaya-mudra The *mudra*, or gesture, of reassurance, in which the palm of the right hand is held outward with the fingers extended upward.

Adi-Buddha The predominant Buddha in Mahayana Buddhism.

Airavata The elephant, that is the mount or vehicle of Indra, usually portrayed with three heads, but occasionally with one only. Known in Thai as Erawan.

Agni The Vedic god of fire, and one of the three principal gods in the Rig Veda (with Indra and Surya). Agni grants immortality and cleanses sin, and mediates between the gods and men.

Amitabha The Bodhisattva of infinite light, who helps those who falter and are weak.

Amrita The elixir of life, or ambrosia, produced by the Churning of the Sea of Milk, and over which the gods and demons fought. Literally, 'non-dead'. Known in Thai as *'amarit'*.

Ananta The endless World Serpent floating in the cosmic sea, and supporting Vishnu as he sleeps through the night of Brahma before the rebirth of the world. Also known as Sesha.

Anantasayin Term used to descibe Vishnu reclining on the back of the Naga Ananta.

Antaravasaka The lower garment (of three) used by Buddhist monks.

apsaras Celestial dancers who entertain the gods and are the sensual rewards of kings and heroes who die bravely. In Hindu mythology they always performed with the celestial musicians, *gandharvas*, but in Khmer mythology they were elevated alone to special importance in temple decoration.

Arishta Demon in the form of an ox, sent to kill Krishna by his uncle Kansa.

Asura Demon, and enemy of the gods. *Asuras* and gods are locked in perpetual conflict, although in the Churning of the Sea of Milk they act, albeit temporarily, in concert. *Asura* originally meant something quite different in the Rig Veda – a divine being.

Avalokitesvara The Compassionate Bodhisattva, also known as Lokesvara. He is the Mahayana Buddhist ideal of compassion, choosing not to pass into nirvana but to help instead to bring enlightenment to humans. Often represented as a young man holding a lotus in his left hand, and wearing an image of the Bodhisattva Amitabha on his head.

Avatar The 'descent' or incarnation of a god, in the form of a human or animal. Rama, for instance, is one of the avatars of Vishnu.

Balarama Half-brother of Rama – the serpent Ananta in human form.

Bali The brother of the monkey-king Surgriva who usurped the latter's throne in the Ramayana epic

Banaspati Mythical animal in Dvaravati art with horns, wings and beak.

Bhadreshvara Alternative name for Shiva.

Bhaisajyaguru A Mahayana Buddha considered the master of medicine, worshipped in the *arogayasalas*.

Bhumidevi Goddess of the Earth and one of Vishnu's two consorts.

Bodhisattva   In Mahayana Buddhism, a being who voluntarily stops short of reaching Buddha-hood in order to help humanity. The stage in the development of a Buddha before Enlightenment.

Bhumisparsa-mudra   The *mudra*, or gesture, of touching the Earth. With this *mudra*, Buddha called the Earth-goddess to witness. From *'bhumi'* meaning Earth.

Brahma   The Creator of all things, and principal deity of the Trimurti (with Vishnu and Shiva). Brahma has four heads and four arms, holding sceptre, rosary, bow and alms-bowl. Brahma is born from Vishnu's navel at the beginning of each world cycle. His vehicle is the *hamsa*, or goose.

Brahman   The transcendent absolute.

Brahmani   See Brahmi.

Brahmi   One of the Sapta Matrikis (Seven Divine Mothers); also called Brahmani.

brahmin   Hindu priest.

Bringin   Legendary disciple of Shiva.

Buddha   The Enlightened One'. Gautama Siddartha, born in 543 BC

Chakra   The wheel, emblem of Buddhist law and of the sun.

Chakravala   The concentric rings of mountain ranges which enclose the world mountain Meru, in Hindu cosmology.

Chakravartin   Universal ruler.

Chenla   The Chinese name for Cambodia before the Khmer era

deva   Deity, one of 33 in the Vedic system.

Devaki   Krishna's mother

Devaraja   Meaning 'god who is king', a cult deriving from Shiva-worship in which the king had divine associations.

devata   Female deity.

Devi   Consort of Shiva in her benevolent form. Phum Tawee in Thai. Also known as Uma, Gauri, Parvati, Jaganmata. See also Durga.

Dhamvantali   Celestial doctor, a minor form of Vishnu.

Dharma   The lows of Buddhism, separately, the doctrine of Hindu moral duty. Also, an ancient *rishi*.

Dharmachakra   The Buddhist Wheel of the Law, representing the dominon of the Buddha's Law over everything.

Dharmachakra mudra   The gesture of teaching, or turning the Dharmachakra, in which the right hand is held in front of the chest, its thumb and index finger joined and touching one finger of the left hand, the palm of which is turned inwards.

Dhana-mudra   The attitude of meditation, in which both hands, fingers extended, rest in the lap, right above left.

Dikpala   One of the eight gods of direction.

Durga   Consort of Shiva in her terrible form. Also called Kali, Chandi, Bhairavi.

dvarapala   Temple guardian, normally sculpted as a door watchman.

Dvaravati, Name given to the culture and art widespread throughout Thailand from the 6th to 11th centuries.

Erawan   See Airavata.

Funan   The oldest Indianised state of Indochina and precursor of Chenla

Gaja   Elephant.

Gajasimha   Mythical creature - part elephant, part lion.

Gana   A servant of Shiva. Ganesha is the leader of the *ganas*.

gandharva   Celestial musician, normally associated with *apsaras*.

Ganesh   Elephant-headed son of Shiva. According to legend, Shiva decapitated his son in a moment of anger, and in remorse replaced the head with the first that came to hand – that of an elephant.

Garuda   Mythical bird-man; the vehicle of Vishnu. Mortal enemy of *nagas*.

Gopala   Alternative name for Krishna; also, the name of a cow-herd (Krishna lived as one when a youth to escape his uncle Kansa).

Govardhana   The mountain that Krishna lifts in order to protect the cow-herds and their cattle from Indra's rain.

guru   Spiritual instructor.

Hamsa   Sacred goose; vehicle of Brahma. In Buddhism, represents the flight of the doctrine.

Hanuman   Monkey general and ally of Rama in the Ramayana.

Hara   Alternative name for Shiva.

Hari   Alternative name for Vishnu.

Harihara   God combining Shiva and Vishnu in one image

Harivamsa   Sacred book containing the genealogy of Hari – that is, Vishnu.

Himavatta   Mythical forest surrounding Mount Meru.

Hinayana   'Lesser Vehicle', referring to the traditional, conservative form of Buddhism which concentrates on the doctrine rather than on the worship of the Buddha or Bodhisattvas. Its adherents use the term 'Theravada' instead.

Hiranya   A Khmer prince, son of Narendraditya and founder of Phnom Rung.

Hiranyakasipu   Demon killed by Vishnu in his avatar Narasimha (man-lion).

Indra   The Vedic god of the sky, clouds and monsoon, and guardian of the East. The principal god in the Rig Veda.

Isuan   See Shiva.

Isvara, -eshvara   Lord, supreme deity

Indrajit   Son of Ravana.

Jataka   'Birth-story', of which there are 547 recounting the Buddha's previous incarnations.

Jatamukuta   Hairstyle in the form of a tall chignon, worn by Shiva and Shivaite hermits; also worn by Bodhisattvas in Mahayana Buddhism.

Jayabuddhamahanatha   Statue of the Buddha made by royal command of

Jayavarman VII to be sent to his vassal cities.

Jina Synonym of the Buddha.

Kailasa, Mount Abode of Shiva, named after the actual mountain Kailas in western Tibet.

Kala Adopted Indian motif; demon commanded to devour itself. Commonly sculpted over a temple entrance as guardian. Name from the Sanskrit for "blue-black".

Kalasa A pot. A *purnakalasa* is a pot filled with water and plants, symbolising prosperity – a kind of cornucopia.

Kaliya Name of the *naga* with multiple heads subdued by Krishna.

Kalkin Future and last avatar of Vishnu.

Kalpa A cycle of time, at the end of which Shiva destroys the world; following this, a new *kalpa* is initiated by the recreation of the world when Brahma is reborn from the navel of Vishnu. Each *kalpa* is a day and a night of Brahma, but 8,640 million human years, and contains 2,000 *mahayugas*, or 'great ages'. See also *yuga*.

Kamrateng añ Khmer term for a high dignitary (lit. 'my lord').

Kamrateng jagat Literally 'lord of the universe', used as reference to a deity, usually Shiva and the representation of Shiva as a linga.

Kamsa Wicked king killed by Krishna.

Kareikalammeyar Female disciple of Shiva.

Kesin Demon in the form of a horse sent to kill Krishna by his uncle Kansa.

Ketumala see Ushnisha

Kirtimukha Term used for *kala* (lit 'glory face').

Krishna One of the avatars, or incarnations of Vishnu, and hero of the Mahabharata epic.

Krut Cambodian and Thai name for *garuda*.

kshatriya Hindu warrior caste.

Kubera The god of wealth and guardian of the North; chief of the yakshas.

Kurma (or kurma-avatara) One of the avatars, or incarnations, of Vishnu, as a giant turtle. Kurma appears supporting Mount Mandara in the Churning of the Sea of Milk.

Kuvalayapida Demon in the form of an elephant sent by Kansa to kill his nephew Krishna.

Lakshmi Wife of Vishnu, goddess of fortune and symbol of Vishnu's creative energy. Her emblem is the lotus.

Lakshmana Brother of Rama.

lalitasana Seated posture with one leg folded in front of the body, the other on the ground – the posture of relaxation for a king.

Lanka Capital city of the demon Ravana, in the Ramayana.

Linga Stylised image of a phallus representing the essence of the god Shiva. In Sanskrit, the word means 'sign' and 'distinguishing symbol'.

Lingaparvata A naturally-occurring mountain, hill or peak in the form of a *linga*.

Lokesvara See Avalokitesvara.

Mahabharata Major Hindu epic written between about 400 BC and 200 AD with a central narrative of the feud between the Kaurava and Pandava dynasties.

Mahakala One of Shiva's guardians (distinguishable by a pair of fangs) standing in a pair at an entrance with Nandikesvara.

Mahayana 'Great Vehicle', referring to the later form of Buddhism in which the Buddha and Bodhisattvas are worshipped as deities.

Maheshvara Alternative name for Shiva.

Maitreya The future Buddha, yet to come.

Makara Sea monster with scales, claws and a large head, often in the form of a crocodile, sometimes with the trunk of an elephant. In Khmer sculpture, acquired from India via Java.

mandala Magic diagram in the shape of the cosmos.

Mandara, Mount Mythical mountain used as a pivot for churning the Sea of Milk.

Mara The master demon of illusion, the Evil One in Buddhist myth.

Maricha Cousin of Ravana who disguises himself as the Golden Deer to lure Rama away from Sita, from the Ramayana.

Matsya (or matsya-avatara) The incarnation of Vishnu as a fish.

Meru, Mount The cosmic or world mountain of Hindu cosmology which lies at the centre of the universe. Its summit is the home of the gods. Also called *Sumeru*.

Mohini Form of Vishnu, in which the god disguises himself as a beautiful woman to tempt the demons and so recover the *amrita* produced by the Churning of the Sea of Milk.

Mon People inhabiting lower Burma and central Thailand from the 6th to 11th centuries. The Mon culture in Thailand is known as Dvaravati.

Muchalinda The giant serpent who shelters the meditating Buddha from a storm with its hood.

mudra The ritual gesture of the hands of a deity or Buddha.

Mukhalinga Linga bearing the face of Shiva.

naga Multi-headed serpent with many mythological connections, associated with water, fertility, rainbows, and creation. Five- and seven-headed *nagas* are common motifs, usually with the basic form of a cobra.

Nagapasa A noose in the form of a naga that mutates from an arrow fired by *Indrajita*.

nagara Hindu city or capital, the origin of the Khmer word 'Angkor'. The Thai derivation is *'nakhon'*.

nagini Serpent goddess.

Nandikesvara One of Shiva's guardians, standing in a pair at an entrance with Mahakala.

Nandi Sacred bull; the mount, or vehicle, of Shiva.

Narai Thai name for Vishnu.

Narasimha (or naraisimha-avatara)   The avatar, or incarnation, of Vishnu as part-man, part-lion.

Nataraja   Shiva as Lord of the Dance.

Padmanabha   Literally 'lotus from the navel', referring to Vishnu reclining on the Naga Ananta; a lotus springs from his navel and Brahma appears from its flower.

Padmapani   'The one who holds the lotus'.

Pala   Indian art style from the eastern Indian dynasty of the same name, 7th-12th centuries

Parvati   Goddess and consort of Shiva.

phnom   Khmer for 'hill' or 'mount'.

pradakshina   Clockwise, and the usual, form of procession around a temple, keeping the shrine to the right. See also *prasavaya*.

Prajñaparamita   Female form of the Bodhisattva Lokesvara.

prasavya   Anti-clockwise procession around a temple, keeping the shrine to the left: the direction if it is a tomb. See also *pradakshina*.

Pratibimba   Hindu concept of making an earthly representation of a heavenly form.

Preah   Khmer word for 'sacred', from the Sanskrit *'brah'*.

Puranas   The sacred Hindu texts, including the Ramayana and Mahabharata.

Purusa   Male person.

Rahu   Demon whose body was cut by Vishnu's discus; responsible for eclipses by his attempts to eat the sun and the moon.

Rama   One of the earthly incarnations of Vishnu and eponymous hero of the Ramayana.

Ramakien   Thai version of the Ramayana.

Ramayana   Major Hindu romantic epic tracing the efforts and adventures of Rama to recover his wife Sita, who was kidnapped by the demon Ravana. The Thai version is the Ramakien.

Ravana   Multi-armed and -headed demon; the villain of the piece in the Ramayana epic.

Rig Veda   The earliest Vedic sacred text, meaning 'Wisdom of the Verses', written about 1400 BC. Its principal myth is the struggle between the major Vedic god Indra and the dragon Vritra.

rishi   Hindu seer, ascetic or sage. Forerunners of the brahmins.

Saivite   Pertaining to Shiva.

Shakti   The creative force in its feminine form.

Samadhi   The deepest from of yoga meditation, in which is achieved the ultimate vision.

Samanakha   Thai name for Surpanakha.

Sampot   Traditional Khmer garment.

samsara   The endless cycle of life and rebirth.

Sangha   Community of Buddhist monks.

Sanskrit Ancient Indian language and script.

Sapta Matrikis 'Seven Divine Mothers'. They comprise Brahmi, Maheswari, Vaishnavi, Kaumari, Indrani, Varahi, Chamundi.

Savayambhu Natural rock linga.

sema Buddhist boundary stone.

Senapati Minister of State.

Sesha See Ananta.

Shiva One of the Hindu Trinity of gods; the God of Destruction, but also of rebirth. Called Isuan in Thai.

Shivaite See Saivite.

Shurpanakha Ravana's sister.

Simha Lion.

Simhamukha Literally 'lion face'. Similar to a kala, but with a lower jaw.

Singh, Singha Thai name for simha.

Sita Wife of Rama.

Soma The drink of Indra, related to the fermented juice of a climbing plant, and to the moon. See *somasutra* under Architectural terms.

Sri Alternative name for Lakshmi, wife of Vishnu. its general meaning is 'auspicious'. In Thai: 'Si'.

stele Upright slab bearing inscriptions.

Surgriva Monkey-king ally of Rama in the Ramayana.

Surya The god of the sun, and one of the three principal gods in the Rig Veda (with Indra and Agni).

Sutra Narrative scripture.

Tandava Shiva's dance in which he brings the universe to destruction and a new beginning.

Tantric Developed form of Hinduism and Mahayana Buddhism in which magic features strongly.

Theravada The traditional form of Buddhism (see Hinayana).

Toranee Thai name for Bhumidevi.

Trailokyavijaya Literally 'victory of the three worlds'; name given to one of the major Mahayana Bodhisattvas.

Trijata Wife of Ravana's brother, Vibeksha.

Trimurti The Hindu trinity of gods: Brahma the Creator, Vishnu the Preserver and Shiva the Destroyer.

Ucchaisaravas Magical horse that emerges from the Churning of the Sea of Milk; later appropriated by Indra.

Uma Shiva's consort.

Umamahesvara Term describing the image of Shiva and Uma together, riding Nandi.

Ushnisha Protuberance on the head of Buddha, symbolising his all-

encompassing knowledge.

vahana Mount or vehicle of a god. For example, Shiva rides the bull Nandi.

Vaisnavite Pertaining to Vishnu.

vajra Diamond, thunderbolt.

Vajradhara Literally 'bearer of lightning'; name given to one of the Mahayana Buddhas and also to one of the Mahayana Bodhisattvas.

Vajrasattva One of the six 'meditation-Buddhas'.

Vamana (or vamana-avatara) The avatar, or incarnation, of Vishnu as a dwarf.

Vara-mudra Gesture signifying benediction, in which the right hand is extended palm outwards.

Varaha (or varaha-avatara) The avatar, or incarnation, of Vishnu as a boar.

Varman, Varman Literallly 'chest-armour', and by extension 'protégé', 'protected by'.

Varuna Originally a universal deity, encompassing the sky, later to become a god of seas and rivers, usually riding the makara. The guardian of the West.

Vasudeva Father of Krishna.

Vasuki Name of the giant naga used by the gods and demons to churn the Sea of Milk.

Vayu God of air and wind, linked with Indra.

Vedas The four religious books that instruct Brahmanic ritual. The most famous is the Rig Veda, composed in the first millennium BC.

Vibeksha Ravana's brother.

Viraba Demon enslaved by Rama.

Vishnu Member of the Hindu Trinity; the Preserver and Protector. The Thai name is Narai. A popular deity among worshippers, he manifests himself on earth in a variety of incarnations, or *avatars*.

Vishnuite See Vaisnavite.

Vitarka-Mudra Gesture of preaching and giving a sermon, performed with one hand or both by joining thumb and forefinger, palm held outwards.

yaksha Demi-god.

yakshi, yakshini Female yaksha.

Yama God of death and guardian of the south.

yogini Mahayanic goddess associated with Vajrasattva.

yuga One of the four ages in the world cycle according to Hinduism. The four ages, and shorter intervening periods of twilight, last 4,320,000 human years, and this is called a *mahayuga*. 2,000 *mahayugas* comprise a *kalpa*.

Architectural Terms

Acroter   See Antefix.

Anastylosis   Integral restoration in which all the elements of a structure are analysed and numbered, following which the building is made structurally sound and rebuilt using original materials as much as possible. Additional materials are used only where structurally necessary.

Antarala   Vestibule connecting the *garbhagrha* to the *mandapa*.

Antefix   Pinnacle or other ornament that stands on a parapet.

Arcature   Niche.

Ardhamandapa   Shallow porch on a *mandapa*.

Arogayasala   Chapel, usually in laterite, that was part of a hospital. Part of a building programme undertaken by Jayavarman VII.

Asrama   Monastery, hermitage (Sanskrit).

Baluster   Circular-sectioned post or pillar, as in a barred window or the uprights of a balustrade.

Balustrade   Railing or similar in which balusters are the uprights surmounted by a beam or coping.

Banteay   Khmer for 'citadel', probably from the Sanskrit 'pandaya' ('fortress')

Baray   Artificial lake or reservoir.

Colonette   Small column, usually decorative in Khmer architecture, standing at either side of a doorway.

Corbel   Deeply embedded load-bearing stone projecting from a wall.

Corbel arch   False arch built from corbels projecting from opposite walls in tiers so that the topmost stones meet in the centre.

Cornice   Decorated projection that crowns or protects an architectural feature such as a doorway. The cornice level is that immediately above the lintels.

Decorative lintel   Rectangular stone slab carrying a carved design with important iconographical features. Attached above any doorway in a Khmer temple; has no structural supportive function.

Dharmasala   Chapel, usually in laterite, that was part of a resting-house or way-station, built along the main roads leading from Angkor. Part of a building programme undertaken by Jayavarman VII.

Fronton   See pediment.

Functional lintel   See structural lintel.

Garbhagrha   The inner chamber in a Khmer sanctuary, in the form of a square cell. Literally 'womb house'.

Gopura   Entrance pavilion, sometimes surmounted by a tower.

Laterite   Red, porous, iron-bearing rock, easy to quarry but very hard when dried.

'Library'   Isolated annexes usually found in pairs on either side and in front of the main entrance to a temple, or the entrance to an enclosuré. This is a traditional name for them, although there is no certainty that they were actually used as libraries.

Lintel   Stone block spanning an entrance, across the two door pillars. May be load-bearing or decorative. Also see structural lintel, decorative lintel.

Mandapa   Antechamber: a pavilion or porch in front of the main sanctuary.

Pancha Yatana   In Hindu religious architecture, a temple with a main central sanctuary surrounded by four other shrines and connected to them by cloisters.

Pediment   The triangular vertical face above the lintel, over a portico or other entrance. Used decoratively.

Pilaster   Square- or rectangular-sectioned pillar that is actually engaged in the wall, so that it becomes a projection.

Portico   Entrance porch.

Prali   Roof finial.

Prang   Thai term for an elongated cone-shaped tower. The central prang is built over the garbhagrha.

Prasat   From the Indian 'prasada', a terraced pyramid temple typical of South India.

Quincunx   Arrangement of five objects in which four occupy the corners and the fifth the centre. See Pancha Yatana .

Redenting   Architectural treatmrnt of a structure in plan whereby the corners are indented (cut back) into successive right angles.

Sala   Rest hall.

Sema   Buddhist boundary stone.

Shikara   Pointed tower in Indian architecture; a tapering superstructure to the chamber of a sanctuary that had its origin in Orissa.

Somasutra   Stone pipe or channel through which the lustral waters used to wash the image inside the sanctuary are drained, projecting outside the temple. Often terminates with a carved *makara* head at the spout. Indicative of a Saivite temple.

Srah   Artficial pond, usually smaller than a *baray*. 'Sa' in Thai.

Stele   Upright slab bearing inscriptions.

Structural lintel   The load-bearing upper member of a stone door-frame. Normally concealed for the most part.

Stucco   Plaster used for covering walls or for decorative purposes. In Khmer architecture, it was used to cover brick and laterite.

Trimukha   Literally, 'three-faced'. Three-lobed design of a platform or structure seen in plan.

Vantail   Leaf of a door.

Vat   Khmer for 'wat'.

Vault   Arch extended in depth.

Vihara   Temple building, rectangular in plan, designed to house a Buddha image (Sanskrit).

Viharn   Thai name for *vihara*.

Vihear   Khmer name for *vihara*.

Wat   General term used in Thai for Buddhist temple, from the Sanskrit 'vatthu'.

Bibliography

Anuvit, Charernsupkul. *The Structure Types and Pattern Bonds of Khmer and Srivijayan Brick Architecture in Thailand.* Bangkok; 1982.

Aymonier, Etienne. *Le Cambodge.* Paris: E. Leroux; 1900 [Vol. II Les provinces Siamoises].

Black, J. *The lofty sanctuary of Khao Phra Viharn.* Bangkok: Siam Society; 1976.

Boisselier, J. *Le Cambodge.* Paris: Picard; 1981.

Briggs, L.P. *The Ancient Khmer Empire.* Philadelphia: The American Philosophical Society; 1951.

Brown, R. *The Ceramics of South-East Asia* (2nd edition). Singapore: Oxford University Press; 1988.

Chandler, David. *A History of Cambodia.* Colorado: Westview Press; 1983.

Chou, Ta-Kuan. *Notes on the Customs of Cambodia.* Translated by J. Gilman D'Arcy Paul from Paul Pelliot. Bangkok: Social Science Association Press; 1967.

Clarac, Achille and Smithies, M. *Guide to Thailand.* Bangkok: Duang Kamol; 1981.

Coedès, George. *The Indianized States of Southeast Asia.* Honolulu: The University Press of Hawaii; 1968.

Coedès, George. *The Making of South East Asia.* Berkeley and Los Angeles: University of California Press; 1966.

Cotterell, A. *A Dictionary of World Mythology.* Oxford: Oxford University Press; 1986.

Craven, Roy. *Indian Art, A Concise History.* London: Thames & Hudson; 1976.

Fine Arts Department. *Report of the Survey and Excavataions of Ancient Monuments in North-Eastern Thailand.* Part Two: 1960-61. Bangkok: Fine Arts Department; 1961.

Fine Arts Department. *The Survey and Excavations of Ancient Monuments in North-Eastern Thailand.* Bangkok: Fine Arts Department; 1959.

Frankel, B. *The Waters, the King and the Mountain: Khmer Cosmology. The Artistic Heritage of Thailand.* (ed. National Museum Volunteers). Bangkok: Sawasdee Magazine. pp 67-69; 1979.

Frederic, Louis. *The Temples and Sculpture of Southeast Asia.* London: Thames and Hudson; 1965.

Giteau, Madeleine. *Histoire du Cambodge.* Paris: Didier; 1957.

Groslier, Bernard Philippe. *Indochina: Art in the Melting-Pot of Races.* London: Methuen (Art of the World); 1962.

Groslier, Bernard Philippe and Chatelet, Albert. *Histoire de l'Art: l'art asiatique.* Paris: References Larousse; 1988.

Hall, D.G.E. *A History of South-East Asia.* London: Macmillan; 1964.

Hammond, S. *Prasat Phnom Rung: a Khmer Temple in Thailand.* Arts of Asia 18(4) pp 51-67; 1988.

Jacob, J. 'The Ecology of Angkor: Evidence from the Khmer Inscriptions'. *Nature and Man in South East Asia.* (ed. P. Stott). pp 109-128. London:

SOAS; 1978

de Lajonquière, Lunet. *Inventaire Descriptif des Monuments du Cambodge*. Paris: Imprimerie Nationale; 1907. [vol 2].

Le Bonheur, Albert. *Art khmer*. Paris: Musee Guimet; 1991.

Manit, Vallibhotama. *Guide to Phimai*. Bangkok: Fine Arts Department; 2504.

Mazzeo, D. and Antonini, C. S. *Ancient Cambodia*. London: Cassells; 1978.

Moore, E, 'Origins of Khmer Naga Legends'. *Sawasdee Magazine* pp 23-28; May-June 1981.

Moore, E. 'Water Management in Early Cambodia: evidence from aerial photography'. *Geographical Journal*, 155(2) pp 204-214; 1989.

Moore, E. and Smitthi Siribhradra. *Palaces of the Gods*. River Books, Bangkok 1992.

National Museum Volunteers Group. *Treasures from the National Museum, Bangkok*. Bangkok: TWP; 1987.

Piriya Krairiksh. *Art Styles in Thailand*. Bangkok: Fine Arts Department; 1977.

Piriya Krairiksh. 'Khmer Ruins in Thailand'. Orientations, 12(12) pp 22-23; 1981.

Pym, Christopher (ed.) *Henri Mouhot's Diary*. Kuala Lumpur: Oxford University Press; 1966.

Smitthi Siribhradra and Mayuree Veraprasert. *Lintels: a comparative study of Khmer lintels in Thailand and Cambodia*. Bangkok: Siam Commercial Bank; 1989.

Srisakra Vallibhotama. *Prasat Khao Phnom Rung*. Bangkok: Silpawatannatham; 1987.

Stern, Philippe. *Les Monuments Khmers du Style du Bayon et Jayavarman VII*. Paris: Presses Universitaires de France/Publications du Musée Guimet; 1965.

Suriyavudh Sukhasvasti. *Stone Lintels in Thailand*. Bangkok: Meuang Boran; 1988.

Wolters, O. W. *History, Culture and Region in Southeast Asian Perspectives*. Singapore: Institute of Southeast Asian Studies; 1982.

Wyatt, David K. *Thailand, A Short History*. pp 24-30. New Haven: Yale University Press; 1984.

Zimmer, Henrich. *Myths and Symbols in Indian Art and Civilization*. Princeton: Bollingen; 1974.

Index

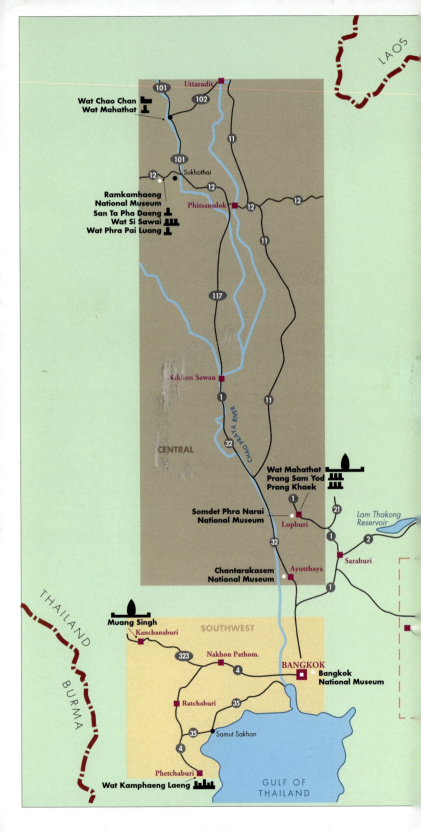